365 SAINTS

SAINTS

YOUR DAILY GUIDE
TO THE WISDOM AND WONDER
OF THEIR LIVES

WOODEENE KOENIG-BRICKER

HarperOne
An Imprint of HarperCollinsPublishers

HarperOne

365 SAINTS: *Your Daily Guide to the Wisdom and Wonder of Their Lives.*
Copyright © 1995 by Woodeene Koenig-Bricker. All rights reserved.
Printed in the United States of America. No part of this book may be
used or reproduced in any manner whatsoever without written
permission except in the case of brief quotations embodied in critical
articles and reviews. For information, address HarperCollins
Publishers, 195 Broadway, New York, NY 10007.

HarperCollins books may be purchased for educational, business,
or sales promotional use. For information, please e-mail the
Special Markets Department at SPsales@harpercollins.com.

HarperCollins Web site: http://www.harpercollins.com
HarperCollins®, 📖®, and HarperOne™ are trademarks of
HarperCollins Publishers.

Library of Congress Cataloging-in-Publication Data
ISBN 978–0–06–067594–3

18 19 LSC(H)   40 39 38 37 36 35 34

≈ ⑥ ≈

TO JSB AND MSB

ACKNOWLEDGMENTS

To all those whose love, encouragement, and support made it possible for me to write this book, more thanks than I can ever express.

To John, who did everything so I could spend all my time in the company of the saints. I couldn't have done it without you.

To Matt, who always said, "You can do it, Mom!" I wouldn't have tried to do it without you.

To Bobbi, Debbie, and Kris, who had more confidence in me than I had in myself.

To the sons of St. Dominic, whose love and prayers constantly sustain me.

And finally, a special thanks to my mother, who always believed I'd write a book one day. One day finally came.

INTRODUCTION

I'll admit it. I love the saints. I've loved them for as long as I can remember. One of the first joys of my childhood was receiving a book about St. Francis of Assisi. (And one of my first great disappointments was not being chosen to play the role of St. Clare in our third-grade production of St. Francis's life.) I can't imagine life without the saints. I don't know what I would do without St. Anthony to help find lost objects, or St. Elizabeth Ann Seton to confer with about child-rearing, or Blessed Diana D'Andalo to consult on maintaining friendships. I know my life would be diminished without a celestial shoulder or two to cry on occasionally or a heavenly companion to share an earthly joy.

But what is a saint?

Anyone who is in heaven is a saint, but a Saint with a capital *S* in the Catholic and Orthodox tradition is someone whose life so exemplifies holiness and virtue that the Church has officially declared them to be in heaven. (Interestingly, although thousands of people are officially said to be in heaven, not one single person has ever officially been declared to be in hell!)

The lengthy process by which a person is named a capital *S* saint is called canonization. If a person has shown great holiness in life, he or she may be called "Venerable" after death. This step in the saint-making process indicates the person may be honored. The next step is beatification. After more investigation and indisputable evidence of miracles worked through the person's intercession, a "Venerable" may be named "Blessed" and assigned an official feast day--usually the day of death (their *birthday* into heaven). Then, after more investigation and more miracles, a "Blessed" may finally be canonized and declared an official capital *S* saint. The only exception to the process is a martyr, a person who is killed for the faith. In those cases, the need for a miracle may be waived. The saints in this book, with a few notable exceptions such as Mother Teresa of Calcutta, are either official capital *S* saints or are in the process of becoming official saints.

So what are the saints really like?

All too often, we think of them as heavenly Goody Two-shoes who did nothing except pray, perform good deeds, and make everyone feel guilty for not living up to their example. While some of the saints did spend all (or most) of their time praying and doing good deeds (and probably making others feel guilty), the majority were real people--with all the foibles, eccentricities, and charm of real people.

That's what makes the saints so appealing--they're ordinary people with one extraordinary difference; they've been so inflamed with the love of God that their entire lives are a celebration of God's love and goodness. They were so passionately in love with God while they were living, they're now believed to be permanently with God for all eternity in heaven.

In writing this book, it was my hope to share some of the saints' successes and failures, joys and sorrows as an encouragement for your own spiritual journey. I hope that you come to discover, by their example, that we each have our own path of spiritual growth and development. The saints were never plaster statues on a heavenly assembly line. They made mistakes in everything from business deals to marriage. They suffered the same heartaches, illnesses, and sorrows that we suffer. And they experienced all the joys of everyday life. They didn't become saints because they were perfect; they became saints because they let God transform their imperfections.

I love the saints, not because of their sanctity—although that is certainly important—but because of their humanity. I hope through this book, you will find at least one heavenly friend to know and love. But more than that, I hope as you discover the love the saints had for God, you will also discover how much love God has for each and every one of us. And I pray that you will realize God is calling each and every one of us to become saints as well.

365 SAINTS

MARY, MOTHER OF JESUS

FIRST CENTURY

Appointment books. Planners. Calendars. We outline our present, plan our future, and review our past. We know exactly where we want to be and how we want to get there. And then it happens—the unexpected, the unplanned, the unforeseen. The death of a family member. A job change. A serious illness. Our neatly ordered lives are shattered and we are left holding the pieces.

How do we react when things happen that we can't control? Do we rail against the heavens, demanding answers, or do we accept, trusting that everything will work out according to divine plan?

Mary certainly wasn't expecting an angel to appear to her and ask if she was willing to become the mother of the Messiah. Naturally, she had a few questions—like, how can this happen when I am neither married nor involved in a sexual relationship? Yet once her questions were resolved, she answered "*Fiat*" ("Let it be done to me according to God's will"). She was willing to trust, even when it entailed mystery and the unknown.

As we begin a new year, let us resolve to accept with joy the twists and turns life brings us. Let us open our hearts to the wonder of each new day and trust that our lives are unfolding the way they ought.

Do I have to be in control of everything? In what areas can I let others have their say?

TODAY, AND EVERY DAY, I WILL TRUST IN THE GOODNESS AND WISDOM OF LIFE.

ST. BASIL THE GREAT

329–379

Do you sometimes feel you can't win for losing? St. Basil the Great could empathize. Archbishop of what is now southeastern Turkey and founder of what was probably the first monastery in Asia Minor, St. Basil was deeply embroiled in leading the fight against the Arians, who argued that Jesus was neither divine nor eternal. In his attempts to defend the faith, Basil was even accused of heresy himself. Frustrated and dismayed, he wrote, "For my sins I seem to be unsuccessful in everything."

Often when life's struggles sap our energy, we also feel unsuccessful in everything. Our past triumphs fade under the weight of the current failure, and we slip into self-pity. We are tempted to give up.

Even a saint as great as Basil the Great wasn't immune to such a temptation. Yet he didn't let his negative feelings rule his life. He continued preaching with such zeal that today he is considered one of the most eminent teachers of the Church.

St. Basil didn't surrender in the face of seeming failure. He kept going, even when he undoubtedly would rather have retreated to the sanctuary of his monastery. His life demonstrates that perseverance is just another name for success. When we feel tempted to give up, let us remember, as Charles Spurgeon said, "By perseverance the snail reached the Ark." May we emulate the example of Basil the Great.

How do I react when I feel like a failure? What keeps me going when I feel the most discouraged?

I GIVE MYSELF CREDIT FOR ALL I HAVE ACCOMPLISHED.

ST. GENEVIEVE

A.D. 500

Most of us spend a good deal of time each day dealing with food. Ironically, one of the times when we have to concentrate the most on food is when we are eating the least—during a diet. Many dieters constantly weigh and measure portions, evaluating fat content and trying to convince themselves that a carrot stick tastes much better than a slice of cheesecake.

St. Genevieve, who lived in Paris at the time Attila the Hun was pillaging most of Western Europe, is said to have eaten only barley bread with a few beans—and that meager meal only on Sundays and Thursdays. While we can't be sure if the story is true, if it is, then she maintained a very stringent diet most of her life.

So why is she the patron saint of Paris? When Childeric, the king of the Franks, blockaded the city, the citizens were besieged by famine. St. Genevieve led a company to find food and brought back several boats filled with corn. She, who ate almost nothing herself, is remembered for having fed a city.

Sometimes in our quest for the perfect body, we treat food as if it were the enemy. Food, in and of itself, is neither good nor bad. It can be a means of discipline, as it was for St. Genevieve, or a source of salvation, as it was for the people of Paris. The key is to know, as did Genevieve, which is which.

How important is food in my life? Do I use food
or do I let it use me?

I GIVE THANKS FOR THE FOOD I EAT, WHICH GIVES ME LIFE
AND SUSTAINS ME THROUGHOUT THE DAY.

ST. ELIZABETH ANN SETON

1774–1821

Elizabeth Ann Seton, the first native-born North American saint, was well-acquainted with loss. Her mother died when she was three; her beloved father died of yellow fever; her husband died when she was only twenty-nine, leaving her with five small children; her sisters-in-law, with whom she founded a religious order, both died young; and in the following decade, her daughters Anna Maria and Rebecca, on whom she doted, also died.

You might think a woman as devout and dedicated as Elizabeth Ann Seton would have been stoic. Each time one of her loved ones died, however, she grieved deeply. Even when we aren't mourning the death of a loved one, we experience the pain of loss. Implied in every beginning is an ending. And yet, in every ending is a beginning. Each day, we are given a fresh chance to love and to be loved.

When we cling too tightly to the people and things in our lives, we have no room for God's new beginnings. After all, we cannot experience the warmth of spring until winter relinquishes its icy grasp. Even in the midst of her grief, Elizabeth Ann Seton never lost sight of that truth. "In heaven we shall know each other by a glance of the soul," she wrote. Only when we let the endings in our life point to new beginnings will our life have real meaning.

What am I clinging to? What has to end so I can begin again?

⟨≈≈≈≈≈≈≈≈≈≈≈≈≈≈≈≈≈⟩

I CELEBRATE EACH DAY AS A NEW BEGINNING AND A FRESH START.

ST. JOHN NEUMANN

1811–1860

How much money would it take for you to feel comfortable? Some studies have indicated that no matter what you earn, your so-called comfort zone is just a little bit higher. Most of us seem to believe we would finally feel content if we earned a few thousand dollars more each year.

Bishop John Neumann, the fourth bishop of Philadelphia, understood the fallacy of such thinking. He took the vow of poverty he made as a Redemptorist priest so literally that he gave away virtually everything he owned. Once, when he arrived home with wet feet, someone suggested he change his shoes. He answered that if he did, it would be to put his left shoe on his right foot and vice versa since he owned only one pair. At his funeral, he was clad in a new suit of clothes for the first time in many years.

St. John Neumann did not choose a life of poverty because he enjoyed deprivation. He chose to divest himself of material possessions because he understood that the real treasures of life can never be purchased.

When we value ourselves merely for what we own, we will always be poor. Only when we realize that God values us for what we are, not what we have, do we become rich beyond measure.

How does my income affect the way I think about myself? What do I consider my greatest treasures?

I AM NOT MY MONEY. I CAN BE RICH, NO MATTER WHAT MY CIRCUMSTANCES.

BLESSED BROTHER ANDRÉ

1845–1937

"A joyful heart is good medicine, but a broken spirit dries up the bones," says the Book of Proverbs. Blessed Brother André, called the "Miracle Worker of Montreal," for the many cures his prayers wrought, would have agreed. Born Alfred Bessette, he entered the Congregation of the Holy Cross at age twenty-five. Over the next fifty years, thousands of people came to him begging for his prayers and guidance. As well known as he was for his devotion to St. Joseph and his down-to-earth advice, Brother André was equally well known for his sense of humor. "You mustn't be sad," he said. "It is good to laugh a little."

Modern medicine agrees with Brother André. Research shows laughter strengthens the immune system and bolsters the body's ability to heal itself. It helps us to share a moment of grace with others. Even more than that, laughter refreshes our souls by allowing us to connect directly with God.

Laughter is one of the tools God uses to break down our walls of defensiveness and isolation. When we laugh, we strip away our conventions and preconceived notions. We allow ourselves to become more open and responsive to the gift of the moment. It is precisely in those moments when we shed our brittle shells that God dances into our lives, transforming and renewing our very beings.

What makes me feel the most joyful? When was the last time I laughed out loud?

TODAY I WILL FIND SOMETHING TO LAUGH ABOUT, EVEN IF IT IS JUST AT MY OWN FOIBLES.

ST. RAYMUND OF PEÑAFORT

1175–1275

Every day we are bombarded with advertisements extolling the virtues of youth. From TV to radio to newspapers and magazines, the advertising industry would have us believe that once we are over twenty-five, life is all downhill. We are told, in subtle and not so subtle ways, that we should do all we can to deny the aging process, for only the young live rewarding, fulfilling lives.

St. Raymund of Peñafort lived at a time when life expectancy hovered around the mid-thirties. When he became a Dominican at forty-seven, he undoubtedly figured his life was virtually over. Little did he know that at sixty he would become Archbishop of Tarragona and at sixty-three he would become the third Master General of the Dominican Order. When he retired at sixty-five, he still had thirty-four more years to live. He died when he was one hundred years old.

Although we can't count on living as long as St. Raymund, we can trust that we will live as many days as have been divinely given to us. As the Psalmist says, "In Your book they were all written, the days that were ordained for me when as yet there was not of them."

How do I feel when I spot a wrinkle or a gray hair? Does it bother me to tell people how old I am?

AGE IS ONLY A STATE OF MIND. I AM NOT GROWING OLDER.
I AM GROWING BETTER.

ST. THORFINN

A.D. 1285

The closest St. Thorfinn, a Norwegian bishop, came to fame occurred when he sided with the archbishop of Norway in a dispute against King Eric and was subsequently banished. He ended up at a Cistercian abbey in Flanders, where he died and was quickly forgotten.

More than fifty years later, when some construction work was being done, his tomb was opened and his remains were said to have given off a pleasant aroma. An elderly monk who had recalled Thorfinn's virtue had written a poem about him which was still hanging above the tomb. These events were taken by the Abbot as signs that Thorfinn should be remembered. And so he has been, for more than seven hundred years.

Most of us will live ordinary lives. We will take care of our families, do our jobs, and be ordinary law-abiding citizens. It doesn't seem like much, but in the heavenly scheme of things, it is more than enough.

God doesn't say we have to perform mighty deeds to get to heaven. We just have to do what we are called to do—no matter how insignificant that might seem. St. Thorfinn lived a very ordinary life, yet it was enough to ensure him a place in heaven. No matter how routine our lives may seem, it is precisely in the forge of the ordinary that the silver of eternal life is fashioned.

What part of my life is the most routine? If I think of my life as normal, rather than ordinary, how does that change my feelings?

TODAY I THANK GOD FOR ALL THE ORDINARY IN MY LIFE.

ST. ADRIAN

A.D. 710

It takes a good deal of self-knowledge and self-confidence to turn down a prestigious position. When we consider the honor and glory, we are inclined to say yes too eagerly. If we then find ourselves in over our heads, we may begin to regret our decision.

St. Adrian didn't fall into that trap. Although Pope Vitalian wanted to make him archbishop of Canterbury, he declined, agreeing instead to be the assistant and adviser to the man he recommended—St. Theodore. In his turn, St. Theodore made Adrian the Abbot of Canterbury, where he instructed students from all over the British Isles in classical languages and virtue.

Although St. Adrian probably would have made a perfectly fine archbishop, he found his success as a teacher. He is said to have "illuminated" England by both his doctrine and his example. Had he chosen the more prestigious path as archbishop, how many lives would have been the poorer?

Knowing our own strengths as well as our weaknesses allows us to make choices that are best not only for our own spiritual growth, but also for the growth of those around us. We can never know for certain, but perhaps Theodore would never have become a saint if he hadn't been named archbishop. Perhaps Adrian himself would not have become a saint if he had been the archbishop.

If someone asks me to list my characteristics, am I more inclined to look at my weaknesses instead of my abilities?

TODAY I SEEK THE WISDOM TO KNOW MYSELF, MY STRENGTHS AS WELL AS MY WEAKNESSES.

ST. PETER ORSEOLO

928–987

Ever wonder what it would be like to run away from home? St. Peter Orseolo did more than wonder. On the night of September 1, 978, Orseolo, who was the doge of Venice, left his wife of thirty-two years and his only son to enter a Benedictine abbey on the border of France and Spain. For a long time his family had no idea where he was.

Running away from home didn't make Peter Orseolo a saint—his life of asceticism and prayer did that—but his desire to escape is something with which many of us can identify. Sometimes the pressure of work and family become so overwhelming we feel like our spirits are being crushed. That's the time to make a retreat.

A retreat is a time set apart from the ordinary routine to reflect, pray, and contemplate. Even if we don't have time for an extended retreat, we all have time for a mini-retreat.

Set aside a block of time—a couple of hours will do. Find a quiet spot where you can be alone. Bring along a few soul-nourishing objects, like a candle, a flower, or a favorite book. Shut the door and leave the cares of the day on the other side. This isn't a time to "do." It's a time to "be." Thank God for the blessings in your life and then rest in the silence.

How do I feel when I take time for myself? If I could run away, where would I go?

I WILL TAKE TIME TODAY TO NOURISH MY SOUL WITH BEAUTY AND SILENCE.

ST. THEODOSIUS THE CENOBIARCH

423–529

Robert Burns wrote: "The best laid schemes o' mice and men/Gang aft a-gley." It was as true in the time of St. Theodosius as it is today.

In the sixth century, the emperor Anastasius held heretical views about the nature of Christ. After trying unsuccessfully to bring Theodosius over to his side, the emperor hit on the scheme of sending Theodosius a large sum of money, ostensibly out of charity but in reality as a bribe. The emperor felt that the money would succeed where other persuasions had failed. Unhappily for Anastasius, Theodosius distributed the money to the poor while maintaining his firm stand against the heresy.

Sometimes we act more than a little like the emperor. We want something so badly that we devise what seems like a foolproof plan to get our own way. Then, when our schemes "Gang aft a-gley", we wonder why. The problem is motive. Anastasius's motive in giving a charitable contribution was not to help the poor; it was to win over Theodosius. The emperor was pretending to do a good deed, when, in fact, he was being dishonest.

When our motives are dishonest, we can end up like Anastasius—frustrated on all counts. We are more than our actions. We are also our hearts. Since God looks at our motives as well as our actions, it is only when we act honestly, without manipulation or deception, that our plans and actions can be blessed.

Do I ever try to manipulate others into behaving the way I want them to? Do I ever deceive myself about my motives?

THE NEXT TIME I WANT SOMEONE TO DO SOMETHING FOR ME, I WILL EXAMINE MY MOTIVES.

ST. MARGUERITE BOURGEOYS

1620–1700

There is something very therapeutic about cleaning. As you scrub away the soap scum that collects on the shower, you can almost feel some of the mental scum that collects on your soul being scrubbed away as well.

For St. Marguerite Bourgeoys, founder of the first non-cloistered teaching sisterhood in Canada, cleaning and keeping house were always essential parts of her life. After her mother died in childbirth, she took over the family's household duties. Later she not only served as a housekeeper herself, she also taught the young girls who were sent from France to be brides for the French-Canadian settlers how to keep their own houses. Even after her girls' school was established, she continued to instruct future brides.

Cleaning our external dwelling places provides a valuable lesson in cleaning our spiritual homes as well. How often we let cobwebs of doubt and fear clutter the corners of our hearts. How frequently we let guilt and regret accumulate in the closets of our mind. Just as it is necessary to give our houses a spring cleaning, it's necessary to periodically cleanse our souls.

St. Marguerite Bourgeoys could have delegated responsibility for teaching young women housekeeping skills, but she realized that cleaning teaches as important a lesson for the heart as it does for the hands.

What areas of my spiritual or emotional life need cleaning? What mental junk drawer can I begin to straighten?

¶ MAKE MENTAL AND SPIRITUAL CLEANING A REGULAR PART OF MY LIFE.

ST. HILARY OF POITIERS

315?–368

St. Hilary of Poitiers was strongly opposed to a group of Christians who denied the divinity of Christ but who enjoyed great political favor. A brilliant theologian, he resisted the conventions of his time to support his beliefs. When the emperor Constantius ordered all bishops to sign a condemnation of St. Athanasius, the great defender of the faith, Hilary refused. He was banished to Phrygia, but continued to defend his position with such vigor that he was finally allowed to return to France.

St. Hilary never ceased to speak out for his beliefs, even though it caused him to be exiled and even exiled from his exile. When we speak up for what we believe, we run the risk of becoming unpopular. We run the risk of offending important and influential people who have, in effect, the power to banish us.

Yet to keep silent is to live a lie. We are called by God to be witnesses to the truth. When we fail to defend our faith, we are, in fact, denying it. If we are asked, like St. Hilary, to support something we don't believe, our refusal need not be unruly. We can politely and civilly state our point of view. But it is both our right and our duty to dissent when we are being forced into a position that makes us spiritually uncomfortable.

How do I react when I am asked to support something I don't believe? Am I willing to stand up for my beliefs, even when they are unpopular?

TODAY I WILL SPEAK ONLY THE TRUTH.

ST. SAVA

1174–1237

If St. Sava, the patron saint of Serbia, were to write out his résumé, it might look something like this:

Established numerous monasteries, including one at Khilandari.

Restored religious vigor to people of Serbia.

Translated books into Serbian language.

Crowned brother, Stephen II, as king.

Was named archbishop of the Serbs.

Not a bad list of accomplishments, but even more than his deeds, St. Sava is remembered for his gentleness. It is said that when he trained young monks, he erred more on the side of leniency than harshness, yet he was equally well known for his effectiveness.

When we try to correct our own bad habits, we can become harsh taskmasters, browbeating and berating ourselves for our failings. For instance, a single missed day of exercise can become a capital offense. How could I be so lazy? we moan and complain about having no self-discipline.

The next time you set out on a self-improvement program, follow the example of St. Sava and his monks. Be gentle with yourself. Instead of criticizing every failure, congratulate every success. Instead of being harsh and demanding, be lenient and forgiving. Instead of hating your inadequacy, love yourself into improvement.

What area of my life would I most like to change? When am I the harshest on myself?

I WILL FORGIVE MYSELF FOR THE TIMES I HAVE BEEN TOO HARSH ON MYSELF.

ST. ITA

A.D. 570

Who was your favorite teacher? Perhaps it was your first-grade teacher who taught you to read and instilled a love of books. Or your grandmother who taught you how to bake a pie or sew a straight seam. Or a mentor who taught you how to survive the rigors of your first job.

Anyone lucky enough to have been profoundly influenced by a teacher owes a debt of gratitude. Teachers do more than instruct; they change lives. They help us see the world in a new way. Most of all, they help us see ourselves and our potential in ways we might never have seen without them.

St. Ita lived in Ireland in the sixth century in what is now the county of Limerick. Among her other ventures, she founded a boys' school. There, for five years, she taught a young lad by the name of Brendan. He, in his turn, grew up to become famous in his own right as an abbot, missionary, and saint. In Brendan's biographies, St. Ita is cited as one of the primary influences of his early life.

One of the greatest gifts we can give those who have taught us is our thanks.

What makes a good teacher? Have I ever thanked the people who have taught me well?

I AM THANKFUL FOR ALL I AM LEARNING AND I AM GRATEFUL TO ALL THOSE WHO ARE TEACHING ME.

ST. HONORATUS

A.D. 429

St. Honoratus and his brother Venantius were from a noble Roman family that lived in the region now known as France. After their conversion to Christianity, they wanted to withdraw from the world, but their father constantly put obstacles in their way.

Isn't that often the way with us? When we feel it's time to concentrate on our spiritual growth and development, the path may suddenly be strewn with obstacles. We decide to get up early to spend time in reflection and prayer but then the alarm clock fails and we oversleep. We plan to donate an afternoon to a charitable cause, but the kids get sick and we have to stay home. We get ready to go to church only to have the car battery die.

If we chafe against the obstacles, which will inevitably come, we do ourselves a double disservice. First, we let the obstacles distract us from our good intentions. Second, by concentrating on the obstacles instead of building our relationship with God, we actually go backward instead of forward in our spiritual development.

St. Honoratus persisted in his desire for holiness. It took him awhile, but eventually he succeeded and even founded a monastery famous for the charity and devotion of its members. When we make a decision to reach for holiness, we are much better prepared to make the journey if we are aware from the onset that the road may be bumpy.

Do I look at obstacles as challenges or roadblocks? What is standing in the way of holiness for me today?

IF I CAN'T GO THROUGH THE OBSTACLES ON MY QUEST FOR HOLINESS, I WILL PRAY MY WAY AROUND THEM.

ST. ANTONY THE ABBOT

251–356

Imagine for a moment what it would be like to have the most famous person of your time write directly to you, asking for your advice and suggestions.

The fourth-century monks who lived under the rule of St. Antony the Abbot in the Egyptian desert were undoubtedly stunned when a letter bearing the mark of the Emperor arrived at their monastery. The letter from Constantine the Great and his sons asked the abbot Antony for his prayers. While the monks marveled, Antony told them: "Do not wonder that the Emperor writes to us, a man even as I am, rather be astonished that God should have written to us, and that He has spoken to us by His Son." Nonetheless, Antony was apparently a little surprised himself, since he said he didn't know how to respond and it was only after being nagged by his monks that he finally got around to answering.

Antony's discomfiture is understandable. When we are asked to do something for someone successful—even if they aren't an emperor—we often feel inadequate. Yet what was asked of Antony is something we can all give—our prayers. When we pray for someone else, we recognize our mutual dependence on God. As John Donne says, "no man is an island, entire of itself." We all have need of God. . . and of each other.

How do I feel when people ask me to pray for them? How do I feel when I ask someone to pray for me?

I AM GRATEFUL WHEN I AM GIVEN THE OPPORTUNITY TO PRAY FOR OTHERS.

PRISCA

FIRST CENTURY

St. Paul first met Prisca and her husband, Aquila, in the marketplace at Corinth where he went to find a job as a tentmaker. Soon, however, Paul learned that he shared more than professional skills with the couple. All three were members of the radical new religion called Christianity. Prisca and Aquila had been banished from Rome by an edict of Claudius which expelled all Jews from the city. Over the next several years, they traveled and preached with Paul, living for a while in Ephesus and eventually returning to Rome.

We don't know much more about Prisca, but we do know this: She was her own person. Although women living in the Roman empire of the first century enjoyed somewhat more freedom than they did in other cultures, it was still a male-dominated world. Paul himself fit comfortably into that world. Nonetheless, there was something about Prisca that so impressed Paul that he listed her name before her husband's when he wrote his letter to the Romans.

One of the hallmarks of maturity is that we know who we are. We don't have to prove anything to anybody. We can be ourselves.

Prisca could have faded into the shadow of her husband, but she was confident enough in her own self-worth and value that she was able to establish an independent identity. If we hope to become fully mature, we need to do the same thing.

Do I run myself down? Do I let other people run me down?

I KNOW I AM A VALUABLE PERSON.

ST. WULFSTAN

A.D. 1095

What is the purpose of prayer? All too often we think it's to change God's mind, when in fact, the real purpose of prayer is to change us.

Not too many years ago, it was the custom for men to tip their hats when they went past a church. St. Wulfstan, who was the bishop of Worcester in the eleventh century, went one step further—it is said that he never passed a church without stopping to pray at the altar.

Today, it wouldn't be possible to enter and pray in every church we pass, but what would happen if, for just one day, we said a quick prayer every time we saw a church, a temple, or a synagogue? Even if the prayer were as simple as "God, watch over those who worship you here," it would change us, for it would remind us that no matter what differences we might have over doctrine or dogma, the one thing we have in common is God.

God is the creator of all. Black or white, rich or poor, male or female, we are children of the same God. When we accept our common kinship, we see a brother or sister in every person we meet. When we view all of humanity as our family, then we can truly begin to see God as our parent.

Whom do I consider my brothers and sisters?

TODAY I WILL SAY A SHORT PRAYER EVERY TIME I SEE A PLACE OF WORSHIP.

ST. FABIAN

A.D. 250

Have you ever been touched by God? There you are, going along, living your ordinary life, when all of a sudden God calls you and nothing is ever quite the same again.

St. Fabian was a Roman farmer who just happened to come to town at the time a new pope was being elected. According to the stories, a dove suddenly appeared and settled on his head, convincing everyone that Fabian should be the new pope. He was duly elected and served for about fifteen years before being martyred during the persecution of the emperor Decius.

One can't help but wonder what Fabian told his family. "You'll never guess what happened to me! I was just minding my own business when a bird sat on my head, and now I'm pope!" While such spectacular (and unusual) events are unlikely to happen to any of us, God does touch each of us every day. The touch is often as subtle as a warm feeling that suddenly washes over us or an unexpected surge of joy in our soul.

How do we recognize the touch of God? When we feel especially alive, especially connected with all living creatures, we can be sure that God is drawing us nearer.

When was the last time I felt God's touch? What was I doing at the time?

I WILL LOOK FOR GOD'S LOVING TOUCH IN MY LIFE TODAY.

ST. AGNES

A.D. 304

If you had to speak publicly about your convictions, would you know what to say? Would you be able to discuss your spiritual beliefs without embarrassment? Apparently, St. Agnes, a young Roman girl of the third century, could.

While virtually all of the details of her life are shrouded in legend, we do know that she was very young—not more than twelve or thirteen—when she was arrested and executed for the crime of being Christian.

In our day and age, virtually every imaginable topic (and a few unimaginable ones) are freely discussed on afternoon TV talk shows. We learn the most intimate details of strangers' private lives, yet we are often reluctant to discuss the mysteries of life and death with even our closest friends and family members. Sadly, they often are similarly reluctant to discuss those topics with us.

While we don't have to become so single-minded about our spirituality that people avoid us at parties, neither should we be ashamed to let people know what we believe. Instead, we should strive to integrate our spiritual and physical lives in such a way that the people around us feel comfortable talking to us about our beliefs. By being open, neither forcing our convictions on someone else nor withholding them, we not only live honestly, we also give others the courage to live honestly.

How does my spiritual life affect my relationships? What can I do to fully integrate my spiritual and my physical lives?

I AM WILLING TO TALK ABOUT MY SPIRITUAL BELIEFS WHEN SOMEONE ASKS ME ABOUT THEM.

ST. VINCENT

A.D. 304

During times of crisis, many people bear up remarkably well. They remain clear-headed and rational, only to fall apart when the crisis is over.

According to the accounts we have of his martyrdom, St. Vincent, a deacon who lived in Valencia, Spain, bore up very well indeed under the tortures devised by the governor Dacian. He survived beating, flaying, broiling, and stretching on the rack. When at last Dacian gave up and allowed Vincent's friends to place him on a soft bed, he died as soon as he was laid on it.

Sometimes we get so geared up for adversity, we don't know what to do with blessing. It's almost as if we don't know how to react when God's favor rests on us. One reason we may struggle more with blessing than with tribulation is our own sense of unworthiness. When we come face to face with divine goodness, we see our own flaws and failures. We recognize that we have done nothing to earn God's love and we feel undeserving.

God reassures us that we don't have to earn love. It is ours from the beginning of time. "In this is love, not that we loved God, but that He loved us. . . " writes St. John. When St. Vincent endured torture without complaint, he demonstrated love for God. When he was finally permitted to die in comfort, God demonstrated love for Vincent.

How does knowing I am loved by God change the way I think about myself?

TODAY I WILL REMEMBER HOW MUCH GOD LOVES ME.

ST. JOHN THE ALMSGIVER

A.D. 619?

"Let not the sun set on your anger," writes St. Paul in his letter to the Ephesians. It's good advice, but difficult to follow. When we are feeling very angry, we usually are also feeling very self-righteous. We're convinced that our position is absolutely right, and the last thing we want to do is back down.

As patriarch of Alexandria, St. John the Almsgiver was a tireless champion of the poor and oppressed. When the governor proposed a new tax, St. John spoke on behalf of the poor. The governor, undoubtedly feeling threatened and insulted, stormed out in a huff. That night, St. John sent him a message, reminding him, "the sun is going to set." The governor, much to his credit, got the hint and apologized.

How much easier it would have been if the governor had controlled his temper in the first place. How much easier our lives would be if we controlled our tempers. When we speak out in anger, we often say things we later regret. Once a word leaves our lips, however, we can't suck it back, no matter how much we try.

The next time you're feeling angry, instead of counting to ten and then exploding, try mentally apologizing ten times. You may find that it's much easier not to blow up than to have to say you're sorry afterward.

What is my first reaction when I get angry? Do I ever substitute anger for other emotions, such as embarrassment or fear?

TODAY I WILL TRY TO LIVE IN HARMONY WITH ALL I MEET.

ST. FRANCIS DE SALES

1567–1622

Recently a study revealed that, contrary to common belief, many rich folk are indeed happy. "Money *can* buy happiness," taunted the headlines.

Well, yes and no. The study didn't claim that wealth was the key to happiness. It merely said that being rich wasn't a barrier to happiness.

St. Francis de Sales observed the same truth more than five hundred years ago. "There is a difference between having poison and being poisoned," he wrote in his famous spiritual classic, *Introduction to the Devout Life.* St. Francis pointed out that pharmacists keep all kinds of poisonous drugs on hand, but they aren't poisoned themselves because the drugs are in their shops, not their bodies. In the same way, as long as wealth is in our purses and our homes and not in our hearts, it cannot corrupt us.

Easier said than done. One of the dangers of possessions is how quickly and easily they can possess us. We've all heard of people who save every Christmas and birthday gift because "they're just too nice to use." The gifts languish in drawers and closets until one day they end up in an estate sale or given to charity.

The things of this life are here for us to appreciate, not to grasp so tightly our fingers turn numb. It is only when we use our possessions for our good and that of others will they contribute to rather than detract from our happiness.

What are you saving that you could be enjoying? Why are you saving it?

TODAY I WILL ENJOY ONE THING I'VE BEEN SAVING FOR A SPECIAL OCCASION.

ST. PAUL

FIRST CENTURY

Nothing matches the zeal of a new convert, be it someone who has just quit smoking, someone who has discovered the benefits of exercise, or someone who has had a religious conversion. Most of the time, however, zeal wears off. The first rush of enthusiasm is replaced by a mundane acceptance.

When we encounter someone who manages to keep the zest alive, we are automatically attracted. Their enthusiasm and excitement is contagious and sometimes, if we are lucky, their joie de vivre rekindles our own.

Saul, the name St. Paul had before he became a Christian, was always zealous. He was so determined to persecute fellow Jews who converted to the new religion that he asked the high priest for permission to arrest all the Jewish converts at Damascus and bring them to Jerusalem.

It was on the road to Damascus that Saul had one of the greatest conversions of all time. Struck to the ground, he heard a voice asking, "Saul, Saul, why do you persecute me?" The speaker then identified himself as Jesus of Nazareth. Saul, soon-to-be Paul, had a complete change of heart. From that time on, the zeal he showed in persecuting converts paled in comparison to his zeal in making converts. What's the most impressive is that his zeal never died. Up to the time of his death, he passionately preached his convictions. In fact, his zeal bridges nearly two thousand years and his letters continue to inspire and convert millions even today.

In what areas of my life do I need to have a conversion experience?

TODAY I WILL TURN FROM THOSE THINGS THAT KEEP ME
FROM CELEBRATING LIFE, AND I WILL REJOICE
IN ALL MY BLESSINGS.

ST. TIMOTHY

FIRST CENTURY

One of the first things parents do when they see their newborn is try to figure out who the baby resembles. As exciting as it is to discover the baby has grandpa's eyes or his dad's dimples, physical characteristics are literally only skin deep. The important characteristics—those that shape personality—take time to develop. Will the child be trustworthy? Will the child be patient? Most important, will the child have faith in God?

St. Timothy's mother, Eunice, and his grandmother, Lois, were women of great faith. Undoubtedly they were delighted when, even as a lad, Timothy took an interest in the Scriptures. Later, when he became one of St. Paul's disciples and closest friends, they must have felt a sense of pride that their own deep faith had been passed on.

Recently the idea that virtue can be taught has made a comeback. However, such virtues as honesty, goodness, and courage cannot merely be taught; they must also be lived.

The old writing adage "show, don't tell" applies to life as well. We can tell our children about virtues, but for them to become a reality in their lives, they must first become a reality in ours.

What legacy are we leaving our families? What values are we passing on to our children?

¶ CHOOSE ONE VIRTUE TO MAKE A REALITY IN MY LIFE.

ST. ANGELA MERICI

1470–1540

St. Angela Merici founded the first teaching order of women in the Church—the Ursulines. By rights, one would think her order would have been named after her. But Angela placed the young women who joined with her under the spiritual patronage of St. Ursula. Hence Angela's order bears the name of her patron saint.

A patron is a benefactor or protector. A patron saint is a *heavenly* benefactor or protector. There are patron saints for virtually every occupation, profession, country, and medical or social condition from abdominal pains (Erasmus) to Zaire (Mary, The Immaculate Conception). Often during baptism or confirmation an individual is given the name of someone who is to be their personal patron saint. Others choose their own patron saints at some significant point in their lives. Each of the saints in this book can serve as a personal friend and individual patron saint.

Patron saints can be wise and trusted guides on our spiritual journey. Although they aren't magic workers, they are always ready to respond when we ask for their assistance. We must, however, be willing to listen and watch carefully for their answer. It might not always come in the time and the place we expect, but if what we have asked is in the will of God, we can be confident that our patron saints will work tirelessly on our behalf. Through their friendship, we can grow in faith. Through the example of their lives, we can grow in love.

Do I have a patron saint? If not, who would I like to choose as my patron?

I PLACE MYSELF UNDER THE PROTECTION OF MY PATRON
SAINT, CONFIDENT THAT HE OR SHE WILL
GUIDE AND GUARD ME.

ST. THOMAS AQUINAS

1225–1274

When the Dominicans list their most famous members, St. Thomas Aquinas is almost always near the top. Called "the dumb Silician ox" by his classmates, St. Thomas went on to write the *Summa Theologica,* one of the greatest of all theological works.

But if his mother had had her way, Thomas would have been a Benedictine instead of a Dominican. Thomas spent most of his youth in the Benedictine abbey of Monte Cassino. It was not until he studied at the University of Naples that he became involved with the Order of Preachers and eventually joined their company.

Theodora, who had had visions of her son becoming the abbot of Monte Cassino, was outraged. She tried many tactics, including having his brothers kidnap him and keep him under house arrest for two years, to try to dissuade him from remaining with the Dominicans. In the end, however, Thomas's resolution won out.

Often we think of resolution as the goals we set on New Year's Day and abandon on January 2. On the contrary, the virtue of resolution lies more in gritty determination than mental pledge. It is stick-to-itiveness, backbone, tenacity. Without resolution, we cannot turn dreams into reality. With it, literally anything we set our minds to is possible. St. Thomas is usually remembered for his profound writings, but without his firm resolution, none of his great works would ever have been possible.

How do I react when family or friends try to dissuade me from doing something I believe is essential to my spiritual growth?

BY EXERCISING THE VIRTUE OF RESOLUTION, I CAN ACCOMPLISH THE GOALS I SET FOR MYSELF.

ST. GILDAS THE WISE

?500–570

Being wise isn't the same thing as being smart. A person can be very intelligent and still be unwise. Wisdom is more than IQ or education. It's the ability to make sound judgments; to know what's best to do in any given situation.

We don't know much about St. Gildas. He apparently wrote a famous work called *De excidio Britanniae* about problems that existed in Britain, and he seems to have spent the last years of his life near Brittany. We do know, however, that through the years the sobriquet 'wise' has been attached to his name. Perhaps St. Gildas was like the apocryphal old man who sits on the top of the mountain dispensing words of wisdom. Perhaps he was just a man of uncommon common sense. At any rate, St. Gildas has come down to us as an example of a *wise* man.

God told the great King Solomon, ask what you wish me to give you. Instead of riches or honor, Solomon asked for wisdom. God was delighted and granted Solomon his request. God is equally delighted when we ask for wisdom, for in doing so, we are asking for the ability to see our lives through God's eyes. We are asking to be able to make decisions that are in harmony with God's will. We are, in essence, asking to become holy. Since God desires our holiness more than anything else, God will never turn down our request for wisdom.

When I have an important decision to make, what do I do? Who is the wisest person I know?

⋅⦅⟨▬▬▬▬▬▬▬▬▬▬▬▬▬▬▬▬▬▬▬▬▬▬▬⟩⦆⋅

I BELIEVE THAT WHEN I ASK GOD FOR WISDOM, IT WILL BE GRANTED TO ME.

ST. HYACINTHA MARISCOTTI

1585–1640

When we're forced to do something we don't want to do, we have two choices. We can either resist with all our might, making ourselves and everyone around us miserable, or we can gracefully accede and make the best of an unpleasant situation.

St. Hyacintha Mariscotti did the former. When her youngest sister married before she did, she became so insufferable her family shipped her off to a Franciscan convent. There she caused enormous grief by living as luxurious a life as she possibly could for at least ten years. It wasn't until she became seriously ill that she finally changed her ways, becoming a model of charity and self-discipline.

St. Hyacintha shows that it's never too late to change. After a decade, most of the sisters in her convent probably figured she was a lost cause. Imagine their surprise when the changes she made were real and long-lasting.

Change is never easy, because it requires intense self-examination. When we look deeply into our souls, we often discover things we don't like: selfishness, pride, arrogance. We are forced to see a side of our nature we would rather pretend didn't exist.

Recognizing our dark side is the necessary first step to change. Once we have done that, then, like St. Hyacintha, we are ready to begin the process of replacing the darkness with the light of truth, hope, and love.

Am I afraid of change? What do I think would happen if I made sweeping changes in my life? What do I think would happen if I did not?

I LOOK AT MYSELF HONESTLY AND WITHOUT GUILE.

ST. JOHN BOSCO

1815–1888

We are all familiar with dreams that occur during periods of deep, restful sleep. There is also another kind of dream: prophetic dreams. Unlike the dreams experienced during sleep, prophetic dreams come from God, outlining the future and showing us our hopes, aspirations, and goals.

St. John Bosco was a prophetic dreamer. At the age of nine he had a vision of Mary showing him his vocation as a priestly leader of poor boys. Throughout the rest of his life, he was guided by his dreams. In fact, later in life he sometimes discerned the state of the souls of the boys at his schools through dreams. Often he dreamed of new projects and missionary work, and even though he seldom had the funds, he began the work, trusting that God would provide.

God always did provide. At the end of his life, Father Bosco, or Don Bosco as he was called, had founded the Salesians, now one of the largest religious orders in the world.

Although our dreams may never be as prophetic as Don Bosco's, all dreams come with a message. When we pay attention to our dreams, we gain insight into our deepest desires and aspirations. Our dreams can help us figure out who we are and what we want. They enable us to wake up to our potential and help us determine our direction in life. All we have to do is pay attention.

Do I remember my dreams? Have I ever had a dream which
seemed to be particularly prophetic? What did
I do about that dream?

I WILL PAY ATTENTION TO MY DREAMS.

ST. BRIGID OF IRELAND

C. A.D. 452–524

St. Brigid of Ireland was born in the middle of the fifth century, somewhere near Dundalk. The daughter of a minor Irish king and a slave mother, she devoted her entire life to God, eventually founding a famous religious community at Killdara. While many legends have grown up around Brigid, one thing is certain: she lived out a life of service while knowing she was born to a higher estate.

Each of us lives with a similar dichotomy. We are creatures of this earth, rooted in its rhythms and struggles. At the same time, we were created for heaven and its glories beyond imagination. Our bodies are subject to the frailties of this existence, but our souls are destined for eternal life.

It is only when we remember that we are created both with a mortal body and an immortal soul that we can live fully and creatively. We forget one at the expense of the other. If, for instance, we concentrate too much on the needs of our bodies, we neglect the needs of our souls. Conversely, if we focus entirely on the soul, we may lose sight of the requirements of the body. What is needed is balance. Through the example of St. Brigid, we can learn to take care of the ordinary tasks of life while always remembering we are destined for greater things.

How much time do I spend taking care of my bodily needs? How much time do I spend on my spiritual needs? How can I achieve a better balance?

TODAY I WILL TAKE TIME TO NOURISH BOTH MY BODY AND MY SOUL.

ST. JEANNE DE LESTONNAC

A.D. 1640

Whoever wrote "Sticks and stones may break my bones, but words can never hurt me" never was on the receiving end of a lie. The damage inflicted by malicious words can be every bit as painful and as long-lasting as any physical wound.

After being widowed and raising her four children, St. Jeanne de Lestonnac tried various forms of religious life, eventually founding her own religious community. All was well until one of her nuns, Blanche Hervé, began a vicious conspiracy that resulted in her election as superior and St. Jeanne's disposition. Blanche then cruelly mistreated her former superior. St. Jeanne bore her trials with great patience until Blanche finally repented. By then, however, St. Jeanne no longer desired to be restored as superior and lived her remaining years in retirement.

Trying to combat a nasty lie is like fighting a will-o-the-wisp. The louder we protest, the more people are likely to believe the falsehood.

When we are the victim of a lie, it helps to remember that actions speak louder than words. Rather than verbally trying to convince others of our innocence, we, like St. Jeanne, would do better to demonstrate our integrity by living with dignity, honesty, and grace. While we can't be guaranteed that our tormentors will repent as did Blanche Hervé, we can be assured that we will not have stooped to their level by dignifying their defamation with our protestations.

Have I ever told a lie? In what ways can I repent for those times when I have failed to tell the entire truth?

IF I CAN'T SAY SOMETHING GOOD ABOUT SOMEONE, I WILL NOT SAY ANYTHING AT ALL.

ST. BLASE

C. A.D. 316

St. Blase is best known as the patron saint of those who have throat complaints. He gained this honor because he is said to have cured a boy who was brought to him with a fish bone stuck in his throat. On this day in many Catholic churches, the practice remains of blessing throats with candles in honor of St. Blase.

Even if the story about St. Blase and the fish bone is apocryphal, the realization that saints are concerned with such mundane aspects of our lives as sore throats is comforting. But it shouldn't be surprising. The love and concern of the saints is a reflection of God's own love and concern. God is so intimately connected with every aspect of our lives that even a sore throat is worthy of divine attention.

When we realize that our entire lives are wrapped in love, we experience tremendous freedom. We begin to understand that even what looks like a calamity can actually be a lesson that will draw us closer to the truth. Such realization doesn't happen overnight, but as we grow, we will feel the presence of love in every aspect of our lives—sometimes even in our sore throats.

How do I react when bad things happen to me? Can I change the way I think so as to find good in all things?

I LOOK FOR LOVE IN ALL AREAS OF MY LIFE.

ST. JOHN DE BRITTO

1647–1693

A company manager once hired an efficiency expert to analyze the office layout. The expert arrived and proceeded to change everything. Desks were moved; work stations altered. Even the contents of desk drawers were shifted. When the expert was done, the office was totally reorganized.

The changes lasted about a week. Then the employees put things back the way they had been originally. The expert had failed to take into account such factors as which employees were left-handed, who smoked and who did not, and who insisted on sitting next to the window. The rearranged office, while terrific-looking on paper, didn't work in real life.

Unlike the modern efficiency expert, St. John de Britto, a seventeenth-century Jesuit missionary, understood that "experts" who come in to change things never stand a chance. Soon after he arrived in southern India, he realized that in order to teach the people, he had to become part of their lives. So he adopted the dress, diet, and, insomuch as possible, the lifestyle of the residents of the region.

While few of us are called to be missionaries, we are all called to be witnesses to the truth. When, however, we think of ourselves— even secretly—as having some special claim on the whole truth, we are bound to be met with disdain and ridicule. It is only when we, like St. John de Britto, are willing to be humble enough to recognize that we are all pilgrims on the same journey that our lives will have long-lasting effects.

What can I do today to show my love to my friends and neighbors?

TODAY I WILL "BLOOM WHERE I AM PLANTED."

ST. AGATHA

C. A.D. 251?

The life of St. Agatha is shrouded in mystery and legend. Like many other virgin martyrs, she is said to have maintained her chastity despite numerous tortures. In the end, she died while giving thanks for the "patience to suffer."

The idea of being thankful for suffering is rather foreign to most of us. We look for ways to end pain, rather than ways to embrace it. Even a simple headache can send us hurrying to the medicine cabinet for a speedy cure.

Ironically, most of our growth and maturation takes place in the midst of our suffering. When we are going through trials, it's hard to see their value. Afterward, we may realize that through our difficulties, we have become stronger and more resilient. It is as if suffering were the flame that tempers the steel of our souls.

That is not to say we need to go out of our way to seek suffering. Each one of us has our fair share of struggle without looking for more. Rather than chafe and resist the pain that will inevitably enter our lives, we can let our suffering make us more empathetic, caring, and understanding. By seeing suffering as part of the way we learn the essential lessons of life, we can, like St. Agatha, let it redeem rather than destroy us.

What has been the greatest difficulty of my life? Has my struggle made me stronger?

I LOOK ON THE SUFFERING IN MY LIFE AS AN OPPORTUNITY TO GROW IN FAITH AND TRUST.

ST. PAUL MIKI AND COMPANIONS

A.D. 1597

One of the great mysteries of creation is the intimate interconnectedness of all life. The relatively new discipline called chaos theory suggests that the flapping of a butterfly wing on one part of the globe can effect massive weather changes in another part.

We don't need chaos-theory scientists to tell us how much our actions can affect others. A careless word. A neglected birthday. A forgotten anniversary. They seem like such minor, unimportant things, but in creating deep rifts and heartache, their effect may last a lifetime. In the same way, the good we do—even when it seems to be quickly forgotten—can create eternal ripples of holiness.

St. Paul Miki was one of twenty-six Christians crucified on a hill overlooking Nagasaki on a cold February morning. Miki, a Japanese native who had been educated by the Jesuits, spoke out before his execution, asking that his blood fall on his fellows "as a fruitful rain."

His last prayer might seem to have gone unanswered, for when missionaries were allowed to return to Japan in the 1860s, all traces of Christianity had disappeared. Yet, once the missionaries were reestablished, they were amazed to discover thousands of Christians around Nagasaki. The influence and witness of St. Paul Miki and the martyrs of Japan had spanned more than two hundred years, preserving not only their own memory, but also the Christian faith.

How have I been influenced by my parents and grandparents? In what ways am I leaving a legacy for those who will follow me?

TODAY I THANK ALL WHO HAVE HELPED ME GROW IN MY SPIRITUAL UNDERSTANDING.

ST. THEODORE OF HERACLEA

C. A.D. 319?

When two people meet, one of the first questions invariably is, What do you do for living? Consider for a moment what your reaction if the response is neurosurgeon or film producer. Now consider what your response would be if the reply were gravedigger or janitor. Although we may like to pretend a person's occupation doesn't influence us, all too often we form judgments about others' education, social status, income—even religious conviction—based solely on their profession.

Making such superficial judgments isn't something new. In the early days of Christianity, being a member of the army wasn't necessarily a positive. Being a general was considered even less of a positive. Yet all we know for sure about St. Theodore of Heraclea was that he was a general in the Greek army. When he was beheaded for his faith by the emperor Licinius, probably more than a few people were surprised to learn that a military official could also be a Christian of deep conviction. St. Theodore's witness shows that no honest occupation is a barrier to holiness. If we perform our tasks with care and diligence—no matter what they are—we will discover God is working alongside us. After all, although our profession is important to us, God cares less about what we do than what we are. In the eternal scheme of things, God looks at our hearts, not our résumés.

What do I like best about my job? How can I use my job as a path to spiritual maturity?

·〘〙·

I REALIZE MY JOB IS AN ESSENTIAL PART OF MY SPIRITUAL GROWTH.

ST. JEROME EMILIANI

1481–1537

Have you ever tried to solve an intricate puzzle? If you have, then you know how frustrating it is to reach what appears to be a dead end. You know there has to be a way out, but you can't find it.

Sometimes real life is like one of those puzzles. We feel trapped and frustrated by our inability to get beyond the circumstances of the moment. Ironically, as long as we concentrate on the obvious, that's all we'll see. It's only when we allow our minds to consider other options—no matter how improbable—that we are able to see the way out.

St. Jerome Emiliani, a soldier for the city-state of Venice, probably thought his life was fairly well set until he was captured in a minor battle and tossed in a dungeon. All of a sudden, he was literally stuck. To his credit, he used his imprisonment to consider his options and reevaluate his life. Once free, he left the military to enter the priesthood and devote himself to the care of the sick and orphaned. The one-time careless and irreligious soldier became a model of sanctity.

St. Jerome realized that what sometimes seems to be a dead end is actually a doorway in disguise. In order to discover the door, however, we have to be willing to open our eyes to its existence.

What do I do when I feel like I'm at a dead-end?

I OPEN MY EYES TO NEW POSSIBILITIES IN EVERY LIFE SITUATION.

ST. ANSBERT

C. A.D. 695

A famous motivational speaker once asked how many people in the audience were doing exactly what they wanted to do. Only a few raised their hands. Then she asked the rest what was stopping them from fulfilling their dreams. For most, the answer was some kind of fear—fear of failure, fear of financial ruin, fear of ridicule. All too often, fear is like a deep freeze, preserving us in the status quo but preventing us from growing and changing.

St. Ansbert was chancellor to King Clotaire III of France. As a member of the court, he enjoyed the privileges of his rank. Ansbert, however, was drawn to the life of a monk. Leaving court life, he entered the monastery at Fontenelle.

We can't know for certain what Ansbert felt when he excused himself from the highest society of his time, but we can guess he must have felt a tinge or two of fear. After all, he was taking a big risk. What if he hated monastic life? What if he wanted to come back to the court? What would people say?

St. Ansbert was willing to take the risk because he knew true happiness comes only when we follow the deepest longings of our heart. He must have understood that when we give up something for a greater good, we receive far more than we relinquish. In St. Ansbert's case, he was returned to a place of honor at court by becoming confessor to King Theodoric III and eventually bishop of Rouen. For Ansbert, life became a case of having your cake and eating it too.

What's keeping you from fulfilling your dreams? Are you afraid of failure or success?

I AM NOT AFRAID TO FOLLOW MY HEART, NO MATTER WHERE IT LEADS.

ST. SCHOLASTICA

480–542?

Sometimes our relatives frustrate us beyond belief. Other times, we wonder what we would ever do without them. While St. Scholastica and her twin brother, St. Benedict, shared much in common, including entering religious life, they didn't always agree. The last time they argued, it even took divine intercession to resolve the issue.

Scholastica's community of women was only about five miles from her brother's monastery, so the two would meet once a year at a nearby house to talk and pray together. At their final meeting, Scholastica, perhaps sensing that her life was ending, begged her brother to stay. He refused, saying that he couldn't break his own rule forbidding monks to spend the night outside the monastery. When Scholastica realized Benedict wasn't about to budge, she asked God to intercede. Immediately a fierce storm broke out and Benedict cried, "God forgive you sister. What have you done?" Scholastica replied, "I asked a favor of you and you refused it. I asked it for God, and He has granted it." Benedict was forced to remain, talking and praying with his sister. He returned to his monastery the next day, and three days later St. Scholastica died.

Sometimes we reach an impasse with family members. In those times, rather than continue to argue and butt heads, let us ask God to intercede with help and healing. As we wait for the answer, however, it might be a good idea to get out our umbrella!

When was the last time I told my family members how much I loved them?

I AM GRATEFUL FOR EACH PERSON IN MY FAMILY.

OUR LADY OF LOURDES

1858

On this day in 1858, the Virgin Mary appeared for the first time to fourteen-year-old Bernadette Soubirous. Eighteen times between February and July, the Virgin appeared to St. Bernadette, the last time telling her, "I am the Immaculate Conception." Today the shrine at Lourdes is one of the most visited Marian sites in the world.

When Bernadette told of her visions, she described a young woman dressed in white with a rosary draped over her arm. She also mentioned that the lady did not use the informal *tu* when she spoke, but the more polite and respectful *vous*. Since Bernadette was the daughter of poor peasants, the formal form of address was all the more impressive to her.

When we are around people whom we consider our equals, it's easy to be respectful. When we are dealing with those we consider inferior, it can be tempting to act just a wee bit supercilious. Anyone who has ever been a waiter knows what it feels like to be on the receiving end of such false superiority. Regardless of our status, we are called to treat every one we encounter with equal respect. We are to accord the street person begging for a handout the same courtesy we would the president.

Being respectful serves a dual purpose: first, it gives the other person their rightful due; second, it ensures that we constantly exercise the virtue of humility.

In what way do I let status and position influence my treatment of others? Do I give others the same respect I ask for myself?

I WILL TREAT EVERYONE I MEET TODAY THE WAY I WOULD LIKE TO BE TREATED MYSELF.

ST. MELETIUS

A.D. 381

There's an old saying, you attract more flies with honey than with vinegar. Although one wonders why a person would want to attract flies in the first place, it's true that honey makes a better lure than vinegar. Similarly, a gentle disposition makes more friends than does an abrasive one.

St. Meletius was born to a distinguished family of Lesser Armenia in the fourth century. Despite being deeply embroiled in controversy over doctrine, "his kindly disposition gained for him the esteem of both Catholics and Arians." St. Meletius apparently mastered the difficult art of disagreeing without being disagreeable.

It isn't easy to stand up for our convictions without knocking others over for theirs. When emotions run high, the real issue can become buried under a barrage of angry words. During such moments, one of the best things we can do is put our own feelings on hold and concentrate on what the other person is saying. In the midst of the argument, we need to look for some sliver of common ground. The simple words, "I see your point," often signal the beginning of a more rational discussion.

Not every disagreement ends in accord, of course. St. Meletius often had both Catholics and Arians mad at him, but as another old saying goes, you can't please all of the people all of the time. You can, however, always please yourself by being agreeable to your opponents.

How do I react when I get into an argument? Do I always have to be right?

I WILL HOLD MY TEMPER WHEN ALL THOSE AROUND ME ARE LOSING THEIRS.

ST. CATHERINE DEI RICCI

1522–1590

Modern medicine is now saying what saints and mystics have known for millennia—meditation is good for you. Regular meditation can lower blood pressure, bolster the immune system, lift depression, and generally improve mental and physical health.

For all its medical benefits, meditation is even more valuable for what it does spiritually: It opens a window in the soul to a higher state of awareness. That's why some form of meditation has long been used by those who have great spiritual insight. For Christian saints, the Passion and Death of Jesus often serves as a foundation for their contemplation. By entering into mystical union with Jesus, the saints are able literally to experience heaven on earth.

St. Catherine dei Ricci, the daughter of a well-known Florentine family, entered a Dominican convent at age thirteen. She meditated daily on Jesus's crucifixion and, at age twenty, began to experience ecstasies in which she not only saw, but actually enacted the events of the Passion. Her raptures, as they were called, created quite a stir, and many people flocked to the convent every Thursday and Friday to watch.

Fortunately, few of us attract crowds when we meditate. By its very nature meditation is supposed to be private and personal. It's a time away from the daily pressures; a time when we don't have to *do* anything. When we meditate, all that is required of us is to *be*. In a busy world with its ever-increasing demands, regular meditation can become not only a means to sanctity, but an oasis of sanity.

When was the last time I took time away from my daily activities to reflect on my life?

TODAY I WILL SPEND FIVE MINUTES, NOT DOING, BUT SIMPLY BEING.

ST. VALENTINE

C. A.D. 269

Only two saints—Valentine and Patrick—have their feast days listed on ordinary calendars. Ironically, we know almost nothing about the real St. Valentine except that he was a Roman priest who was martyred for his faith. Why a celibate priest should be associated with love and lovers since as far back as Chaucer's time is a good question. For whatever the reason, Valentine's name has become virtually synonymous with expressions of affection.

Although we may not understand why a priest is the patron of lovers, it's easy to know why we have a saint especially assigned to the virtue of love. Love is an essential ingredient for life. Experiments have demonstrated that infants who are provided with adequate food and warmth but denied human contact and affection will literally die. Even plants and animals respond positively to love. In fact, love might be said to be the life blood of all creation. Although the astronomer Carl Sagan calls us "star stuff," we are more than that: We are love.

One of the immutable laws of the universe is that the more we love, the more we will be loved. If we try to hoard our love, we will end up with nothing, for love cannot exist in the same space as possessiveness, dependency, or selfishness. The very essence of love demands that we give it away.

How does knowing that I was created both to love and be loved make me feel?

I KNOW I AM LOVED.

BLESSED JORDAN OF SAXONY

A.D. 1237

BLESSED DIANA D'ANDALO

C. 1201–1236

There's something wonderful about a real, honest-to-goodness letter. Opening the mailbox and seeing familiar handwriting amid the bills is sure to brighten even the gloomiest day. Unlike phone calls, letters are meant to be read and reread, savored and saved. In a disposable world, they are tangible reminders of the reality of friendship.

Jordan of Saxony, the second master general of the Dominican Order, and Diana D'Andalo, a nun at St. Agnes's convent at Bologna, were close friends for more than fifteen years. Although they seldom saw each other in person, they maintained a deep friendship through their letters. Given that they lived in a time when postal services were poor to non-existent, the extent of their correspondence is truly remarkable. Of the fifty-six letters written by Jordan that have survived the centuries, thirty-eight are written to Diana.

In his letters, Jordan talks about his successes and failures, as well as his aspirations and dreams for the Dominican Order. He consoles Diana when family members die and he exhorts her to works of charity and prayer. Although we don't have her responses, it's clear from Jordan's letters that she offered him the same encouragement and consolation.

Sometimes we think letters have to be flawless before we send them. We think so much about what we want to say and how we want to say it that we never get the letter written. Better to jot a short note that actually gets mailed rather than a massive tome that never gets composed.

Whom should I write to? What's stopping me from sending them a note?

TODAY I WILL WRITE THAT LETTER I HAVE BEEN PUTTING OFF FOR SO LONG.

ST. ONESIMUS

FIRST CENTURY

Lay a six-foot-long board on the ground and try to walk its length without losing your balance. You can probably reach the end without much stress or difficulty. Now imagine that same board is suspended eighty feet in the air. Suddenly it seems impossibly long and ridiculously narrow. The board hasn't changed, but your perception of it has. In the first instance it seems safe; in the second it appears risky. It's all in how you look at it.

St. Onesimus, a runaway slave, was sent back to his master, Philemon, with a letter from St. Paul asking that he be accepted "no longer as a slave, but as . . . a beloved brother." Apparently, Philemon did as Paul requested since tradition says Onesimus returned to Rome and eventually became a bishop.

Although Onesimus is celebrated on this day, perhaps Philemon should be honored as well, for he was able to change his perception of Onesimus from that of a worthless slave deserving death to the "beloved brother" of Paul's letter.

When we aren't willing to change our perceptions, how different— and difficult—our lives and the lives of those around us become. We find ourselves locked into old patterns of thought and behavior, even when they no longer serve a useful purpose. It's only when we are willing to look at things in a new way that we can uncover the options that always exist.

What prejudices do I cling to? What habits and behaviors do I keep, even when I know they are not in my best interest?

I LOOK AT ALL MY OPTIONS BEFORE MAKING LIFE-CHANGING DECISIONS.

SEVEN FOUNDERS OF THE
SERVITE ORDER

C. A.D. 1240

When Terry Anderson, the former Mideast Associated Press correspondent, was being held captive in Lebanon, one of his fellow hostages was Fr. Martin Jenco, a Servite priest. Through the long hours of imprisonment, Anderson and Fr. Jenco talked about faith and the meaning of life. Anderson credits Fr. Jenco with helping him renew his faith in a "kind and gentle God."

In fulfilling his role as priest, even in the most horrific of circumstances, Fr. Jenco followed the divine call to service first heard by the founders of his religious order more than seven hundred years earlier. In the mid-thirteenth century, seven Florentine noblemen banded together to lead a life of prayer and penance under the name Servants of Mary, or Servites.

While the Servites acknowledge their need to serve by their very name, we are all called to be servants. We are placed on earth, not to amass wealth and prestige, but to care for and minister to our fellow human beings. Although most of us wouldn't want to leave our homes and families to join a religious community as the founders of the Servites did, we can always find ways to serve others in our everyday lives. Even when it's as simple as thanking the clerk checking out our groceries or holding open the door for someone with a package, we can always find a way to serve.

Which is easier—to serve or be served? How do I feel when
I know someone wants to help me?

I HELP THOSE WITH WHOM I LIVE AND WORK.

BLESSED FRA ANGELICO

1400–1455

Fra Angelico, one of the most prolific and influential painters of the Italian Renaissance, entered the Dominican Order when he was about twenty. Although he was ordained a priest, he worked as a professional artist until his death. His work now graces many museums, and his frescoes of scenes from the lives of St. Stephen and St. Lawrence decorate the private Vatican chapel of Pope Nicholas V.

At Fra Angelico's beatification, Pope John Paul II quoted from an early biography, "His painting was the fruit of the great harmony between a holy life and the creative power with which he had been endowed."

What creative power have you been given? You may think that when creativity was being handed out, you were standing in another line, but every one of us is overflowing with creative energy. Just for fun, let your imagination wander. What do you like best? Maybe it's cooking (or eating!). Or gardening. Or skydiving. Don't be afraid to admit your passion. Every one of us has something that makes our hearts skip with the sheer joy of life. The key to becoming more creative is to recognize that passion and creativity are inseparably entwined. When we are involved in our passion, we can't help but be creative. If you don't feel creative, it's only because you haven't given yourself permission to explore your passion.

When do I feel the most alive? What brings me
the most joy in life?

I DO WHAT I LOVE, AND I LOVE WHAT I DO.

ST. BARBATUS

A.D. 682

Are you reluctant to walk under a ladder? Do you panic if a black cat crosses your path? Are you afraid to break a mirror for fear of seven years of bad luck?

Superstitions are a part of most cultures. The idea that future events can be controlled (or not controlled) by present actions is very appealing. It can be comforting, for instance, to believe that throwing salt over your right shoulder will avert bad luck. It can also be distressing to think that a simple accident, such as breaking a mirror, can alter the course of the next several years.

Superstitions aren't limited, however, to feelings about black cats and ladders. Sometimes even faith itself can become muddled with superstition.

St. Barbatus lived in Italy during the end of the reign of Pope Gregory the Great. When he came to work in Benevento, he was distressed to learn the people of that city venerated a golden viper. It was only through his earnest prayer and preaching that the populace agreed to melt the golden serpent into a chalice for the altar.

While there's nothing wrong with using religious objects to enhance our faith, the danger lies in losing focus. If we begin to think an object itself has some kind of inherent ability to act on our behalf, we tread dangerously close to idolatry. The only way to keep our faith from sliding into superstition is to remember that spiritual blessings come not from created matter but from the Creator of all matter.

Do I consider myself to be superstitious? Do I ever let superstitions control my life?

I AM IN CONTROL OF WHAT I BELIEVE.

ST. WULFRIC

A.D. 1154

Medieval saints often performed what seems like most peculiar penances. St. Wulfric of England, for instance, is said to have sat at night in a tub of cold water reciting the entire psalter. While such behavior strikes us as bizarre, some of the things we do may strike our descendants as equally strange. For instance, what might a historian of the twenty-eighth century think upon reading that people of our time would rise before sunup to run long distances in the dark, just to keep their bodies thin? If jogging were no longer a popular activity, such an account might seem as laughable as St. Wulfric sitting in his cold tub.

All too often, we judge others' behavior by our own cultural and temporal limitations. Yet we are warned, "Do not judge lest you be judged yourselves. For in the way you judge, you will be judged; and by your standard of measure, it shall be measured to you." (Matthew 7:1–2)

The real danger in judging others lies in what it does to us. We begin to believe that the way we do things is right and proper. From there it's an easy slide to thinking of our way as being the *only* way.

One of the greatest lessons the saints have to teach us is to mind our own business. St. Wulfric sat in the cold water of holiness. May we never find ourselves sitting in the hot water of judgment.

When do I find myself becoming judgmental? Do I feel I am responsible for other people's behavior?

¶ LET OTHER PEOPLE MAKE THEIR OWN DECISIONS.

ST. PETER DAMIAN

1007–1072

St. Peter Damian would undoubtedly agree with the proverb, idle hands are the devil's workshop. When he wasn't working or praying, he kept himself occupied by making useful objects, such as wooden spoons.

Being idle is hard on both mind and body. When we have nothing worthwhile to do, temptations automatically rush in to fill the void. Some are relatively harmless—maybe I'll just have a couple more cookies. But others are more destructive—my spouse will never find out I'm having an affair. Even when we don't act on our temptations, we make life more difficult than it has to be by constantly exposing ourselves to their lure.

One of the best ways to escape the snare of temptation is to keep busy. Keeping busy does more than hold temptation at bay. It also allows us to feel better about ourselves. Almost nothing gives a greater sense of accomplishment and self-worth than completing a task we enjoy. It doesn't matter whether it's planting a garden, making a quilt, or carving wooden spoons. As long as we have done it to the best of our ability, we can take legitimate pride in our accomplishment.

The next time you find yourself being enticed by temptation, check to see if you're feeling bored or idle. If so, find something constructive to do and watch the temptation evaporate.

When I'm bored, what tempts me the most?

∙ꝑ⸺⸺⸺⸺⸺⸺ꝑ∙

I KEEP BUSY ENOUGH TO AVOID UNNECESSARY TEMPTATION.

ST. MARGARET OF CORTONA

1247–1297

For as long as twenty-five thousand years, dogs have been an intimate part of human life. Amazing in their diversity (if you didn't know it, would you really believe that a Pomeranian and a St. Bernard are family members under the fur?), dogs are our loyal, devoted companions. While we can safely assume that many saints must have enjoyed canine companionship, such details aren't usually part of standard hagiography. St. Margaret of Cortona is one of the rare exceptions. A dog is even represented in the church where she is buried.

Margaret lived as a wealthy man's mistress for nine years. One day, while waiting for him to come back from one of his estates, she saw the dog that had been with him returning alone. The animal led her to the base of an oak tree, where she discovered the body of her murdered lover. Margaret was so overcome with remorse, she spent the rest of her life performing stringent acts of penance and charity on behalf of the poor and sick. So complete was her conversion, early biographies call her the perfect penitent.

While it's stretching things to credit Margaret's change of heart to her dog, it is clear that a dog played an important part in her life. Likewise, dogs can play an important role in our lives by showing us examples of unconditional love and undivided loyalty.

How do I feel about owning a pet?

I WELCOME THE PRESENCE OF ANIMALS, BOTH WILD AND DOMESTIC.

ST. POLYCARP

A.D. 155?

In the heat of a dispute, one of the most difficult things to do is agree to disagree. Although we may finally say, let's just drop it, secretly we cling to our position. If the opportunity arises to press our point, we gladly jump on it. Letting a legitimate disagreement continue without antagonism or animosity is a sure sign of great wisdom and maturity.

St. Polycarp was one of the earliest leaders of the Christian Church. Taught directly by St. John the Evangelist, he himself trained many famous disciples, including St. Irenaeus.

When a controversy arose over the date for Easter, St. Polycarp was selected by the Asiatic churches to travel to Rome to confer with Pope Anicetus. Although St. Polycarp and Pope Anicetus could not come to accord on the date, they did agree that local tradition should be maintained. Their agreement to disagree has continued even to the present, with Eastern and Western churches celebrating Easter on different days.

When we are involved in an argument, let us remember that we don't live in a black-and-white world. Not every question has a single right answer. If we feel certain we've found the right answer, we must allow others that same freedom of conscience.

That's not to say we have to be doormats. We can express our views. We can even try to convince others. But if we realize we will never be able to agree, then, like St. Polycarp and the Pope, we must politely and respectfully agree to disagree.

Do I like to argue for argument's sake?

I STAND UP FOR MY CONVICTIONS, BUT I ALSO ALLOW OTHERS TO STAND UP FOR THEIRS.

ST. MONTANUS

A.D. 259

If champions of censorship were ever to read the expurgated accounts of early martyrs, they would wear their blue pencils to the nubs. While references to sex are so veiled they are almost unrecognizable (one saint who in her youth lived with a man she did not marry is said to have had a "propensity to vice" and their relationship was referred to as "the greatest disorders"), torture is another story. Modern horror films have little over early martyrologies.

St. Montanus was an early martyr. Along with several others, he was executed for his faith during the persecution of Valerian in the third century. The account of their trial and execution is extensively detailed. Actually, they got off easy. They were only imprisoned, dragged through the streets in chains, deprived of food and water, publicly humiliated, and beheaded. Many other early martyrs were subjected to ingenious torments, including the rack, flaying alive, and burning at the stake before finally being killed.

While such accounts are difficult to read, they serve as a powerful reminder that evil is not just a figment of our collective unconscious. It's not just an illusion that can be explained away. Evil is real.

But that's not the end of the story. As real as evil is, goodness is even more real. The stories of the early martyrs like St. Montanus are reports of the triumph of faith and the resiliency of the human spirit even in the face of the greatest of evil.

Have I ever encountered real evil? What do I think is the greatest evil in the world today?

I KNOW EVIL EXISTS, BUT I DO NOT LET IT HAVE A PLACE IN MY LIFE.

BLESSED SEBASTIAN DE APARICIO

1502–1600

Of all the inventions that have altered history, the wheel must be considered one of the most important. The modern road would be a close second. Without good roads, civilization as we know it is impossible. One of the reasons the Roman Empire was so successful in maintaining peace throughout its far-flung provinces was because of its extensive road system.

In the New World, roads were slower in developing. In fact, the first passable roads in Mexico weren't built until the middle of the sixteenth century. One man—Blessed Brother Sebastian de Aparicio—is credited with building those roads. Even today, many of the highways of Mexico, including that from Mexico City to Zacatecas, follow much the same route as did Sebastian's original road.

The roads we use for transportation aren't the only roads in our lives. We are all pilgrims on a journey that starts at birth and ends in eternity. The road we travel on this journey is seldom without difficulty. For most of us, it is filled with bends and twists, forks and impasses. Often the way is so obscure we can barely see far enough to put one foot in front of the other. One thing is certain, however. We are never alone on our journey. God is always with us, encouraging us in the mountains, refreshing us on the plains, carrying us across the rivers. Ultimately, when our road ends, God will be there, too, welcoming us home.

How does it change the way I think about my life when I know
I am never alone on the journey?

I KNOW GOD IS ALWAYS WITH ME.

ST. ALEXANDER

A.D. 328

St. Alexander, the bishop of Alexandria in the middle of the fourth century, is best known for his resistance to a doctrine maintaining, among other things, that Jesus was capable of sinning. It's hard for us to picture the furor such theological disputes could cause. Not only did theologians get involved, but both church and civil authorities and even ordinary citizens were divided by the controversy.

Hatred and division because of religious beliefs didn't end sixteen hundred years ago. Even today hair-triggers are pulled over what seems like hair-splitting. When we aren't involved in the controversy, it's easy to see how ridiculous the whole thing can become. When our emotions are involved, however, it isn't so easy to be an unbiased observer.

While emotions are an essential part of being human, over-reliance on feelings can be exhausting. We've all known people who wear their hearts on their sleeves. Like dandelion tufts in a windstorm, they are blown every which way by their feelings. If we get caught in their downdrafts, we, too, can get tossed and turned. We can find ourselves becoming overwrought and upset by events and people that don't really involve us. When that happens, we need to stop and ask, is this really my problem? Am I trying to fix something that isn't mine to fix? Life gives all of us more than enough emotional challenges. We don't need to assume more than our share.

When someone I love is hurting, do I try to fix things?

⋅◖⟪▰▰▰▰▰▰▰▰▰▰▰▰▰▰▰▰▰▰▰⟫◗⋅

I ACCEPT THE FACT THAT I CANNOT SOLVE EVERYONE
ELSE'S PROBLEMS.

ST. GABRIEL POSSENTI

1838–1862

A famous folktale tells the story of a poor man who went to work for a stingy farmer. The poor man worked all day and when night fell, the farmer told him he would pay him for his labor "tomorrow." The next day the poor man returned, asking for his pay, but the farmer pointed out that he had agreed to be paid "tomorrow" and this was "today." Of course, "tomorrow" would never arrive.

When it comes to doing what we should, many of us act just like the farmer. We procrastinate as long as we can.

St. Gabriel Possenti understood procrastination. Although he felt a call to enter religious life, he kept putting it off. When he was seriously ill, he promised to enter a religious order if he recovered, but once he was well, his resolve disappeared. A year or two later, he once again was seriously sick, once again promised to enter religious life, and once again delayed after the crisis passed. It wasn't until his sister died of cholera that he finally ended his procrastination, becoming Brother Gabriel-of-our-Lady-of-Sorrows. Sadly, he himself did not have long to live. Within four years, he contracted tuberculosis and died.

St. Gabriel reminds us that since we cannot know how long we have to do our good deeds, we need to act before it is too late.

Why do I put things off? How do I feel when people around me procrastinate?

TODAY, I WILL DO ONE GOOD DEED (AND NOT TELL ANYONE ABOUT IT).

ST. ROMANUS

A.D. 460

Do you ever get the feeling you could make great strides spiritually if you could just have some time to yourself? It's a real temptation to believe we would continually concentrate on the essentials if we weren't distracted by all the demands of life.

St. Romanus thought the same thing. At age thirty-five he headed to the Jura Mountains between Switzerland and France to live as a hermit. For a time, he was blissfully alone, then his brother arrived, followed by a couple of other men. Then his sister and a group of women joined them. Soon there were enough men and women to build two monasteries and a nunnery. St. Romanus, who wanted nothing more than to be left alone, spent the rest of his life surrounded by people.

The lesson St. Romanus learned is one that many of us must also learn: Most spiritual development takes place in the crucible of everyday existence. It's easy to feel kind and generous when there's no one else around. But what good does feeling kind do if we have no one with whom to be gentle? How can we be generous when no one challenges our selfishness? Unlike vice, which grows best in the dark, dim corners of our soul, virtue requires interaction with others to blossom and flourish.

Am I an introvert or an extrovert? How do I feel when people intrude on my space?

I SHARE MY TIME WILLINGLY WITH OTHERS AND DO NOT SECLUDE MYSELF FROM THOSE WHO NEED MY HELP.

ST. DAVID

520–589

Here's a quick test. Which is more holy?

A. Scrubbing the bathroom or B. Preaching a sermon

If you chose B, St. David would suggest you reconsider your definition of holiness. David, the patron saint of Wales, did a good many things we normally consider holy—he spent long hours in prayer, performed severe penances, preached eloquent sermons. On his deathbed, however, his final words included: "Keep your faith, and do the little things you have seen and heard with me."

Holiness does not lie in doing great things. As Mother Teresa of Calcutta says, it lies in doing little things with great love.

Love is the one true alchemy. Unlike the pseudoscience of the Middle Ages, which unsuccessfully tried to change base metals into gold, love actually works. It transforms ordinary activities—even things as ordinary as mopping the bathroom floor—into the gold of redemption.

One of the immutable laws of creation is that everything we do has consequences. Every action, when we do it out of love, has the power to bring us into closer union with God and our fellow human beings. Conversely, every time we act out of selfishness, hate, or anger, we create a barrier to union with God and others. The good thing about all of this is that the choice is always ours. No matter how insignificant or unimportant our actions may seem, when we make the conscious, deliberate decision to act in and with love, all the saints rejoice with us and support our decision.

How does it change my feelings about mundane tasks when I do them with love?

I DO MY DAILY ACTIVITIES CHEERFULLY AND WILLINGLY.

BLESSED PETER MANRIQUE
DE ZÚÑIGA

1585–1622

"His parents and relatives objected vigorously; but, eventually he overcame their opposition, and he received the Augustinian habit at Seville on October 2, 1604," wrote a biographer of Blessed Peter Manrique de Zúñiga.

What were his parents' objections? Why would they be so opposed to their son's decision to become a priest? If his family had known Peter was destined to become a missionary to Japan and be burned at the stake, their unhappiness would be understandable. But it's unlikely they could have seen into the future. With rare exceptions, most of us have to take each day as it comes.

Although we might believe it would be wonderful to know what the future holds, it's probably a good thing we can't. Just think back over the past year. If you had known in advance all the difficulties you would have to face, you might have wanted to hide in bed with the covers pulled up over your face. Or maybe, if the trials were stringent enough, you might have been tempted not to go through with them all.

The only way we can live life is one day at a time. Even when we are in the midst of great suffering, if we focus on each moment as it comes, we will find the grace we need to keep on going.

Am I afraid of the future? How do I feel when things happen that I didn't anticipate?

⁓⁓⁓⁓⁓⁓⁓⁓⁓⁓⁓⁓⁓⁓⁓⁓⁓⁓⁓⁓⁓⁓⁓⁓⁓⁓⁓

I TAKE EACH DAY AS IT COMES.

BLESSED KATHARINE DREXEL

1858–1955

When there's a job to be done, are you the first to step forward, or do you hang back, waiting to see if someone more qualified takes the initiative? The problem with waiting for someone else to volunteer is that the job might never get done.

The daughter of a wealthy Philadelphia banker and heir to an enormous fortune, Blessed Katharine Drexel met Pope Leo XIII while on a European tour. When she asked the pope to send more missionaries to help poor blacks and Native Americans, he suggested she become a missionary herself. After overcoming her shock at his suggestion, she did, using her twelve-million-dollar fortune to build missions and schools across America. In 1915, she founded Xavier University in New Orleans, the first university for African-Americans in the United States.

While we may not feel we are the best person for a particular job, God often has a different idea. It doesn't matter that someone else might be able to do the job better or easier. What does matter is that we do what we can with what we have been given.

Katharine Drexel was able to do much because she was given much. While few of us have million-dollar fortunes at our disposal, we all have the wealth of our time and talent. When we put our lives at God's disposal, miracles will happen.

What do I do best? How can I use my abilities to make life easier for others?

I WILLINGLY SHARE MY TIME AND TALENTS.

ST. CASIMIR

1461–1484

"Blessed are the peacemakers." (Matthew 5:9)

What does it mean to be a peace-maker? Does it mean to hammer out an international peace agreement like the Camp David accord? That may be one definition, but it isn't the only one, and it isn't the one that fits St. Casimir.

St. Casimir, the third of thirteen children of the king of Poland, is called The Peace-maker, not because he masterminded a resolution between warring factions but because he refused to take part in a war between Hungary and Poland. Initially, out of obedience to his father he led an army into Hungary, but when his own officers advised him to return home, he did so. Nothing anyone could say or do could ever induce him to pick up arms again.

Peace-making doesn't happen because high-ranking government officials sign important documents. Peace-making is a process, a process that begins with each one of us. We are peace-makers every time we listen to another person's point of view, every time we think before we speak, every time we choose not to become embroiled in strife. We are peace-makers when we build up rather than tear down, when we praise rather than criticize, when we hope rather than despair.

How can I be a peace-maker in my family or place of work?

I AM AT PEACE WITH MYSELF AND THEREFORE I CAN BE AT PEACE WITH OTHERS.

ST. JOHN JOSEPH-OF-THE-CROSS

1654–1734

Recreation is serious business. We work very hard at play. Our weekends are often so filled with activity that when Monday comes we need a day off to recuperate. In the midst of it all, sometimes we forget that the purpose of recreation is to refresh and restore us so we can return to our regular duties with renewed enthusiasm. We forget that without proper recreation, we become bored and boring.

St. John Joseph-of-the-Cross is an unlikely champion of recreation. As a boy on the island of Ischia, off Naples, he showed such unusual piety that he entered the Franciscans when he was only sixteen. Noted for his austerity, he insisted on equally strict austerity from the novices under his charge. He even came up with the idea of building hermitages away from the main building of the monastery so he could practice greater self-discipline. Despite his exacting observance of the rules of his order, he was also especially careful that the novices had regular times of recreation. He understood that far from being a luxury, recreation is a necessity for the human spirit.

This spring, spend less time working at having fun and more time just having fun. Blow bubbles. Eat an ice cream cone. Sing a silly song. Kiss a baby. Walk a dog. Rejoice in a rainbow. Celebrate a saint.

Do I use my time wisely? Do I feel guilty when I "waste" time?

I GIVE MYSELF PERMISSION TO WASTE AS MUCH TIME
AS I NEED.

ST. COLETTE

1380–1447

By the early fifteenth century, the Poor Clares, the order of nuns founded by St. Clare under the direction of St. Francis of Assisi, had lost much of its original spirit. St. Colette felt divinely called to restore the order to its initial severity. On the advice of her spiritual director, she set out on her mission. Needless to say, she was not greeted with enthusiasm. You can hardly blame the nuns. If a young woman showed up at your doorstep, claiming St. Francis appeared to her in a vision and telling you to clean up your act, how would you react? As one biographer says, "she was met with the most violent opposition and was treated as a fanatic."

Little wonder. None of us like to be told our faults. We are often like the emperor of fairy-tale fame. He wanted to hear how handsome he looked in his new suit of clothes when, in fact, he was parading around town naked. It was only after a little boy had the courage to say aloud what everyone else was thinking that the emperor had the sense to get dressed.

When someone like St. Colette or that little boy comes into our lives, do we react with indignation and dismiss them as fanatics or do we consider the possibility they may be right? While recognizing our faults can be embarrassing, it isn't as bad as walking around thinking we are dressed when we are really stark naked.

Am I oversensitive? Do I have to defend my position even when I know I'm wrong?

1 ACCEPT CORRECTION WHEN NECESSARY.

STS. PERPETUA AND FELICITY

A.D. 203

Sequels to movies are so common, it almost seems as if the original film were merely cut in half, with a "to be continued" sign stuck at the end. It's too bad early historians didn't feel the same way about the lives of the saints. The little we know about the martyrs who died during the Roman games tantalizes more than it informs. Take Perpetua and Felicity. We know Perpetua was a noblewoman of Carthage and the mother of an infant son. Her companion, Felicity, was a slave who gave birth to a daughter just before her death. We also know they were beheaded as part of a public spectacle.

Where were their husbands? What happened to their children? Did they grow up to be Christians? Did they know each other?

The questions surrounding Perpetua and Felicity show how important it is to leave a record of our lives for our descendants. We may not think we have much to share, but we are an essential part of the fabric of our family. Without us, the quilt of life would lose much of its color and texture.

Leaving a record doesn't mean writing a six-volume life history complete with footnotes. It can be as simple as labeling the pictures in the photo albums before we forget who is who. Or jotting a note next to a name in an address book ("Carrie's godmother") so that someday someone will know why that person was important. The essential thing is to do one thing today, no matter how insignificant it may seem.

What do I know about my grandparents and great-grandparents?
What do I wish I knew about them?

I KNOW I AM AN IMPORTANT PART OF MY FAMILY.

ST. JOHN OF GOD

1495–1550

St. John of God was nothing if not enthusiastic. Moved by a sermon of St. John of Avila, he ran through the streets of Granada, beating his breast and crying for God's mercy. Unimpressed, the townsfolk threw him in an insane asylum. It was only after John of Avila admonished him to start doing something constructive for the poor that John of God calmed down. Earning money by selling firewood, he rented a house to care for the sick and destitute.

John of God's enthusiasm got him started, but it was his hard work chopping wood that saw him through.

If enthusiasm were a racehorse, it would be a good starter but a poor finisher. We all know what it's like to become excited by a project. Let's say we find an antique table that would be just perfect for the living room—if it were refinished. Chances are, by the time we've stripped, sanded, and stained, we aren't quite as excited by the job as we were when we began. If we relied on enthusiasm alone, the table would probably never get finished. It's only when we add hard work to the mix that we are able to keep going. After all, it isn't always the first out of the starting gate who wins the prize, and it isn't always the person who is the most enthusiastic at the beginning who ultimately completes the job.

Do I start things I don't finish? What do I do with projects I know I'm never going to complete?

TODAY I WILL FINISH WHAT I START.

ST. FRANCES OF ROME

1384 – 1440

Ever met people who are so busy working for the church that they overlook the needs of their own families? They spend hours serving on this committee and chairing that project. They organize food drives and rallies and lead prayer services. They help anyone who comes asking for help. All the while, their own families feel neglected and forgotten. The saddest part about such people is that they often believe they are doing just what God expects them to do.

St. Frances of Rome has different advice. Although she dedicated much of her life to prayer, penance, and good deeds, she was also an exemplary wife and mother. Part of the reason she was so loved by her family was that she kept her priorities straight. "A married woman must, when called upon, quit her devotions to God at the altar, to find him in her household affairs," she said.

God doesn't expect us to spend all our time working for the church. God resides with us in our homes, amid the ebb and flow of everyday life. God is found in the laundry, the dishes, the car pool, the bills, the grocery shopping. Although we may feel more holy when we are surrounded by stained-glass windows and sacred music, St. Frances of Rome urges us to remember that wherever duty calls, there God will be found.

Where do I look for God? Where have I found God?

I BELIEVE THAT GOD IS WITH ME AT ALL TIMES AND
IN ALL PLACES.

ST. JOHN OGILVIE

1579–1615

One of our greatest—and most underrated—blessings is a good night's sleep. In *Macbeth*, Shakespeare writes that sleep "knits up the ravell'd sleave of care". Modern science has proven the Bard right. Adequate sleep not only restores our psychological reserves, it also strengthens our immune system. Without sufficient rest, we begin to literally break down. It's no wonder that sleep deprivation is a classic form of torture.

St. John Ogilvie endured many torments for his faith, but none was more difficult than eight straight days without sleep. John, the son of a Scottish baron, became a Catholic at seventeen while studying in Europe. He entered the Jesuit order and, despite the ban on the entry of priests to the British Isles, secretly returned to Scotland as a missionary. When his identity was revealed, he was arrested and tried for high treason. Before he was hanged, however, he was kept awake for eight days and nights in a futile attempt to wring out a confession. Only after the doctors said that three more hours without rest would be fatal was he given a reprieve.

Sometimes we unwittingly subject ourselves to the torture of sleep deprivation. Recent studies indicate that most of us get at least one to two hours less sleep each night than we really need. We may think we are getting more done when we sleep less, but in fact we become less productive and more accident-prone. So the next time you feel weary, do the natural thing. Go to sleep!

How much sleep do I get each night? Would I feel better if I started going to bed a few minutes earlier?

I ALLOW MYSELF TO GET THE REST I NEED.

ST. OENGUS

C. A.D. 824

St. Oengus, an Irish monk and scholar, was nicknamed the Hagiographer, the Culdee, and God's Vassal. These nicknames aren't the run-of-the-mill saintly sobriquets, like St. Oengus the Good or St. Oengus the Wise. His nicknames are creative. (Can you imagine his friends calling out, Hey there, God's Vassal! Want to go down to the well?)

Nicknames often reflect what others think of us. Although they may be based on physical characteristics such as hair color (Red) or size (Shorty), nicknames may also mirror some aspect of our personality. What would you guess a person nicknamed The Professor would be like? How about The Terminator?

Although we may not be able to control the names others give us, we can mentally give ourselves nicknames that indicate a virtue or characteristic we would like to acquire. By hearing the virtue associated with our name, we come one step closer to making it a reality. For example, if you start thinking of yourself as Patient or Understanding, you'll soon find yourself living up to those qualities. Likewise, if you run yourself down by using nicknames such as Fatso or Jerk, those negative pictures will insinuate their way into your self-image.

The words that echo in our minds have a lot to do with our self-worth. Let us make them as positive and uplifting as possible.

Do I have a nickname? What nickname would I like to have? How does it make me feel when I hear a virtue associated with my name?

·⟨░░░░░░░░░░░░░░░░░⟩·

I WILL GIVE MYSELF A NICKNAME I REALLY LIKE.

ST. MAXIMILIAN

A.D. 296

Our culture glamorizes the extraordinary. We are so captivated by the exceptional that the word *average* has taken on a pejorative connotation. If you live in an average house, your investment is not worth much. If your weight is average, you had better cut out desserts. If your income is average, you are probably looking for a second job. Somehow, average has come to mean substandard.

But how many of us are really exceptional? Don't most of us live ordinary—dare we say it—average lives?

For all of us who feel more average than we might like, St. Maximillian offers hope. While many saints did amazing and wondrous deeds, St. Maximilian simply entered the army at age twenty-one. About the only thing we know about him is that he was "of due stature . . . about five feet and a half of our measure." In other words, the only fact we have about St. Maximilian concerns that most average and ordinary of things—his height. And even that was average.

When we are feeling particularly average and believing everyone we know is more talented, more attractive, and more interesting than we are, we need to remind ourselves that average isn't bad. It merely means standard or usual. When we consider that the usual standard of living in most Western cultures includes such things as indoor plumbing, central heating, a safe water supply, and access to education, not to mention a life expectancy of over seventy, average begins to sound pretty good. So, the next time you're feeling like a brown paper sack in a gift-wrapped world, ask St. Maximilian to help you remember that average isn't so average after all.

Are my feelings hurt when people think of me as average?

AVERAGE IS NOT A FOUR-LETTER WORD.

ST. EUPHRASIA

C. A.D. 420

Most of us have experienced "buyer's remorse." After we've made a purchase, particularly something large and expensive like a house or a car, we are filled with instant regret. We spent too much money. We didn't get the value we expected. We should have shopped around a little longer.

When we're feeling the sour taste of buyer's remorse, St. Euphrasia can help.

Euphrasia had been betrothed at age five, but when her day of marriage approached, she asked to be allowed to join a convent instead. Since she was a wealthy heiress, she also asked that her fortune be given to the poor and her slaves freed. Amazingly, she got her wish. That's when buyer's remorse set in. Euphrasia was immediately stricken with temptations to know more about the life she had given up.

The same is true for us. Once we have made an irrevocable decision, we begin to have doubts and questions. We wonder if we've made a big mistake. At that point, we have two choices: We can make ourselves miserable or we can, like St. Euphrasia, get on with life.

One of the best ways to stop fretting is with good, old-fashioned physical labor. St. Euphrasia stopped second-guessing her decision by moving piles of rock until she was exhausted. Although we may not have access to a quarry, we all have ways to get our muscles moving—working in the yard, scrubbing the bathroom, washing the car. While we can't always be sure we've made the best decision, we can always decide to make the best of our decisions.

Do I ever second-guess my decisions? How impulsive am I?

I THINK THROUGH MY DECISIONS BEFORE I MAKE THEM.

ST. LEOBINUS

A.D. 558

One of the great secret pleasures of childhood is reading under the covers with a flashlight. From comics to classics, many a page has been devoured in the wee hours of the night. Children think they are putting something over on their parents by this clandestine act, but parents know—because they did the same thing themselves.

What is it about reading at night that gives the written word such life? Are our inhibitions lower? Our imaginations more vivid? Perhaps it's because we have fewer distractions and can concentrate more fully. Whatever the case, a ghost story at noon just isn't the same as a ghost story at midnight.

If you love to read at night, you may identify with St. Leobinus, a French monk who lived in the sixth century. Because he had to work all day, the only time he could read was after dark. To make things more difficult, his fellow monks complained that his lamp kept them awake. Nonetheless, he kept on reading.

Reading—whether at night or during the day—is one of the great joys of life. It doesn't matter whether it's a novel or a biography, a best-seller or an academic tome, books are the one sure portal to knowledge and growth. Tonight, curl up with a good book and watch your world expand.

What's my favorite book? When was the last time I read it?

TODAY I WILL READ SOMETHING I REALLY ENJOY.

ST. LOUISE DE MARILLAC

1591–1660

St. Louise De Marillac was a very busy woman. Along with St. Vincent de Paul, she founded the Vincentian Sisters of Charity. Because of her extensive work on behalf of the needy, Pope John XXIII proclaimed her the patron saint of social workers in 1960.

With that kind of background, one might think St. Louise was a "professional religious"—one of those women who dedicate themselves to God during childhood and spend their entire lives in convents. Louise, however, was happily married for twelve years before her husband died.

One of the few things St. Louise worried about was the spiritual welfare of her only son, Michael. Her biographer says, "With all her occupations, she never forgot him."

Would our families be able to say the same thing about us? It's all too easy to shortchange the ones closest to us when we become pressed for time. St. Louise might have had legitimate reason to let her adult son fend for himself, but she didn't. He remained close to her heart, and on her deathbed, one of her last actions was to bless him, his wife, and her grandson.

No matter how busy we become, let us not forget the example of St. Louise. While we work to bring blessings to others, let us also remember to be a blessing to our own families.

Is there someone in my life I've been neglecting lately?

TODAY I WILL TELL THE PEOPLE I LOVE HOW MUCH THEY MEAN TO ME.

ST. JOHN DE BRÉBEUF

A.D. 1649

It takes a special kind of person to be an explorer. Heading out into uncharted territory, braving the elements, seeking new horizons . . . many of us would rather read about such deeds than perform them.

St. John de Brébeuf and his fellow missionaries were among the first white explorers to settle in what is now Ontario. Following the fur traders, Fr. Brébeuf and his fellow priests had come to the New World to try to convert the Native Americans to Christianity. To say they met with resistance is an understatement—they were tortured and killed and their missions wiped out. As missionaries, their success was problematic. As explorers they fared a little better, becoming part of the annals of history.

Most of us will never be explorers of new worlds. The opportunities are much more limited today than they were in St. John de Brébeuf's time. No new continents await our discovery, and unless we head to outer space or the deep sea, we are probably out of luck.

But exploration isn't limited to physical adventure. We are all called to become explorers of the truth. Like all explorations, seeking the truth can be dangerous. We may face great opposition. We may suffer the torture of doubt and despair. We may even have to die to our old way of life.

Exploration always has its cost, but it also has its rewards. St. John de Brébeuf may have lost his life, but he gained the reward of heaven. When we seek the truth, we will discover our own rewards as well.

How much am I willing to risk for the truth?

I AM A SEEKER OF TRUTH.

ST. PATRICK

389–461?

Today, everyone, no matter what their heritage, can be a little bit Irish. For someone whose life contains as much fiction as fact, St. Patrick is arguably one of the most famous saints of all times. Although he is probably best known for shamrocks (and green beer), he is also believed to have written the hauntingly beautiful prayer entitled "The Breastplate of St. Patrick." Containing the request, "Christ shield me this day: Christ be with me, Christ before me, Christ behind me, Christ in me, Christ beneath me," the prayer goes on to say, "Christ in quiet and in danger, Christ in hearts of all that love me, Christ in mouth of friend and stranger."

Although we can't be absolutely certain Patrick is the author, this ancient prayer is a perfect reflection of his life and beliefs. Like all the saints, Patrick centered his life in Christ. Everything he did was done out of a passionate belief in the message of Jesus Christ. In a time when few people could read and write, Patrick's life became a living gospel.

Likewise, our lives reflect the gospel we espouse. If we adhere to the gospel of materialism and consumerism, our actions will demonstrate our conviction. If we follow the gospel of self-interest, it will be apparent to all we meet. If like St. Patrick, however, we embrace the true gospel, which calls for selflessness and sacrifice, we become messengers of life and hope for a fallen world.

When people meet me, what message do I convey? Do I reflect my beliefs in both word and deed?

I ADMIRE ST. PATRICK'S TOTAL DEDICATION.

ST. CYRIL OF JERUSALEM

315?–386

St. Cyril of Jerusalem could probably appreciate the expression, damned if you do; damned if you don't. As archbishop of Jerusalem, he was not only ensnarled in a heated controversy over doctrine, he was also condemned for having sold church property to help the poor. He didn't deny making the sale, but many other saints had sold church holdings to help the poor. St. Cyril was caught between his duty to help the less fortunate and his responsibility to care for church property. Although he acted in good conscience, he was in a no-win situation. No matter what he did, someone was going to get mad.

When we follow our consciences, we may find ourselves in similar straits. Those who disagree with our decisions may be quite vocal and vociferous in their condemnation. The saints, including St. Cyril, offer many examples of the difficulty of following our consciences, especially when it goes against the expected.

While no one can tell you what you should do in every situation, one rule holds fast: when in doubt, err on the side of charity. For St. Cyril, that meant selling church holdings to avert the effects of famine. In our lives it may be as simple as refraining from gloating when we are right or as difficult as taking an unpopular political stand. Whenever we follow our conscience, however, we can be sure that the saints understand our struggle and are ready to support us with their prayers and encouragement.

Do I follow the crowd or do I follow my conscience?

WHEN I FOLLOW MY CONSCIENCE, I DO SO OUT OF CONVICTION.

ST. JOSEPH

FIRST CENTURY

Stories about Jesus, Mary, and Joseph often mention their poverty. While they were hardly rich, picturing the Holy Family dressed in rags living in a tumbled-down shanty with only crusts of bread to eat does St. Joseph a grave disservice. Unless we want to believe that he was utterly incompetent at his job, maybe we ought to reconsider our definition of poverty.

First, Joseph was a carpenter, a skilled professional akin to a building contractor, who would have been a respected and necessary member of his community. Second, he was probably paid for some of his labor with grain, livestock, and other nonmonetary goods. Although he didn't have a stockpile of coins, that doesn't necessarily make him poverty-stricken. Finally, the middle class did not exist in first-century Israel. Being called poor didn't make you a beggar; it made you ordinary. Everyone, with the exception of nobility and government toadies, was poor. Jesus, Mary, and Joseph were no exception.

None of this is to say that Joseph was a wealthy man. He wasn't. But Joseph was "a just man." In other words, he was a man of faith who trusted God would help him provide for his family.

God honored his faith. Jesus, Mary and Joseph were not so poor that they lived on the street, but not so wealthy that they were possessed by their possessions.

What makes me feel wealthy? What makes me feel poor?

I BELIEVE GOD WILL ALWAYS PROVIDE
ALL I TRULY NEED.

ST. CUTHBERT

636?–687

In the comic strip "Peanuts," Snoopy often begins his latest novel with the words, "It was a dark and stormy night . . . " Although we don't know if it was a dark and stormy night when St. Cuthbert first arrived at the gate of Melrose Abbey, it should have been. Picture the scene . . .

It's early evening. The monks have just finished vespers and are getting ready to retire for the night when a solitary figure crests the hill just outside the abbey walls. Astride a noble warhorse, the battle-weary figure rides to the gate, brandishing his spear. "I've come from fighting the Mercians," he announces. "I am sick to death of battle and wish to be admitted to your company." In amazement, the gatekeeper rouses the abbot, who quizzes the young man. Convinced of his sincerity, the abbot orders the gate to be opened. St. Cuthbert is home at last.

While we know that St. Cuthbert arrived at Melrose Abbey on horseback armed with a spear, the rest is just a story, and stories aren't to be trusted. Or are they? We are creatures of story. Stories and story-telling are welded into our souls. It's the way we as human beings learn. Even Jesus taught his followers primarily through stories.

When we attempt to reduce truth to a mere recitation of facts, we strip it of much of its power. Only when we allow our imaginations to fill in the blanks can we begin to incorporate the fullness of truth into the deepest recesses of our being.

How can I best tell my own story? Do I listen when others want to share their stories?

I AM GRATEFUL FOR THE GIFT OF IMAGINATION.

ST. SERAPION OF THMUIS

C. A.D. 370

If you were making up a list of creatures the world could do without, what would you include? Many people would probably put mosquitoes, snakes, and a few other creepy crawly things on the list.

While we may think of creatures such as mosquitoes and snakes as "bad" because they annoy or frighten us, nothing God has created is bad. In fact, the book of Genesis explicitly says everything God has created is good. The refrain throughout the entire story of creation is: "and God saw that it was good."

When we look closely at the miracle of life, we discover every entity has its own unique place in the balance of nature. If we interrupt one area, either deliberately or accidentally, the repercussions may be greater than we ever imagined.

Although the saints warn us against worshipping nature, they do remind us that we are to respect God's creation by being good stewards of the world. St. Serapion of Thmuis, a bishop who lived in Egypt during the fourth century, commented on that responsibility when he said, "there is no creature of which a good use may not be made."

The problem lies in how we define "good use." If we are to pass on the heritage of creation, we must learn the difference between making good use of our world and exploiting it.

Do I use more than my fair share of the world's resources? Could I live more simply?

I RESPECT GOD'S CREATION BY TAKING CARE OF THE EARTH.

ST. NICHOLAS OWEN

A.D. 1606

Keeping a secret is difficult. As soon as we've been entrusted with a confidence, it's almost as if a little demon jumps in our brain whispering, "It's okay if you share this with just one other person." But, of course, once we tell one person that person will tell someone else, and before we can blink, the secret is no longer a secret.

St. Nicholas Owen knew how to keep secrets.

When the Catholic faith was outlawed in England during the reign of James I, Nicholas saved the lives of countless numbers of Catholic priests by hiding them behind walls, in underground chambers, and in inaccessible passageways. He eluded the authorities for nearly twenty years until he finally allowed himself to be captured in the place of a priest he had concealed.

While knowing something can make us feel important, it also bears a grave responsibility. When someone wants to share a confidence with us, we need to be ready to accept that responsibility. We need to be prepared to keep that secret no matter how tempting it is to tell.

Of course, some so-called secrets, such as knowledge of abuse or criminal activity, must be told to the proper authorities, but most of the time the confidences we are asked to keep are small and personal. Revealing them accomplishes nothing except to hurt the person who shared them with us.

The next time someone wants you to be the guardian of a secret, ask yourself if you are prepared to accept the responsibility. If you are, remember to honor it as a sacred trust.

How good am I at keeping secrets? How do I feel when someone reveals a secret I've shared?

I CAN KEEP CONFIDENCES CONFIDENTIAL.

ST. TURIBIUS DE MOGROVEJO

1538–1606

When the bishop of Lima, Peru, died in 1575, St. Turibius de Mogrovejo was appointed to the post even though he was a layman. Over his initial objections he was ordained as a priest, consecrated as a bishop, and shipped off to the New World where, among other things, he confirmed St. Rose of Lima.

A man of great faith and deep love for the poor and sick, St. Turibius was also gravely concerned about the proper use of time. "Time is not our own," he said. "We will have to give a strict account of it."

We all have the same twenty-four hours in a day, but some people seem to accomplish much more in their allotted portion. If you find your time melting like sugar in hot coffee, consider keeping a time log for a day or two. Before you object that you have no time to keep a time log, remember it doesn't have to be formal or extensive. Every couple of hours, jot down the things you have been doing. Don't censor yourself, though. The idea is to find out *how* you spend your time, not how you *think* you should spend your time.

In the evening, take a look at the entire day. Are you more concerned with the urgent or the important? Do you control your time or does your time control you? What can you eliminate so as to have more time to do the things you really want to do? Remember, all growth begins with recognizing the need for change.

What would you do if you could have one more hour each day?

٠ ⟨⟨⟨⟨⟨⟨⟨⟨⟨⟨⟨⟨⟨⟨⟨⟨⟨⟨⟩⟩⟩ ⟩ ٠

🕇 USE MY TIME WISELY AND EFFICIENTLY.

ST. IRENAEUS

A.D. 304

St. Irenaeus lived during the infamous persecution of the emperor Diocletian. When the authorities decreed that St. Irenaeus should be drowned because he refused to denounce his Christian faith, he protested, saying that such an end was not fitting for the worthy cause for which he had suffered. Whether or not the authorities agreed with his assessment of Christianity, they gave him his wish, beheading him before throwing his body off a bridge.

While we may not be prepared to go to the lengths St. Irenaeus did to defend our causes, we do have an obligation to make sure the causes we back are worthy. We need to be certain we are placing our time, talent, and resources behind something or someone who is deserving. In order not to be duped, we need to do our research. We need to investigate a cause from as many angles as we can and ask as many questions as possible. Once we have done that, however, we have one more thing to do. We need to analyze the cause under the light of our faith. We need to ask, how does this fit with my beliefs? Am I being asked to compromise in ways that make me uncomfortable? What do I have to give up in order to support this?

If we have done our homework on the practical aspects *and* answered these questions to our satisfaction, then we can put our support behind the cause, confident that we have done all that we can.

What is my favorite cause or charity? How much do I really know about it?

I INVEST MY ENERGY IN WORTHWHILE CAUSES.

BLESSED MARGARET CLITHEROW

1556?–1586

Margaret Clitherow converted to the Catholic faith during the English persecution of the 1500s. Along with other Roman Catholic friends, she hid priests and arranged for secret masses until she was arrested, later to be executed by being pressed to death with an 800-pound weight. Her husband, who was a Protestant, loved her dearly and said, "Let them take all I have and save her, for she is the best wife in all England, and the best Catholic."

Marriage isn't easy. No matter how much we love our spouses, we will have differences. They may be as minor as where to squeeze the toothpaste tube or as serious as being willing to die for our religious convictions.

John Clitherow did not share his wife's religious faith, but he did respect her right to have that faith—even when it led to her execution.

Learning to respect differences is an essential component of any relationship, but it is especially important in marriage. Sometimes we assume our spouses should automatically think and act the same way as we do. Such assumptions inevitably create stresses and, left unchecked, can even strangle the love from the relationship.

The greatest gift we can give our spouse is the freedom to become the person God intends him or her to be. Granting that freedom can be frightening. It may mean that our husband or wife will travel a path we cannot follow. But in granting such freedom, we also gain ours.

In what ways do I try to control the behavior of my family members?

I GIVE THOSE I LOVE THEIR FREEDOM.

ST. BRAULIO

A.D. 651

A friend is someone who brightens our joys and bears our sorrows; who stands by us in good times and bad; who loves us even when we do not love ourselves.

St. Braulio was a brilliant scholar and alumnus of the college in Seville founded by St. Isidore. He was also one of Isidore's close friends, despite what must have been a fair difference in age.

Our closest friendships tend to be with people who are close to us in terms of income, social standing, and age. It's only natural that we would enjoy the company of those who share our interests and stage in life. If we limit our friendship to those who are like us, however, we will miss out on many of the true gifts of friendship.

Having an older friend can give us perspective. He or she may have lived through similar situations and can offer insights from practical experience. Likewise, having a younger friend can restore a sense of enthusiasm and excitement about life's potential.

For those of us who do not live in extended families that offer automatic contact with several generations, it can be difficult to find friends of different ages. Difficult, but not impossible. There's an old saying, if you want to have a friend, you've got to be a friend. The next time you meet someone interesting, no matter what their age, why not extend your friendship? You may be rebuffed, or you may find your life enriched. You'll never know unless you try.

What qualities do I look for in a friend?

·◖⟨▬▬▬▬▬▬▬▬▬▬▬▬▬▬▬▬⟩◗·

I AM OPEN TO THE POSSIBILITY OF FRIENDSHIP WITH EACH PERSON I MEET.

ST. JOHN OF EGYPT

304–394

Generally when we look to the saints for advice, it's about religion. Sometimes, though, we forget that the saints were real people. Although they're always ready to help us with our spiritual growth, they can also provide us with practical help for daily living.

Take diets, for instance. Modern cardiologists promote low-fat, high-fiber foods as the key to health and longevity. They urge us to eat as many fruits and vegetables as possible and to avoid red meat and empty calories.

St. John of Egypt would concur with their advice. For fifty years he lived only on dried fruits and vegetables. Admittedly, he took things a bit further than we need to, since he avoided all cooked food. Nonetheless, his diet must have been healthy because he lived to be ninety.

The saints know that one of the keys to a happy, healthy life is self-discipline. Our bodies and souls are intimately interconnected. A life of indulgence, while initially pleasant, leaves us physically and spiritually flabby.

If you are having trouble sticking to a diet, doing your exercises, or improving your lifestyle, remember you don't have to do it alone. Heaven is filled with friends waiting to lend their help and inspiration. All you have to do is ask.

What area of my life would I like the saints to help me change?

I AM BECOMING MORE SELF-DISCIPLINED.

ST. TUTILO

A.D. 915

What makes a genius? If you go on I.Q. alone, Albert Einstein would certainly qualify, yet he is said to have often forgotten to put on socks. He might have been extremely intelligent, but he wasn't always very bright.

As we begin to recognize the intricacies of the human brain, the definition of genius has expanded. Genius is no longer limited to intellectual prowess. We now realize people may be athletic geniuses, or musical geniuses, or mechanical geniuses, to name only a few.

St. Tutilo, a Benedictine monk in the monastery of Saint-Gall, qualified as a genius on many counts. A poet, orator, architect, painter, sculptor, metal worker, mechanic, and musician, he was also said to be "handsome, eloquent and quick-witted." It's a good thing he was also humble or he might never have become a saint!

Although we may not be as talented as St. Tutilo, we each have our own area of genius. You may already know exactly where your special talent lies. If you do, then give yourself permission to celebrate your gift in all its fullness. If you aren't so certain what your talent is, you might ask St. Tutilo to help you uncover it. Remember though, when you ask the saints for assistance, their help may turn up in ways you least expect.

If I could learn one new skill, what would it be? What's stopping me from starting today?

I AM COMPETENT AND CREATIVE.

ST. RUPERT

C. A.D. 710

St. Rupert, the bishop of Salzburg around the turn of the eighth century, built several churches and established at least one nunnery. He also encouraged his faithful to develop several salt mines.

Developing salt mines seems like a rather odd occupation for a saintly cleric, especially because the expression 'working in the salt mines' usually means slaving away at a difficult and unrewarding job. Yet encouraging people to work in salt mines is considered one of St. Rupert's virtues.

Whether we see a salt mine as a negative or a positive is a lot like much of life: It depends on what you're looking at. Take salt itself, for instance. While we tend to view it as something to be eliminated from our food, in ancient times it was so valuable it comprised part of a Roman soldier's pay.

How do you feel about the difficult and seemingly unrewarding tasks of your life? If you see them merely as salt mines, everything associated with the task will be laborious and stressful. If, on the other hand, you focus on the goal at the end, the work will not seem so onerous.

Since we all have our own personal salt mines, we really have only two choices—we can grumble and complain and make things miserable for ourselves and everyone around us or we can look forward to the end result and flavor our lives with joy and optimism.

What one task do I hate the most?

·⟨༚༚༚༚༚༚༚༚༚༚༚༚༚༚༚༚༚༚༚༚༚༚༚༚༚༚༚༚༚༚⟩·

I STICK TO TASKS I HAVE TO DO UNTIL THEY ARE ACCOMPLISHED.

ST. ZOSIMUS

571?–660

How do you feel about growing old? Do you think of aging as getting better, like fine wine, or running down, like an expired battery?

Sometimes as we mature, we may believe our best years are behind us. The future, which once appeared so limitless, seems tight and closed. We feel discouraged by all we haven't accomplished, and we begin to think life has nothing new to offer.

St. Zosimus could easily have felt that way. The son of Sicilian landowners, he was placed in Santa Lucia monastery by his parents when he was seven. For the next thirty years, he watched over the relic of St. Lucy and tended the door. Then one day things changed. The abbot of Santa Lucia died, and the monks couldn't agree on his successor. The bishop of Syracuse was called in to make a decision. Looking over the assembly, the bishop asked if any monk was missing. Someone remembered Zosimus, who was still watching the relic and tending the door. As soon as the bishop saw him, he declared, "Behold him whom the Lord hath chosen."

But that wasn't the end of surprises for Zosimus. When the bishop died in 649, he was named to the position by Pope Theodore.

No matter how old we are or how obscure we may feel, life is filled with surprises. Sometimes we have to seek them out; other times, as with St. Zosimus, all we have to do is be faithful in our duties and the surprises will find us.

Do I like surprises? Would I rather surprise someone or be
surprised myself?

I LOOK FORWARD TO ALL LIFE HAS TO OFFER.

ST. GUY OF POMPOSA

A.D. 1046

We've all met people who can't pass a mirror without primping and preening. While it's one thing to be well-groomed, it's quite another to be so preoccupied with the way you look that it becomes the most important thing in your life.

As a young man, St. Guy of Pomposa is said to have been very careful about the way he looked and dressed. One day, however, he changed his attitude. As part of his spiritual awakening, he gave away his fine clothes and set off for Rome to become a monk. His parents were horrified when he began to dress like a beggar, but St. Guy realized that clothes do not make the man—or woman.

Fashion designers would have us believe that unless we revamp our wardrobes every year, we will become social pariahs. By trying to convince us that we need to have the latest styles the industry preys on our insecurity and desire to conform. Yet the message of the saints is the direct opposite of conformity. Rather than fit in and follow the crowd, the saints tell us to throw off convention. They remind us that God doesn't love us because we fit the mold. God loves us because we design our own molds.

How important is my appearance? Am I satisfied with the
way I look?

I KNOW THAT I AM BEAUTIFUL IN THE SIGHT OF GOD.

ST. HUGH

1052–1132

Of the seven dwarves from *Snow White*, do you identify most with Bashful? If you do, then you know being shy can be a real trial. You might like to be a bit more outgoing, but being reserved and timid is part of your fundamental nature.

St. Hugh, bishop of Grenoble in the twelfth century, knows what it's like to struggle with shyness. He wasn't just bashful; he is said to have been "*extremely* bashful."

Being bashful isn't a great asset for a bishop. In fact, it's probably a liability. St. Hugh, however, managed to put his shyness to good use by transforming it into the virtue of modesty. Instead of showcasing his talents—something his timid nature would most likely have prevented anyway—St. Hugh honored his basic inclination toward shyness and downplayed his abilities. In doing so, he not only won the admiration and respect of his colleagues, but was also widely praised for his humility.

Sometimes we think that in order to be holy we have to revamp our entire natures. St. Hugh shows us the fallacy of that way of thinking. He converted his shyness into the modesty for which he is remembered today. We do the same thing with our basic personality traits when we use them as the building blocks of holiness.

What one word would I use to describe myself? How can I transform that trait into a virtue?

· ⟨⟨⟨⟨⟨⟨⟨⟨⟨⟨⟨⟩⟩⟩⟩⟩⟩⟩⟩⟩⟩ ·

I LOOK FOR WAYS TO DEVELOP VIRTUES IN ACCORD WITH MY OWN PERSONALITY.

ST. FRANCIS OF PAOLA

1416–1507

King Louis XI of France had an inordinate fear of death. When he learned he was dying, he tried everything to forestall the inevitable, including prayers and pilgrimages. As his health continued to fail, he begged the holy hermit St. Francis of Paola to come to him. When Francis refused, Louis finally beseeched Pope Sixtus IV to order Francis to make the trip. Having no choice, Francis set out, arriving at the French court in April 1482.

King Louis immediately begged Francis to extend his life. In reply, Francis said that the lives of kings, like the lives of their subjects, are in the hands of God alone. While the message probably wasn't what King Louis had hoped for, over the next four months, Francis helped the king prepare for death. On August 30, 1482, the king died peacefully in Francis's arms.

None of us knows when we are going to die. We may have a few months' warning, like King Louis, or we may die as suddenly as do victims of airplane disasters. The only certainty about death is that it will happen to each and every one of us.

The saints urge us to live today as if we were to die tomorrow. That doesn't mean we should be paralyzed by fear, but rather that we should never put off doing good deeds, saying kind words, or forgiving those who hurt us, for it is only when we accept the reality of death that we can live the fullness of life.

Am I afraid of death? How do I feel when I think about my own death and the death of those I love?

¶ DO NOT LET THE FEAR OF DYING ROB ME OF THE JOY OF LIVING.

STS. AGAPE, CHIONIA, AND IRENE

A.D. 304

Agape, Chionia, and Irene were three sisters who were martyred for their faith under the persecution of the emperor Diocletian. During their trial, Agape explained that they would not eat the meat sacrificed to the Roman gods, adding, "I believe in the living God and will not by an evil action lose all the merits of my past life." It's hard to imagine that a single evil action could have such enormous consequences, but it can. A one-night stand can destroy a marriage. A lone bribe can demolish a political career. A solitary lie can ruin a reputation.

When we see the results of our sinful actions, we are often overwhelmed with "if only." If only I hadn't lost my temper! If only I hadn't had that affair! If only . . . if only . . . if only . . . The problem with "If only" is that it doesn't change the past. All it does is erode today's gladness and tomorrow's hope.

When you find yourself caught in the spiral of "if only," it's a sure sign you need to ask for forgiveness. First, ask God to forgive you, trusting in divine mercy and understanding. Then, insofar as possible, ask whomever you have hurt to forgive you. Finally, forgive yourself. You may still have to live with the consequences of your actions, but by asking for threefold forgiveness you lift the burden of unresolved guilt from the load.

Do I keep rehashing my past mistakes? Have I asked for forgiveness? If not, why?

⸱⟨⟨▬▬▬▬▬▬▬▬▬▬▬▬▬▬▬▬▬▬▬⟩⟩⸱ ⸱

I ASK FORGIVENESS OF THOSE I HAVE HURT AND I FORGIVE THOSE WHO HAVE HURT ME.

ST. ISIDORE OF SEVILLE

560?–636

Time management books are filled with suggestions on how to squeeze more productive time out of each day. Although the ideas are often creative, they're all based on the same premise—doing more than one thing at the same time. So we prop up the book we've been meaning to read on the handlebars of our exercise bikes with the latest self-help tape on our headsets and the television tuned to CNN, just in case something earth-shattering happens while we are puffing our way through the required 20 minutes of aerobics. No wonder we feel exhausted and overwhelmed. Our energy is so scattered that we accomplish far less than we might with more focused attention.

St. Isidore of Seville was one of the most focused (and accomplished) men of his time. A brilliant scholar, prodigious writer, and noted educator, he hated schoolwork as a youth. Then, one day, he noticed an old stone well. In its walls were grooves worn by the constant friction of wet rope. St. Isidore realized that just as rope can wear away stone, so too could he succeed in his studies with focused concentration.

If we want to succeed, we need to follow the example of St. Isidore's rope. Rather than trying to do as many things as possible, becoming a jack of all trades and master of none, let us focus our attention on one thing at a time. In doing so, we may find that we accomplish more than we ever expected.

Do I find myself scurrying from one thing to the next? Do I accomplish as much as I think I should?

I PAY ATTENTION TO WHAT I AM DOING.

ST. VINCENT FERRER

1350?–1419

The Church of the 1300s and 1400s was, to put it mildly, in a mess. Two popes reigned—Urban VI in Rome and Clement VII at Avignon. When Clement died, Peter de Luna (Benedict XII) was elected as his successor. Everyone from the king to the peasants squabbled over who was the legitimate pope.

Square in the middle of this controversy was a Dominican priest—St. Vincent Ferrer. St. Vincent's loyalty originally lay with Benedict, who had ordained him, but eventually Vincent was convinced that his former friend had no claim to the papacy. He tried to persuade him to step down, but when Benedict refused, Vincent finally denounced him publicly. His base of support eroded, Benedict was forced to resign and flee for his life.

Our lives are often filled with difficult choices. Deciding to confront a friend who is wrong is one of the most difficult. If the issue is serious enough, we must either compromise our conscience by denying what we know is right or sacrifice our friendship by speaking the truth. When we are placed in a position where we must choose between our conscience and our friends, let us remember that honesty is the basis of all true friendship. If we can't be honest with our friends, perhaps they are not really our friends.

Have I ever had to confront a friend? What effect did that have on our friendship?

I AM HONEST WITH ALL MY FRIENDS.

ST. WILLIAM OF ESKILSOË

1125?–1203

St. William's reputation for holiness was so widespread, the bishop of Roskilde asked him to restore discipline to the Danish monasteries. St. William agreed and emigrated from France to Denmark about the year 1170. Once there, he spent the rest of his life reforming religious houses.

Moving to a new place can be frightening. Leaving behind friends and family can be difficult. But moving can also be exciting. It's a chance to start over, to correct the mistakes of the past and create new opportunities. Throughout history, people have emigrated to new lands with the hope of building a better future.

We can't always physically move to a new place, but every morning we are given the chance to create a new future. Mornings provide us with a clean slate. No matter what we did—or didn't do—the day before, the sunrise marks a new beginning. Each one of us gets to start life anew every morning.

Tomorrow, when you wake up, take a few minutes to thank God for the miracle of a new day. Ask God to direct your hours and to give you the insight you need to move in new directions.

Do I view each day as a fresh start or as just more of the same old thing?

I WILL LOOK FOR THE BLESSINGS GOD INTENDS FOR ME THROUGHOUT THE DAY.

ST. JOHN BAPTIST DE LA SALLE

1651–1719

St. John Baptist de la Salle was a wealthy young man. Giving away his fortune, he founded the Brothers of the Christian School (Christian Brothers). While his emphasis was always on the poor, St. John Baptist de la Salle also established schools for wealthy young delinquents so they would not be sent to prison.

We read a lot about juvenile crime these days. It's not unusual to hear about children dealing drugs, committing armed robbery, or even murdering other children. While we all agree that something must be done, we can't always agree on what that something should be. It would be interesting to hear St. John Baptist de la Salle's opinion. He was familiar with both crime born from poverty and crime bred from boredom. In a time when punishment was often swift and harsh, he looked to strict religious education as the answer. Boys in his schools attended daily Mass, studied religion, and were taught according to Christian principles.

Although it would be a grave violation of the separation of church and state to add religious training to public education, the idea that schools should not only prepare students for careers but also help shape character is an idea that extends back to the ancient Greeks. As we look at the challenges facing society today, perhaps it would be a good idea to consider how similar problems were solved in the past. After all, those who do not remember history are doomed to repeat it.

What was the most important lesson I learned in school?

·⟨𝖆𝖆𝖆𝖆𝖆𝖆𝖆𝖆𝖆𝖆𝖆𝖆𝖆𝖆𝖆𝖆𝖆𝖆𝖆𝖆⟩·

WHEN FACED WITH A PROBLEM, I LOOK TO SEE HOW
OTHERS, INCLUDING THE SAINTS, HAVE DEALT WITH
SIMILAR ISSUES.

ST. JULIE BILLIART

1751–1816

The link between our minds and bodies is complex. We all know that when we're stressed, we're more likely to get sick. Conversely, when we're in a buoyant mental state—such as falling in love— our immune systems receive a massive boost. A positive mental attitude can sometimes even change the course of serious illness. For instance, breast cancer patients are known to live longer when they are involved in a support group. While a positive attitude can work wonders, faith can work miracles.

When St. Julie Billiart was a young girl, someone fired a gun through the window of her house. As a result of the shock, she gradually became paralyzed. After more than twenty years as an invalid, Julie met a missionary priest who asked her to pray a novena to the Sacred Heart. On the fifth day, he approached her, saying, "Mother, if you have any faith, take one step in honor of the Sacred Heart." Julie stood up and began walking.

The lives of the saints abound with stories of miraculous healings. Although God doesn't operate like a cosmic vending machine (put in your prayers and out comes your exact request), somehow, in ways we don't quite understand, our faith plays a key role in healings. When we believe God *will* heal us, God *does* heal us. Sometimes the healing is physical—as in the case of St. Julie—but sometimes it is spiritual or emotional. The one thing we can be sure of is that when we ask in faith for healing, we will receive a divine answer.

How do I act when I am sick?

I BELIEVE THAT GOD ANSWERS PRAYERS FOR HEALING.

ST. WALDETRUDIS

C. A.D. 688

We've all known families in which everyone looks alike. They may all have the same hair color or the same nose, but whatever makes them look alike, when you've seen one, you've seen them all.

St. Waldetrudis's family was alike, too, but not physically. Her family was alike in its remarkable holiness. She was not only the daughter of two saints, but her sister, her husband, and her four children all became saints as well!

What was it about her family that resulted in such sanctity? Certainly the personal desire to please God and an emphasis on spiritual growth were present, but living with people who admired holiness couldn't have hurt. The people we choose to let enter our lives have a profound effect on our innermost being. Consider for a moment the following scenario: you've just started a new project and you're filled with enthusiasm. You share your news with two friends. The first says, that's terrific! I know you'll do great. How can I help? The second says, when we tried that it didn't work. It doesn't take much to figure out which friend is better for your soul.

One of the best things about the saints is that they're always ready to be the best kind of friend. When you're in the company of the saints, you will always be supported, encouraged, and loved. While we can't always be certain the people on earth will give us the help we need, we can have total confidence in the care and concern of the saints.

What help do I need from the saints right now?

I KNOW THE SAINTS ARE ON MY SIDE.

ST. BADEMUS

A.D. 376

Have you ever stayed up all night? Maybe cramming for an exam by drinking endless cups of strong coffee. Or perhaps pacing the floor with a sick child. Or maybe suffering the tortures of insomnia. But have you ever spent an entire night in prayer?

St. Bademus was a wealthy Persian who founded a monastery on his estates. He practiced various penances and, like many other saints, is said to have watched whole nights in prayer.

Praying all night isn't easy. Maybe that's why only saints are inclined to try it. Long about 3 A.M., circadian rhythms take over, your eyes grow impossibly heavy, and even the floor begins to look mighty comfy. Doubts about the wisdom of getting exhausted begin to surface, and the temptation to give up becomes almost impossibly strong.

At that point, it's sort of like hitting the wall when running. You can give up or you can push through. If you do persist, you may find something incredible happening. As your natural barriers erode, God comes leaping into your emptiness. You may feel God's presence in a way you've never experienced before. It may be subtle—an enhanced awareness—or it may be more dramatic—a definite sense of being enveloped in God's love. Even if you don't think anything is occurring, it is. God will reward the sacrifice you made of your sleep by blessing you in ways you may never have considered.

Am I a morning person or a night person? When is it easiest for me to pray?

THE NEXT TIME I'M AWAKE LATE AT NIGHT, I WILL USE THAT TIME TO PRAY.

ST. GEMMA GALGANI

1878–1903

The saying, beauty is only skin deep, doesn't apply to St. Gemma Galgani. Although it is obvious from her photographs that she was an extraordinary beauty, St. Gemma was a woman of equally extraordinary holiness. One of the most remarkable things about St. Gemma was her ability to converse directly with her guardian angel. They were on such familiar terms that she often sent her angel on errands, usually to deliver a message to her confessor in Rome.

Like St. Gemma, each of us has our own individual guardian angel, a messenger of light and hope sent directly from heaven to be our friend, guide, and companion. These blessed spirits accompany us throughout life, lending their assistance and offering their love. Although they are always with us, we aren't always aware of our angels' presence. Learning to communicate with the angels is a lot like learning to communicate with the saints. The first step is to acknowledge that both saints and angels are real. The second is to watch for evidence of their proximity.

Although a few saints like St. Gemma have been given the gift of seeing their guardian angels face to face, most of us have to settle for subtler signs. Have you ever felt a tiny flutter of warning? Your angel was nearby. Have you ever felt a profound sense of awe and wonder? Your angel was nearby. Have you ever experienced an unexpected surge of joy? Your angel was most certainly nearby.

If I could send my angel on an errand, what would it be?

I LOOK FOR SIGNS OF MY GUARDIAN ANGEL'S PRESENCE.

ST. JULIUS I

A.D. 352

St. Julius I was Pope during one of the greatest turmoils of the early Church. Bishops were accusing other bishops of heresy. Councils were being convened with and without papal approval. Theological controversy was tearing the church apart. Yet, during all the strife, St. Julius is said to have exercised "apostolic vigor and resolution tempered with charity and meekness."

'Meekness' conjures up the image of a milquetoast sort of person who doesn't have enough gumption to stand up for anything. Assertiveness, confidence, self-assurance—these are the qualities that bring happiness, right?

Well, maybe. And maybe not.

Being meek doesn't mean we let others push us around. Rather, being meek means we bring a sense of calm and peace to all our actions. It means we are patient and forbearing. In short, it means we follow the Golden Rule. Treating others with respect is an important part of the Golden Rule, but sometimes we forget we can apply the rule to ourselves as well. Today, pause for a few moments and pay attention to how you treat yourself. Listen to your mental tone of voice. Watch the way you attend to your body. Ask yourself if you're being as kind to yourself as you are to others. If you aren't, ask yourself why not.

How critical am I of myself? In what ways do I fail to give myself the respect I deserve?

·⟨⟨⟨⟨⟨⟨⟨⟨⟨⟨⟨⟨⟨⟨⟨⟨⟨⟩⟩⟩⟩⟩⟩⟩⟩⟩⟩⟩⟩⟩⟩⟩·

I APPLY THE GOLDEN RULE TO MYSELF AS WELL AS TO OTHERS.

BLESSED MARGARET OF CASTELLO

1287–1320

When Margaret of Castello's parents learned they were to have a child, they were delighted. When they saw their daughter, however, their joy turned to disgust. Margaret was blind, dwarfed, hunchbacked, and permanently lame. Her parents refused to see her and eventually imprisoned her in a small cell attached to a church in the hopes she would die there.

Margaret didn't die. In a desperate attempt to find a cure, her mother persuaded her father to take her to a tomb where miracles were said to be happening. When Margaret wasn't healed, her parents abandoned her. Eventually she was taken in by various poor families where she finally found the love and acceptance her parents could not give her.

Someone once said, tongue in cheek, that every family is dysfunctional. Most of us don't come from a family quite as dysfunctional as was Blessed Margaret's, but few of us come from picture-perfect families. We all bear scars from the things our parents did—or didn't do—as we were growing up.

Blaming our parents for the way our lives turned out does little except inhibit our own spiritual growth. Eventually we have to face the fact that we are no longer children. If we are to become whole, healthy adults then we must let go of the past and be willing to forgive our parents for everything they did—or didn't—do.

Do I still harbor resentments from my childhood? Do I blame my parents for the way I am today?

·⟨⟩·

I MAY NOT LIKE EVERYTHING MY PARENTS DID,
BUT I FORGIVE THEM.

ST. BÉNÉZET

A.D. 1184

Bridges are fascinating structures. Often appearing to hang in mid-air, they fling themselves over open water, tying two distant banks with a ribbon of roadway.

St. Bénézet was an unlikely candidate to be a bridge builder. A shepherd by trade, he heard a voice during an eclipse telling him to build a bridge near Avignon. After many trials, he finally convinced the bishop to let him try, and for the next seven years he oversaw the construction of a stone bridge across a particularly dangerous part of the Rhône. When he died, in 1184, the bridge was almost, but not quite, finished.

Bridge building is a difficult and dangerous occupation. It requires steady nerves, sure footing, and a fair amount of faith. Maybe that's why bridge building is often used as a metaphor for reconciliation. When people are seriously at odds with one another, it takes steady nerves, sure footing, and a fair amount of faith to attempt to bring them back together.

As treacherous as it is to be a bridge builder, it is even more dangerous to leave a gulf of anger unspanned. Although anger is often thought of as being hot and burning, it is more like an untamed river—cold, relentless, and unforgiving. Everything that comes near its banks is swept into its all-consuming current. Since anger runs deep and swift, often the only way to get around it is to go over it; to fling a ribbon of forgiveness from one bank to the next. To build a bridge.

Do I need to build a bridge in my life? What do I need to start the construction?

I BUILD THE NECESSARY BRIDGES IN MY LIFE.

BLESSED DAMIEN DE VEUSTER

1840–1889

For most of the world's history, lepers were among the most feared and loathed of all creatures. Because no one understood how the illness was spread, its victims were ostracized. All known lepers were shipped to leper colonies, places where no one in their right mind would willingly go. If you've ever seen the classic movie *Ben Hur*, you know what life was like for the lepers.

Damien de Veuster not only willingly came to the leper colony on the Hawaiian island of Molokai, but he spent the rest of his life there working with and for the lepers. Eventually he contracted leprosy himself and died at age forty-nine, his body hideously ravaged by its effects.

Although leprosy is uncommon today, other diseases—like cancer and AIDS—elicit similar reactions of fear and revulsion. We often shun their victims, shuddering at the very thought of physical contact. Yet the loving touch of another human being is often what people suffering from terminal illness need the most—a gentle hug, a handclasp, a back rub. It's natural to want to protect ourselves from illness, but ironically, the diseases we fear the most are not usually transmitted by touch. Shaking hands with an AIDS patient will not give you AIDS, and no amount of hugging will cause you to "catch" cancer. Withholding your touch won't keep you well; extending it might be a means of healing for another. Which will you choose?

How does being in the presence of someone who is terminally ill make me feel? Am I frightened for them or frightened for me?

EVEN IF I AM AFRAID OF AN ILLNESS, I AM NOT AFRAID OF ITS VICTIMS.

ST. BERNADETTE

1844–1879

St. Bernadette was only fourteen when the Virgin Mary appeared to her at Lourdes. Never considered very bright, St. Bernadette was often asked why the Virgin would have visited her. Bernadette said, "Don't I realize that the Blessed Virgin chose me because I was the most ignorant? If she had found anyone more ignorant than myself, she would have chosen her. The Blessed Virgin used me like a broom. What do you do with a broom when you have finished sweeping? You put it back in its place, behind the door."

We generally don't like the idea of being used. Most of the time it means being taken advantage of, being duped and deceived. In the heavenly plan, however, being used is part of a creative act—a little like being a glass. A glass sitting on the shelf may be attractive, but it doesn't serve the purpose for which it was made. Only when we take the glass down from the shelf, fill it with water or milk or wine, and share it with our partners, our children, or our friends does it become all it was intended to be. Likewise, it is only when we allow ourselves to be filled with love that we become the people God created us to be.

If I were a glass, where would I be right now? Would I be sitting on the shelf or out on the table in the middle of life?

I ALLOW MYSELF TO BE USED, BUT NEVER USED UP.

ST. STEPHEN HARDING

A.D. 1134

St. Stephen Harding was educated in a monastery, traveled a bit, had a conversion experience, and eventually believed that God intended him to found his own monastery. His new order didn't fare well due to a lack of novices plus the appearance of a mysterious disease. The order would have ceased operating if it weren't for a young man who showed up at the monastery gates with thirty of his relatives and friends, asking to be admitted to religious life. St. Stephen, knowing a good thing when he saw one, quickly welcomed them. From that dubious beginning grew one of the greatest religious orders of all time—the Cistercians, or Trappists—for the young man at the front gate was none other than St. Bernard of Clairvaux, one of the greatest mystics and writers of the Middle Ages.

When St. Stephen founded his monastery, he believed he was following God's will. As things careened from bad to worse, he must have wondered if he had misinterpreted the message. As St. Stephen was on the verge of giving up, St. Bernard arrived. Sometimes when we undertake what we believe is the will of God, everything seems to fall apart. If that happens, St. Stephen encourages us to wait and trust that if what we have begun really is in accord with God's plan, all will work out for the best.

When I start something new, am I willing to wait and see what happens or do I get anxious when success eludes me?

I AM WILLING TO BE PATIENT, EVEN WHEN THINGS AREN'T GOING MY WAY.

ST. GALDINUS

A.D. 1176

In the twelfth century, Milan was believed to be the final resting place for the three kings who visited the infant Jesus. Although gospel accounts do not say how many Magi there were, and despite the improbability of three of them being buried in Milan, public opinion about the reputed relics was so heated that Emperor Frederick ordered them removed to Cologne, Germany, when he sacked Milan.

St. Galdinus was the archdeacon to Archbishop Hubert during this period of history. Not only were the relics of the three kings taken from his city, but he was forced into exile with the archbishop. Eventually, he was appointed a cardinal and took over the archbishop's position. In the midst of such radical change in his life, St. Galdinus must have felt he was the victim of the Chinese curse, may you live in interesting times.

We currently live in very interesting times. From covered wagons to satellites, quill pens to e-mail, more has happened in the past 150 years than in the previous 1500. Every day new inventions are presented that result in even more change. The next time the rapid rush of technology leaves you feeling a bit like you've been exiled while the technocrats ransack your comfortable world, ask St. Galdinus to help you go with the flow. If you do, you may find that living in interesting times isn't such a curse after all.

Am I a technocrat or a technophobe? Do I cling to the past, or do I embrace the future?

I WILLINGLY ACCEPT NEW THINGS AND NEW IDEAS.

ST. LEO IX

1002–1054

When St. Leo IX was born, his body was marked with little red crosses, which were believed to have been the result of his mother's intense meditation on the Passion of Jesus. Although his birthmarks probably had a much less fanciful origin, it is true that a mother's actions while pregnant can have a dramatic effect on her child's later life. For instance, pregnant women are encouraged to avoid alcohol, cigarette smoke, and caffeine.

Preborn babies can be positively as well as negatively influenced. It is now known, for example, that babies respond favorably to music as well as to their mothers' voices.

In some ways, our life here on earth is like our prebirth existence. While we are in utero we have no idea what life outside the womb will be like. The process of birth is painful and frightening. Yet, who would choose to remain unborn after having experienced even some of the riches of life?

Similarly, we have no firsthand experience of what the next life will be like. The transition from this life to the next through the process we call death is often painful and frightening. If the analogies between birth and death hold true, however, we have nothing to fear, for just as this life surpasses existence within the womb, so too will the next life surpass all we have experienced here on earth.

Does thinking of death as a form of birth relieve some of my fears?

I BELIEVE LIFE DOES NOT END, BUT WILL BE TRANSFORMED.

ST. AGNES OF MONTEPULCIANO

1268–1317

Measuring pain is an inexact science. Since we can never really know what another person is feeling, we can't accurately judge how much pain they are experiencing. Nonetheless, observation tells us that pain thresholds are quite individual. Some people collapse while removing a sliver while others can undergo complex surgery with a minimal anesthetic.

St. Agnes of Montepulciano apparently had a high pain threshold since she spent fifteen years sleeping on the ground with only a rock for a pillow—definitely not a practice for the faint of heart.

While we may not think so when we are in the middle of it, pain is one of heaven's blessings. Our body's early warning system, it alerts us that something is wrong, in time—we hope—to take corrective action. Without the ability to feel pain, we would never know we were seriously ill or injured until it was too late.

When we ignore our body's warning signals, we run the risk of permanent damage. Although pain thresholds vary from person to person, we all know when we've crossed our boundary. After fifteen years, St. Agnes finally reached hers and gave up sleeping on the ground. When you reach your limit, don't just grit your teeth and keep going. Pay attention to the message pain is sending you and find out what's wrong.

Do I know my pain threshold? Do I ever push myself beyond my limits?

WHEN I'M IN PAIN, I PAY ATTENTION TO THE MESSAGES MY BODY IS TRYING TO SEND ME.

ST. ANSELM

1033–1109

St. Anselm is known for many things, including being archbishop of Canterbury and a doctor of the Church, but perhaps his most remarkable achievement was getting the national council at Westminster to pass a resolution in 1102 forbidding the sale of human beings as if they were cattle. In a time when virtually no one questioned slavery, St. Anselm became the first champion of human freedom in the entire Church.

Freedom is one of the fundamental rights of all human beings. We have the right to be free, not only from slavery, but also from fear, oppression, doubt, and criticism. We have the right to live openly, creatively, and positively. These things are our divine birthright, but no one is going to come along and hand them to us on a silver platter.

If we want them, we have to get them for ourselves by drafting our own personal Declaration of Independence.

Today, become the champion of your own freedom. Pass a mental resolution that from this day forth, you will not let yourself become enslaved by negative people or negative influences. Make a conscious decision to throw off the shackles of worry and doubt and cast away the chains of discouragement. Finally, ask the saints, especially St. Anselm, to help you break through the bondage of sin and evil so that you can draw nearer to the true and lasting freedom of heaven.

Do I really believe that I have the right to be free? Am I a slave to a bad habit or negative thought pattern?

I REFUSE TO BE ENSLAVED BY ANY PERSON OR THING.

ST. OPPORTUNA

C. A.D. 770

Very little is known about St. Opportuna except that she was Abbess of Montreuil in Normandy during the eighth century. Her brother, a bishop, was murdered in 769 as he was returning from a pilgrimage to Rome. She died a year later, after a life of humility, obedience, mortification, and prayer.

While her life isn't terribly interesting, her name is: Opportuna, or *Opportunity.*

The word *opportunity* is defined by the Oxford American Dictionary as "a time or set of circumstances that are suitable for a particular purpose."

Although the popular saying that opportunity knocks but once indicates we get only a few chances in life, the saints teach us otherwise. Throughout our lives we are presented times and circumstances suitable for choosing between good and bad, light and darkness, hope and despair. Every day we are given chances to make choices that bring us a little bit closer to heaven or draw us a little bit farther away.

These opportunities do not always present themselves with trumpets and fanfare. Often they appear small and insignificant, but do not be deceived. What appears to be minuscule actually may be monumental in God's eyes. As St. Thérèse of Lisieux says, "Miss no single opportunity of making some small sacrifice, here by a smiling look, there by a kindly word; always doing the smallest thing right and doing it all for love . . . . Remember that nothing is small in the eyes of God."

Have I ever missed an opportunity because I thought it was too small?

THE NEXT TIME I CAN DO A GOOD DEED I'LL JUMP
AT THE OPPORTUNITY.

ST. GEORGE

A.D. 303

When it comes to stories, St. George has one of the best. The tale goes something like this: St. George, a Christian knight, was searching for adventure when he happened upon the city of Sylene, which was being held hostage by a dragon. To keep the dragon appeased, the townsfolk fed it two sheep every day. When they ran out of sheep, they began offering the dragon young maidens. These innocent virgins were chosen by lot; it just so happened that the day St. George arrived in town, the king's own daughter had drawn the short straw. As she was heading off to be devoured by the beast (which had not only dreadful eating habits, but also very bad breath), St. George rescued her, slew the creature, and to top off his day, converted the village to Christianity.

Obviously this is one of the more fanciful saint stories.

The real St. George was probably beheaded during the time of Constantine—much less exciting than the tale of dragons and maidens. But then, most of us have much less exciting lives than are found in fiction.

If we base our notion of what real life is supposed to be like on movies and television, we're bound to be disappointed. Reel life is never the same as real life. It's a good thing it isn't. All the reel St. George got to do is fight a dragon. The real St. George got to go to heaven.

If my life were perfect, what would I be doing right now?

THE MORE I LIVE REAL LIFE, THE LESS I AM ATTRACTED TO REEL LIFE.

ST. FIDELIS OF SIGMARINGEN

1577–1622

Entering religious life often prompts changing one's name from the ordinary. A Bill becomes a Reginald, a Carlo becomes a John-Joseph-of-the-Cross, and a Mark Roy becomes a Fidelis of Sigmaringen.

Mark Roy was a seventeenth-century lawyer who specialized in cases involving the poor and oppressed. Disgusted with corruption in the legal system (some things never change!), he entered the Capuchin branch of the Franciscans, where he became noted for his vigorous preaching.

Mark Roy changed more than his name when he entered the Franciscans; he also changed his profession. It used to be that once you were established in a career you stuck with it until you retired. Your job became the center of your life. Now experts say that the average person will change not just jobs, but careers, as many as four or five times. With that many changes, trying to center your life in your profession can be a serious mistake.

One lesson the saints encourage us to remember is that we weren't created to *do*. We were created to *be*. Of course we can't sit around all day just *being*. But we shouldn't put so much emphasis on our jobs that we forget to enjoy other important things in life—the mud-puddle reflection of a cloud, the first daffodil of spring, the sound of a baby's laughter.

What would I do if I no longer had to work?

I WORK WHEN I WORK AND I PLAY WHEN I PLAY.

ST. MARK

FIRST CENTURY

St. Mark, the author of the shortest and oldest gospel, is mentioned at least ten times in the Bible, most often as a missionary companion of Paul. Because the events recounted in the Bible happened so long ago, we may have a hard time imagining the people. Add to that the overly pious pictures and saccharine Biblical stories that are often presented to us as children, and it's a wonder any trace of real personality has made it through the centuries. Yet hidden between the lines of Biblical stories are hints of intrigue and controversy. One of the biggest centers on St. Mark.

Mark was apparently a teenager when Jesus was teaching. About the year 46, Paul and Barnabas took him with them on their first missionary journey. Sometime later, Mark decided to return to Jerusalem, much to Paul's disgust. Mark and Paul could not reconcile their differences, and Paul refused to take him along on his second missionary journey.

Why did Mark go home? What made Paul so furious? Although those questions are intriguing, they just skim the surface of the controversy, for it is apparent that later on Mark and Paul were reconciled. In fact, Mark even visited and comforted Paul in prison.

The questions surrounding their reconciliation are even more intriguing than is their initial argument. Who made the first move? What prompted them to make peace? When we are involved in an angry dispute, let us remember the incident with Mark and Paul. It really doesn't matter who makes the first move, so long as we are willing to meet the other person somewhere in the middle.

Do I find it harder to ask forgiveness or to give it?

I AM AS WILLING TO FORGIVE AS I AM TO BE FORGIVEN.

ST. RICHARIUS

A.D. 645

Have you ever been so wrapped up in a project or activity that time seems to evaporate? You become so absorbed in what you are doing that literally hours can pass without your being aware of the time. It's as if you had been transported to a place where time doesn't exist; a place where your mind, body, and soul are in total harmony. Although you may have been working very hard, you aren't tired. In fact, you feel totally alive and renewed.

That kind of complete absorption happens most often when we are involved in a highly creative act, such as writing poetry or painting or praying. Praying?

Yes, praying. Prayer isn't something we do only in church, and it certainly isn't merely the dull recitation of set formulas. For the saints, prayer is the most creative act of life. St. Richarius, a French abbot, spent much of his adult life in contemplation and prayer. When praying, he became so totally absorbed that "he seemed almost to forget he had a body." For St. Richarius, as for all of us, real prayer is a total surrender into the all-encompassing love of God. When we enter into deep prayer, we cease to be aware of ourselves or our surroundings. We are transported into another realm, a realm where time stops and love becomes tangible; we enter into an intimate, personal interchange with the Creator of all life. What could possibly be more creative than that?

How do I pray? Am I more comfortable with formal prayers, or do I prefer to make up my own prayers?

I REALIZE THAT CREATIVITY AND PRAYER ARE CLOSELY LINKED.

ST. ZITA

1218–1278

Nowadays, many kids expect that when they get out of school, they'll be in high-paying professions, such as medicine, law, or professional athletics. The few kids who do plan to enter less glamorous careers usually assume they'll own their own businesses or become high-level managers within a few years.

Youthful aspirations are wonderful, but most of us have had to settle for something other than what we originally planned. One of the watersheds of maturity comes the day you realize that even though things didn't work out the way you hoped they would, life is still filled with wonder and blessings.

No telling what St. Zita wanted to be when she was growing up. She might have dreamed of marriage and children. Or she could have desired to follow in the footsteps of her older sister, who became a Cistercian nun. Despite Zita's dreams, at age twelve she became the servant of an Italian wool and silk-weaving merchant and worked as the family's housekeeper and nanny for forty-eight years.

Although St. Zita didn't have much choice in her work, she made her work into a blessing. When she died at age sixty, she was far more than a mere servant to the di Fatinelli family. She was friend, advisor, and saint.

What did I want to be when I was growing up? Can I still make that choice?

I VALUE MY WORK.

ST. PETER MARY CHANEL

1803 – 1841

St. Peter Chanel was one of the first missionaries to the New Hebrides. With effort, he mastered the native tongue and began to teach the islanders. His efforts, however, were short-lived. When the chief's son asked to be baptized, the chief sent a band of warriors to club St. Peter to death. Although the chief silenced St. Peter, the saint's words continued. Within two years the entire island had converted to Christianity. Today, St. Peter Chanel is not only the first martyr of Oceania, he is also its patron saint.

Words have enormous power. Take the words *I* and *you*. Put the word *love* between them. Now put the word *hate* between them. *Love* and *hate* are both four-letter words. They both express strong human emotions. But think how you different it makes you feel to say I love you rather than I hate you. Even more, think how different it makes you feel to hear them.

The words we use not only give others a clue as to our level of education and depth of knowledge, they also indicate our sensitivity and awareness. Today be mindful of the words you use. Are they words of encouragement or words of criticism? Are they harsh or are they gentle? Do you use different words with friends and family than you do with strangers? Do you use profanity or obscenities on a regular basis? Finally, how comfortable are you with silence?

*What is my favorite word? When was the last time I learned a
new word?*

I CHOOSE MY WORDS WITH CARE.

ST. CATHERINE OF SIENA

1347–1380

St. Catherine of Siena was a remarkable woman. Although she was almost illiterate, her four dictated treatises ("Dialogue of St. Catherine") have earned her the title Doctor of the Church. She and Teresa of Avila are the only women to be so designated. A woman in a male-dominated society, she changed history by convincing the papacy to return to Rome after nearly three-quarters of a century in Avignon. In frail health, she tirelessly cared for the sick, including victims of the plague.

She was also the youngest in a family of twenty-five children. Being the baby of an enormous family, Catherine would understandably be little inclined to marry and have a family of her own. Yet, in one sense, she did. As her reputation for holiness grew, a group of priests, religious, and lay people gathered around her, seeking her spiritual advice and wisdom. She called them her family, and they in turn called her Mamma.

One of the principle qualities of a good parent is the ability to nurture. Even if we aren't parents in the biological sense, we can all become spiritual parents to those around us. By offering our encouragement, our experience, and our insight, we can help others find and fulfill their potential. And that, after all, is what parents do best.

Whom do I consider my spiritual parents? Is there anyone I would consider my spiritual child?

⸙

I REALIZE THAT IN ORDER TO DISCOVER MY FULL POTENTIAL, I MUST HELP OTHERS DISCOVER THEIRS.

ST. PIUS V

1504–1572

"The Mole had been working very hard all the morning, spring-cleaning his little home. First with brooms, then with dusters; then on ladders and steps and chairs, with a brush and a pail of whitewash; . . . Spring was moving in the air above and in the earth below and around him, penetrating even his dark and lowly little house with its spirit of divine discontent and longing." Thus opens the magnificent children's classic *The Wind in the Willows*, by Kenneth Grahame.

About this time of year, we all get the bug to start spring cleaning. We feel cooped up after the long dark days of winter and want to throw open the windows, literally and figuratively.

St. Pius V must felt that way about the Church after he was elected Pope in 1566. He immediately began monumental reforms, ranging from prohibiting bull-fighting to ordering all bishops to live in their dioceses.

What in your life needs a good spring cleaning? Maybe it's your personal relationships, which have grown stale and stagnant from lack of attention. Perhaps it's your spiritual life, which has become buried under cobwebs of worry and fear. Perhaps it's your intellect, which has been dulled by too many hours of mindless entertainment. Whatever it is, now is an ideal time to get out of the winter rut and into the spirit of spring by cleaning out old habits and negative thoughts.

What bad habit can I begin to change today?

I LET THE WONDER OF SPRING FILL ME WITH ENERGY AND RENEWED HOPE.

ST. PEREGRINE LAZIOSI

1260–1345

One of the truisms of spiritual life is that we get what we ask for in prayer. "Ask and you shall receive," says Jesus. "Yeah, right," you may be thinking. "If that were true, we'd all have won the lottery by now."

It's true, all right, but most of us don't know how to ask. Oh, we know how to put in our requests, as if God were a short-order cook in a fast-food restaurant, but that isn't *asking*. Asking isn't merely the act of articulating our desires and then sitting back and waiting for God to deliver. Asking is the total surrender of our will to the will of God. We bring our needs to God, believing they will be fulfilled, not because we want them, but because God wants to grant them to us.

St. Peregrine suffered from cancer of the foot. When all medical treatment failed, the doctors decided to amputate. St. Peregrine spent the night before the surgery asking God to heal him, but only if God was pleased to do so. When the surgeons arrived the next morning, he was completely healed.

Learning the difference between *asking* and asking takes time. It requires a fearless examination of our motives. If we make our requests out of fear and selfishness, it's unlikely that God will grant them. It is only when we are totally and completely willing to accept whatever God gives us that we can be certain we are really *asking*.

When I pray, do I ask God for help or do I ask God for help?

───

I TRUST THAT GOD WILL GIVE ME EXACTLY WHAT I NEED
AT EXACTLY THE TIME I NEED IT.

ST. ATHANASIUS

297?-373

The popular saying, garbage in, garbage out, is appropriate in a lot of situations. It's perhaps most applicable to our reading material. For example, if all our reading consists of tabloids at the grocery-store checkout, we're going to end up with a fairly peculiar view of the world. If we want to grow and mature in our thinking, then we have to read material that is intellectually and mentally stimulating.

More than sixteen hundred years ago, St. Athanasius understood the principle of garbage in, garbage out as it applies to spiritual growth. "You will not see anyone who is really striving after his advancement who is not given to spiritual reading," he pointed out, "and to him who neglects it, the fact will soon be observed in his progress."

By having picked up this book, you show that you're willing to work on your spiritual advancement. The words of the saints throughout the centuries provide a wonderful place to begin learning what great men and women have thought about God, creation, sanctity, and prayer. This book, however, can provide only those tidbits of saintly wisdom that have appealed to the author. If you want to know more about the saints, what motivated them to holiness, and how their insights can help you on your own spiritual journey, then you need to seek out and read their writings for yourself.

When was the last time I read something that expanded my worldview or changed my way of thinking?

TODAY I WILL MAKE TIME TO READ ONE THING THAT IS DIFFICULT OR CHALLENGING.

ST. PHILIP

FIRST CENTURY

Ever tried really hard to make a good impression and say just the right thing, only to make a fool of yourself? If you have, St. Philip understands.

One of the twelve apostles, Philip was present at the Last Supper. Jesus had just said that he was going to prepare a place for his followers. Thomas interrupted, asking, "Lord, we do not know where you are going. How can we know the way?" Jesus answered, "I am the way. . . . If you knew me, you would know my Father also."

One can almost see what's coming next. Thomas is chagrined, so Philip tries to make things better by asking, "Lord, show us the Father and that will be enough for us." The frustration Jesus must have felt spilled out in his answer. "Philip, after I have been with you all this time, you still do not know me?" Philip must have wanted to join Thomas under the cushions at the table.

Foot-in-mouth disease isn't just a veterinary complaint. We've all suffered from it at some time or another. When we've embarrassed ourselves beyond belief, the only thing we can do is take a deep breath and remind ourselves that to err is human, to forgive divine. We can also take comfort from the example of St. Philip. Although he publicly embarrassed himself in front of Jesus, he was also publicly honored when the Holy Spirit descended on him at Pentecost and gave him the courage to spread the teachings of Jesus throughout the world.

What lessons have I learned from my most embarrassing moments?

WHEN I FIND MY FOOT IN MY MOUTH, I TAKE IT OUT CAREFULLY SO AS NOT TO CHOKE ON MY WORDS.

ST. GOTHARD

A.D. 1038

St. Gothard was born in the Bavarian village of Reichersdorf. As a Benedictine monk, he reformed several monasteries throughout Bavaria. When St. Bernwald, bishop of Hildesheim, died in 1022, the emperor Henry named Gothard as successor.

One of his greatest deeds as bishop was to build a hospice on the outskirts of the city for the sick and poor. Anyone in genuine need could stay there, but St. Gothard had little patience with able-bodied, professional tramps and would not let them remain for more than a few days.

St. Gothard understood that although we are required to lend assistance to those in need, we aren't obligated to be foolish or naive about it. Had he turned his hospice into a hobo haven, the truly needy would have been crowded out.

Nevertheless, St. Gothard let the virtue of charity rule at all times. He let everyone into the hospice and gave them food and shelter for two or three days, long enough to figure out if they were faking it.

St. Gothard's wisdom in dealing with a thorny situation teaches us another lesson. By insisting that professional tramps get off the dole, so to speak, he reminds us that when we are in genuine need, there is no shame in asking for assistance, but when we ask for help in order to avoid our own responsibilities, no one is obliged to help us.

Do I do my fair share of work at home and on the job? Do I ever expect anyone else to do my work for me?

I DO NOT SHIRK MY RESPONSIBILITIES, AND I AM NOT AFRAID OF HARD WORK.

ST. HILARY

A.D. 449

St. Hilary had a difficult time making up his mind whether to enter religious life. On the one hand, he had great potential for a successful secular career; on the other, his kinsman, St. Honoratus, the founder of the monastery of Lérins, tried to convince him he had a religious vocation.

St. Hilary couldn't figure out which way to go. "My will swayed backwards and forwards, now consenting, now refusing," he wrote. Eventually he made a decision and went to join his relative.

Indecision is one of the greatest of all energy sappers. As we struggle to make up our minds, we may find ourselves losing sleep, becoming preoccupied, and generally being downright miserable.

While the saints would never recommend you leap before you look, they don't suggest you hem and haw unduly. When you have a decision to make, it's always a good idea to look at all sides of the issue. Investigate your choices as much as possible and weigh the pros and cons. You might even take a night or two to sleep on it. Eventually, though, pondering must give way to action. Fish or cut bait, as the saying goes.

Once you've made up your mind, don't second-guess yourself and try to remake the decision. Go forward, knowing that you did the best you could and trusting in Providence to take care of the rest.

How good am I at making decisions? After I've made a decision, do I keep going back over it in my mind, worrying that I've made a mistake?

AFTER I'VE MADE A DECISION, I STICK TO IT AND DON'T SECOND-GUESS MYSELF.

ST. JOHN BEFORE THE LATIN GATE

FIRST CENTURY

Etymologists explain that many surnames, especially those from Northern Europe, were originally descriptive terms. For instance, the name Baker probably originally referred to a family of, yes, bakers. Other surnames hearken back to family members—Davidson, meaning, literally, the son of David. Consider for a minute what it would have been like if St. John Before the Latin Gate had had descendants. Would there now be a family of BeforeTheLatinGateson's? Of course not, because St. John (also known as St. John the Evangelist) never married. Even if he had, his descendants would have had Latin or Greek names. The appellation "Before the Latin Gate" was attached to the name supposedly because the emperor Domitian ordered him boiled in hot oil outside the gate of Rome leading to the town of Latinum.

Shakespeare wrote, " . . . a rose by any other name would smell as sweet." Is that really true? You might ask Alan Alda, Brigitte Bardot, or Tom Cruise. They were born Alphonso D'Abruzzo, Camille Javal, and Thomas Mapother.

No rule says that we have to keep the name given to us at birth. If you don't like your name, pick one that suits you better. You might even read about the saints to find one who especially appeals to you and take his or her name as your own. Then whenever you hear your new name called, you can recall the saint who inspired you and ask for his or her special protection.

Why was I given the name I have? Is there any special meaning behind it?

·⟨�⟩·

I AM FREE TO CALL MYSELF ANYTHING I LIKE.

ST. JOHN OF BEVERLEY

A.D. 721

One of the nicest gifts we can give ourselves is a free day. Not because it's a holiday or a special occasion, but just because.

St. John of Beverley was the bishop of York in the eighth century. Then as now, bishops didn't have much free time. St. John, however, would steal away as often as he could for spiritual refreshment. For a while he went to an abbey, but later he spent his free days in a forest.

Free days are just that—free. You don't have to pay for them by running errands or cleaning closets or paying duty visits to elderly relatives. They are days to let the little kid in you come out to play. Remember when you were little and you wanted to play? You called up a friend and said, can you come out? You didn't worry if your friend would think you were foolish or irresponsible or pushy. You just asked, can you come out? And if they could, they did.

Once we are grown-ups, we assume our friends are all too sophisticated to just play. So we make plans and have lunch and do other important things. Underneath it all, we are afraid that if we said all we really want to do is throw stones in a stream and climb a tree and talk, our friend would laugh at us and turn us down. So we stop asking. And we stop playing.

When was the last time I took an honest-to-goodness, genuine free day? When was the last time I went out to play?

⊱⸺⸺⸺⸺⸺⸺⸺⸺⸺⸺⊰

SOMETIME SOON, I WILL CALL UP A FRIEND AND ASK,
CAN YOU COME OUT TO PLAY?

BLESSED JULIAN OF NORWICH

1343–1423

Dame Julian of Norwich isn't one of the official saints of the Roman calendar, but she is one of the most beloved mystics of all times.

Julian was apparently well-educated, but she was not a happy child and even prayed for an early death. She says, "[I was] weary of my life and irked with myself, so that I kept the patience to go on living only with difficulty . . . " But go on she did, becoming renowned for her wisdom and holiness.

When we realize Julian knew firsthand what it is like to feel great despair, one of her most famous sayings becomes even more poignant. "All shall be well and all shall be well and all manner of thing shall be well."

When we are feeling oppressed and weary with life, the words of Julian of Norwich act like a balm to the soul. "All shall be well and all shall be well." No matter what is happening, no matter how bleak things look at the moment, our life is unfolding as it ought. We don't have to *do* anything to make it happen. All we have to do is trust.

"And all manner of thing shall be well." Even when we look around and see all the horrors of war, disease, and disaster, we don't have to worry, because everything, not just some things or the things we can control, but *everything* will turn out for the best.

Do I really believe that things turn out for the best?

THE NEXT TIME I'M FEELING FRIGHTENED, I WILL
REMEMBER THE WORDS OF JULIAN OF NORWICH AND TRUST
THAT ALL WILL BE WELL.

ST. CATHERINE OF BOLOGNA

1463

A thing of beauty is a joy forever:
Its loveliness increases; it will never
Pass into nothingness; but still will keep
A bower quiet for us, and a sleep
Full of sweet dreams, and health, and quiet breathing.

John Keats

St. Catherine of Bologna appreciated the inherent need of the human soul for things of beauty. Because she spent many hours illuminating her breviary, she is considered the patron saint of artists.

Without art we would survive, but we would not live.

It is said that beauty is in the eye of the beholder. If that's true, then it isn't necessary to spend thousands of dollars on an original piece of art to own a thing of beauty. All of us, no matter what our income, can grace our home with something we find particularly beautiful. It may be an object from nature—a particularly pretty pebble or shell, or it could be a project a child has created with love as the main ingredient. It might be a photograph or a plant or an antique. Whatever it is, the main criteria is that it gives us a sense of pleasure and wholeness when we see it.

Today, take a look at your surroundings. Do they nourish your need for beauty? If they don't, ask St. Catherine to help you find just the right thing to introduce to your environment to make it truly your own quiet bower.

Do I let other people's idea of what makes good art influence what I like?

I WILL MAKE SURE I ALWAYS HAVE AT LEAST ONE THING
IN MY ENVIRONMENT THAT NOURISHES MY SOUL.

ST. ANTONINUS

1389–1459

Despite being small and frail, St. Antoninus longed to enter religious life. At age fifteen, he asked the prior of Santa Maria Novella for admittance to the Order of Friars Preacher. The prior, believing the lad to be too frail for the rigors of the life, sent him home, telling him once he had memorized the *Decretum Gratiani*, his request would be considered. Much to the prior's surprise, St. Antoninus returned within a year, ready to recite the entire formidable tome. Needless to say, he was promptly admitted.

Memorization is hard work. Most of us haven't memorized anything since we were in school . . . and that probably wasn't willingly. Yet committing pieces of poetry or literature to memory is the only way to be certain you will always have them with you.

Some people like to memorize Scripture or poetry. Others prefer passages from plays or movies. Still others want to remember famous speeches. Whatever it is, begin by making a copy and putting it someplace where you can refer to it often throughout the day. (When actors are learning lines, they often take their scripts with them wherever they go.) At first, just read it a few times. Then gradually try to remember the first line, then the second. Don't be discouraged if it takes some time. If you stick with it, before you know, you'll have the entire piece stored in your memory, where you can recall it any time you want.

What would I like to be able to call up from my memory any time I wanted it?

TODAY I WILL BEGIN MEMORIZING SOMETHING THAT HAS MEANING FOR ME AND MY LIFE.

ST. MAMERTUS

A.D. 477

Although the saints are always ready to listen to our requests and help us in often miraculous ways, they are the first to remind us that they are powerless without God. When we ask them for their help, it's not like they can go behind God's back to grant our requests. No saint can answer any prayer, perform any miracle, or grant any favor without divine approval. If what we are asking isn't divinely ordained, not even the greatest saint in heaven can give it to us. If what we are asking *has* been divinely ordained, then not even the greatest saint in heaven can prevent it from occurring.

St. Mamertus, the archbishop of Vienne in the fifth century, was well known as a miracle worker. Like all the saints, he attributed his miracles, including extinguishing a mysterious fire by prayers alone, to the grace of God.

The process of saint-making has become much more stringent than it was in the times of St. Mamertus. In order to be officially declared a saint, certifiable miracles are required. Since the miracles must meet exacting standards, medical cures with extensive documentation are the most common. Because of these rigorous standards, the causes for canonization of many holy men and women are awaiting proof of miracles. Among these people are those listed in this book as Blessed. If you have a particularly urgent request for a miracle, you might try asking one of these saints-in-waiting for their help. In having your request granted, you might just help them attain the official status of saint.

If I could ask the saints for a miracle, what would it be?

I BELIEVE IN MIRACLES.

STS. NEREUS AND ACHILLEUS

FIRST CENTURY

Although we know very little about St. Nereus and St. Achilleus, we do know they were soldiers in the Roman army who persecuted the early Christians as part of their duties. We might imagine such deeds to have hardened their hearts, but the opposite occurred. Nereus and Achilleus felt God calling them to become Christians themselves. It was a decision that would cost them their lives. Tradition says they were beheaded on the island of Terracino.

Nereus and Achilleus had to have known the risks when they converted to Christianity. They were willing to face the danger because they also knew God would be there for them. They understood that no lasting reward comes without deep personal sacrifice. As Pope Damasus said in his epitaph for the two soldier saints, "Confessing the faith of Christ, they rejoice to bear testimony to its triumph."

While we may never be martyred for our faith, we are called to die to our own selfishness and greed. We are called to let go of material possessions so that we can create room for eternal wealth. Like St. Nereus and St. Achilleus, we can only have the courage to make those sacrifices when we trust enough to turn our lives and hearts completely to God.

In what areas of my life am I afraid to trust God? What sacrifice is God asking of me today?

TODAY I WILL TRUST THAT NOTHING WILL HAPPEN TO ME WITHOUT GOD'S KNOWLEDGE AND APPROVAL.

BLESSED IMELDA LAMBERTINI

1322–1331

Tradition says Blessed Imelda Lambertini was a devout and pious child who entered religious life at age nine. Her greatest desire was to receive Holy Communion, but she was too young. She was turned down time and again because of her age. Finally, on the Vigil of the Ascension, as she knelt in prayer, a host appeared over her head. The chaplain gave it to her. Sometime later, when the prioress came to check on her, she was dead—still kneeling at the altar.

Regardless of what really happened (or did not happen) with Blessed Imelda, one thing is clear—Imelda was willing to wait patiently for her prayers to be answered.

When we pray, we often want an immediate answer. We want God to say yes or no and to say it right now. If we can't have an immediate answer, we want some sign that God has heard our request and is at least giving the subject serious consideration. All too often, though, we fling our prayers heavenward, never certain if they are actually received.

Our major difficulties with prayer occur because the answers don't usually come the way we expect. We stare in one direction, while the answer comes from the other side. Take Blessed Imelda. She was praying to receive Communion, not to have a miraculous host appear. But look what she got!

When we pray, we need to keep our eyes and hearts open to watch for the answer. It will always come, but almost never in the way we are expecting.

Have I been praying for something for a long time? Could the answer have come without my seeing it?

WHEN I PRAY, I KNOW I AM HEARD.

ST. MATTHIAS

FIRST CENTURY

Taking over where someone else left off is tricky. When the sequel to *Gone with the Wind* was filmed, consider the pressure on the actors who had to recreate the roles played by Vivian Leigh and Clark Gable. Not only did they have to give credible performances in their own right, they were constantly being compared to the original Scarlett and Rhett.

It's difficult enough to try to live up to your predecessor's glorious reputation, but it's even more difficult to have to live down a bad one. St. Matthias had that problem. The only thing we know about him is that he was chosen to take Judas Iscariot's place among the twelve apostles. Imagine going through history known as the one who replaced Judas. No matter what Matthias did, the first thing people were bound to remember was that he took over from the person who betrayed Jesus.

We can have similar difficulties. If we replace a person who was well liked and left under favorable circumstances, we can end up being constantly reminded that our predecessor did things differently. Conversely, if the person was fired, we become known as the one who took over so-and-so's job. In either case, it's difficult to establish our own identity in the shadow of our predecessor.

The best—and only—thing we can do when we're faced with that situation is to focus our attention on the task at hand. We can't change what the person who had the job before us did or didn't do. All we can control are our own actions.

How does it make me feel when I take over someone else's job?

·⟨⟩·

I FIND MY OWN WAY AND MAKE MY OWN REPUTATION.

ST. ISIDORE THE FARMER

1070–1130

Taking care of the earth is a divine trust. If we don't protect our planet, where else are we going to go? *Star Wars* and *Star Trek* fantasies notwithstanding, we haven't perfected the technology that would allow us to colonize any of our neighboring planets, and we don't possess spacecraft capable of carrying us to other solar systems. For the foreseeable future, this world is all we've got to work with.

Caring for the earth is more than just a noble sentiment. If we fail to protect the land, we can't grow crops. If can't grow crops, we'll never have to worry about traveling to Alpha Centauri. In a very real sense, our future rests on the shoulders of our farmers.

It's true that in the interest of mass production, farming has become less of a holy trust between humanity and the soil and more like manufacturing food in a factory. To meet the ever-increasing demands for more and cheaper food, the change was probably inevitable. However, we don't have to let that attitude pervade our thinking. We can still have respect for the food we consume and for the farmers who are responsible for its growth.

St. Isidore is the patron of farmers. A Spanish laborer, he worked hard all his life, combining a deep love of God with a deep love for the land. His reverence for the soil he tilled is a wonderful example for all of us of the delicate balance and intimate relationship we all must have with the earth and its bounty.

Have I ever grown any of my own food?

THIS SPRING, I WILL PLANT ONE THING, EVEN IF IT'S JUST A TOMATO ON THE WINDOW SILL.

ST. BRENDAN

A.D. 577?

Many stories are told of St. Brendan, including tales of his adventures as an explorer. The one fact we know about him was that he founded a monastery around the year 559. His biographers say that its basic founding regulations, called the rule, were dictated to him by an angel.

Have you had an angel speak to you? Maybe you have and you weren't aware of it. "Do not neglect to show hospitality," says the Bible, "for by that means some have entertained angels without knowing it." Angels aren't the chubby little cherubs we see on cards. Real angels are awesome and awe-inspiring. In virtually every account of an encounter with an angel—in the Bible or in the lives of the saints—the first thing the angel says is, "Do not be afraid." If angels all looked like innocent babies, the warning wouldn't be necessary.

Angels are sent to earth for a particular purpose. St. Brendan's angel came to dictate the regulations for governing his monastery. (Could it be the angel was part of a heavenly bureaucracy?) The angels we encounter may come to warn us, enlighten us, or just remind us that there is more than meets the eye in this world and the next.

Although angels are creatures of pure spirit, they may take on human form for a particular purpose. That means an angel could look like the clerk at the check-out counter or the driver in the car next to you. One thing's for sure: you can't judge an angel by its wings!

Do I believe I've ever met an angel?

·〰〰〰〰〰〰〰〰·

↑ THANK GOD FOR SHARING THE ANGELS WITH ME.

ST. PASCHAL BAYLON

1540–1592

There are no coincidences in heaven. Everything happens either because God ordains it or because God permits it. When we strive to live our life in accord with God's will, there are no coincidences for us either. Everything that happens to us has its reason and its purpose.

St. Paschal Baylon was born on a Whitsunday at Torre Hermosa, Spain. A shepherd in his early years, he joined the Friars Minor at age twenty-four. For the rest of his life he had a special devotion to the Eucharist, kneeling for hours before the Blessed Sacrament. He died at the moment of consecration at High Mass on a Whitsunday in 1592.

One tool to help us see the threads and connections in our own lives is a journal. Keeping a journal isn't the same as keeping a diary. A diary records the mundane events of life. (Dear Diary, today I got up, brushed my teeth, took a shower, and had corn flakes for breakfast.) A journal records events of personal significance.

In your journal, concentrate not on events, but on how events make you feel. Write about your emotions, your dreams, and your fears. You can always figure out *when* things happened. Your journal will help you figure out *why* they happened. It may even help you discover that what appeared to be a coincidence was really an essential part of your life path.

Have I ever kept a journal? Does keeping a journal seem like too much work? Am I afraid that someone will read it and discover things about me that I would prefer to keep secret?

I BELIEVE THAT EVERYTHING THAT HAPPENS TO ME HELPS ME GROW SPIRITUALLY.

ST. THEODOTUS

A.D. 303?

When G. K. Chesterton wrote, "The righteous minds of innkeepers/Induce them now and then/To crack a bottle with a friend/Or treat unmoneyed men," he could have been referring to St. Theodotus.

St. Theodotus was a vintner and innkeeper in fourth-century Galatia. When the governor of the area ordered that all food and wine had to be offered to the gods before it could be sold, the Christian community was aghast. Obeying the law would mean that even Communion wine would have to be submitted to pagan rituals. So, at great personal risk, St. Theodotus kept back a supply of wine which he provided to the Christians.

We often go to great lengths to make sure the food we eat every day is pure and safe. However, we may not always take as much care with the food we use to nourish our souls.

We feed our spirits in many ways (the books we read, the music we listen to, the conversations we have), but the primary way we nourish our souls is through prayer. Prayer enables us to tap into the endless resources of the divine, giving us strength for the journey of life. With all its variety of forms—intercessory, petitionary, individual, communal, contemplative, audible, silent, formal, and conversational—prayer provides a veritable smorgasbord for our spiritual growth. Since there is no single right way to pray, just as there is no single perfect food, we are free to sample the various forms until we find the one that suits us best.

What different kinds of prayer have I tried? Is it time for me to try something new?

I NOURISH MY SOUL WITH REGULAR PRAYER.

ST. DUNSTAN

C. 910–988

Many of us think the vice of sloth has gone the way of the dodo. After all, who has time to be lazy?

Sloth, however, has at least as much to do with denial as it does with laziness and misuse of time. When we are slothful, we know what we should be doing, but we try to ignore it. We know, for instance, that we should eat more fruits and vegetables, but we still order a burger and fries for lunch. We realize our heart would be happier if we used the stairs instead of the elevator, but we punch the "up" button anyway.

Most of us would never think of St. Dunstan as slothful. Born near Glastonbury in the tenth century, he spent much of his life closely linked with the ruling family. He was chief adviser to the throne and even directed the country during the reign of young Edward the Martyr. Yet St. Dunstan recognized that even in the busiest of lives, the tendency to sloth can creep in. Thus, as a young monk, he spent as much time as he could doing manual labor as a way to prevent the vice of sloth from taking over in his life.

Like St. Dunstan, we all can be tempted to sloth. If we deny its possibility, we open the door a little wider for its admittance. It's only when we recognize that sloth is as much a covert failing as it is an overt one that we can prevent it from entering into our lives.

What should I be doing that I don't want to do?

I KNOW THE DIFFERENCE BETWEEN NECESSARY REST AND SLOTHFUL LAZINESS.

ST. BERNARDINO OF SIENA

1381–1444

We still use the phrase, avoid it like the plague, but we seldom stop to consider its origin. The plague, or the Black Death as it was called, literally decimated Europe during the Middle Ages. So pervasive were its effects, many people were convinced the world was coming to an end. Because the plague was so often fatal, people would go to almost any lengths to avoid contact with people or places that had been infected.

In 1400, the scourge arrived in Siena. As many as twenty people a day died in the local hospital. Into this pit of death came a group of young men led by Bernardino Albizeschi. For four months, Bernardino and his followers nursed the dying. Although many of his companions died, Bernardino escaped the illness, only to fall victim to a fever that incapacitated him for several months. No sooner had he recovered, than a favorite aunt of his became blind and bedridden. He devoted himself to her nursing care until her death fourteen months later. It was only then that Bernardino was free to enter the Franciscans and to become one of their most famous preachers.

In our lives there are times when we are nurses and times when we need nurses. May we be as gracious and loving when we are the ones doing the service as we are when we are the ones receiving it.

What kind of care do I want when I am sick? When someone I love is sick, how do I respond?

I AM GRATEFUL FOR ALL THE TIMES SOMEONE HAS NURSED ME THROUGH AN ILLNESS.

ST. FELIX OF CANTALICE

1513 – 1587

Ever been around someone who has to have the last word on everything? You say something like, "Last Sunday afternoon about three," and they interrupt, saying, "I believe it was 2:30, not 3:00." You smile politely, and continue, "Last Sunday about *2:30,* I was reading the paper." Again they interrupt, "If memory serves, you were reading a magazine, not the newspaper." Pretty soon you're about ready to scream, but when you react, the person looks offended and says, "But I was just trying to be helpful."

That kind of help we can all do without.

St. Felix of Cantalice offers us one way to respond to people who must have the last word. When anyone contradicted him in unimportant matters, he politely agreed with what they said and never said another thing.

The next time you encounter a person who must have the last word, you might try St. Felix's technique. People who are constantly contradicting and correcting often are just spoiling for a fight. They want to disturb your peace and get you into an argument over something that doesn't really matter anyway. When you fall into their snare and begin to defend your position, you let them win the round. Rather than giving them that satisfaction, refuse to play their game. Be utterly polite as you say, "Why, I believe you are right." By agreeing with them, you not only puncture their pugnacity, but you maintain your own peace of mind.

How do I react when someone tries to push me into an argument?
Can I acquiesce in things that really don't matter?

BECAUSE I VALUE MY COMPOSURE, I REFUSE TO PLAY GAMES.

ST. RITA OF CASCIA

1381–1457

When St. Rita of Cascia's husband was murdered, her two sons vowed to avenge his death. St. Rita prayed that they would die rather than commit murder. She got her wish. The boys contracted a fatal illness and died before they were able to act.

St. Rita got exactly what she prayed for, but fortunately for most of us, God gives us what we need, not what we think we want. Because we have limited insight and vision, we ask for what appears best at the time. God, on the other hand, sees what is best for eternity.

Let's say you interview for a job you really want. It's with a good company and has great benefits. You storm the gates of heaven, begging that you get the position. Then the letter comes: Thank you for your interest, but . . . . You naturally feel disappointed and angry. Why didn't God let you have the job? Maybe the job wouldn't have lasted. Maybe God wants you to change careers. Maybe there would have been temptations that would have proven disastrous to your spiritual development if you had been given the position.

We probably will never know the answers to our questions, but at times like these, all we can do is trust that God has other plans in mind—plans that are always in our best interest.

The next time you don't get what you pray for, give thanks for having been protected from misjudgment and give thanks for the blessings you know will come.

Has there ever been a time that not getting what you wanted turned out to be a blessing in disguise?

I BELIEVE THAT GOD KNOWS WHAT IS BEST FOR ME.

ST. JOHN BAPTIST ROSSI

1698–1764

Saints may be heavenly companions, but sometimes they can make life on earth a bit hellish for those who don't share their drive. St. John Baptist Rossi is one of those saints who probably drove everyone around him to distraction with his good deeds. For instance, when he was given an ecclesiastical post that had been held by his cousin, he promptly gave away the salary to buy an organ for the church and to pay an organist. He donated the house that came with the position to his religious order, the Capuchins, and moved into an attic. He used the stipends he received at Mass to rent a house for homeless women.

When we are wrapped up with enthusiasm for our projects, we need to remember we always have the right to spend our own time and money as we choose, but we don't have the right to insist that others make the same investments.

It's only natural to want others to be involved in the things that interest us, but we need to be charitable with those who aren't on our same spiritual or emotional plain. It's unfair to insist that others make sacrifices for causes they don't believe in. We need to be especially mindful of those projects that entail financial contributions. No matter how excited we are about a cause, we need to give others the room to make their own decisions and come to their own conclusions. If we're lucky, we'll be able to share our excitement. If not, well, then let charity prevail.

How do I feel when I'm solicited for a cause I don't support?

I DO NOT FORCE MY PET PROJECTS ON ANYONE ELSE.

ST. VINCENT OF LÉRINS

C. A.D. 445

Do you sometimes think that you would lose your head if it weren't attached? Do you make lists to help you remember and them forget where you put the list?

If you have trouble remembering things, St. Vincent of Lérins is your saint. He wrote the *Commonitorium*, the book that ensured his sanctity, to aid his own poor memory. In this famous work, St. Vincent outlines the principles he discerned for distinguishing Christian truth from falsehood. His book became his safe place to store the truth.

We all can create our own safe place for storing the truths we've learned about life. For many people such a safe place is a journal, but if you aren't a writer, you can select another type of safe place. Perhaps it's a location, a special area where you go to be alone and to think. Just being there will trigger a flood of memories. Or maybe it's a particular piece of music that will release its memories each time you hear it played. Whatever your safe place is, it is yours alone. It's a place that will jog your memory and refresh your soul; it's a place where you can sort out your feelings and renew your dreams. We all need a safe place. If you don't have a safe place where you can store your feelings and thoughts, why not choose one today?

Where is my safe place? What kinds of things do I store there?

¶ RESPECT MY NEED FOR PRIVACY AND SECURITY.

ST. MADELEINE SOPHIE BARAT

1779–1865

Although things are gradually changing, 150 years ago opportunities for intelligent, ambitious women were definitely limited. St. Madeleine Sophie Barat, who lived during the tumultuous days of the French Revolution and the Reign of Terror, did her best to change that. The foundress of the Society of the Sacred Heart, St. Madeleine devoted herself to the education of women, both rich and poor. She founded numerous schools, starting in France, but spreading throughout the world. At the time of her death, she saw her sisters established in twelve countries. Stressing the importance of literacy, she also firmly believed in balancing the education of the intellect with that of the body and the moral character.

Ahead of her time in many ways, she said, "A woman cannot remain neutral in the world," adding that women must be "strong in every battle of life."

St. Madeleine's spunk and feminism may seem better suited to the twentieth century than to the nineteenth, but she didn't let the obstacles of her time and place keep her from doing what she knew had to be done. When we are called to correct a wrong or to change the way things have always been, let us remember the example of St. Madeleine and realize that strength and courage come not from self-pity, but from determination and action.

Is there some wrong that I know I could correct but that presents a seemingly overwhelming challenge?

⊹⊱━━━━━━━━━━━━━━━━━━━━━━━━━━━━⊰⊹

I BELIEVE THAT GOD HELPS THOSE WHO GET OFF THEIR
DUFFS AND GET GOING.

ST. PHILIP NERI

1515–1595

We make assumptions all the time. Some of them are logical and natural—such as assuming that the sun will rise in the morning or that the law of gravity will continue to operate. We get into trouble, though, when we make assumptions about other people.

The saints are often on the losing end of assumptions. Because they are held up as models of holiness and because holiness is serious business, we sometimes assume they are a rather stuffy lot—good at praying but a real drag at parties.

Take St. Philip Neri, for instance. If we looked merely at a few facts of his life, which include his being spiritual director to such famous saints as St. Francis de Sales and St. Charles Borromeo, we might assume he was a paragon of seriousness. While he did say serious things—like, "Humility is the safeguard of chastity. In the matter of purity, there is no greater danger than not fearing danger"—he is much better known for his sense of humor. In fact, his two favorite books were the New Testament and a joke book. Even when counseling penitents, he was light-hearted. Once he told a gossipy women to toss a bag of feathers in the air and then collect every one of them. When she protested that such a penance was impossible, he pointed out that wanton words are like those feathers; once loosed they are impossible to collect.

As we go through our days, let us be careful of making assumptions about other people, lest they make assumptions about us.

Have I ever assumed something about a person, only to find out later that I was completely incorrect?

I RESERVE JUDGMENT UNTIL I HAVE ALL THE FACTS.

ST. GONZAGA GONZA

1885–1887

Saints have been martyred for their faith in every land and every nation of the world. Between 1885 and 1887, about thirty Ugandan Anglicans and Catholics were tortured and killed. One was St. Gonzaga Gonza.

St. Gonzaga had received his religious instruction from the White Fathers. When the king of Buganda, now part of present-day Uganda, ordered him to recant his faith, he refused. Along with his fellow martyrs, he was marched toward the village of Namugongo, about thirty-seven miles from his home. As was the custom, a victim was executed at each crossroads. St. Gonzaga was one of the first to die. He was speared to death, and his body was tossed on an ant hill, but he died so bravely that even his executioners admired his courage.

Although most of us probably will not have to die for our convictions, we know what it's like to be accused and attacked for our beliefs. Maybe it's because of our political views. Or perhaps we hold to a position that isn't currently politically correct. Or possibly we have chosen a direction for our lives that the people around us can't comprehend. Whatever it is, few of us will get through life without encountering resistance from those around us. When that happens, we have a choice of keeping true to our own tenets or recanting. The latter may keep the peace, but the former maintains our faith.

Have I ever caved in under pressure to say or do something
I didn't believe in? Can I forgive myself for my human frailty?

·⟨᠁᠁᠁᠁᠁᠁᠁⟩·

WHEN I TAKE A STAND, I AM WILLING TO STAND UP FOR IT.

ST. MARIANA OF JESUS

1618–1645

One temptation most of us face is to stick our finger through the fence of someone else's life. The only problem with poking a finger through the knothole is you can't be sure what you'll encounter on the other side! If you're really unlucky, an alligator might be waiting to nibble on your knuckle.

St. Mariana of Jesus, often called the national heroine of Ecuador, lived in Quito during the seventeenth century. Born on Halloween, she spent her short life imposing extraordinary penances on herself, while always being gentle with those who came to her for prayers and advice. In contrast, many of us are very harsh on others, while being quite understanding and forgiving of our own failures. We see other people's faults quite clearly, while being oblivious to our own.

One of many lessons the saints urge us to learn is to pay attention to our own business. They point out that we have enough to do in taking care of our own lives, without becoming the guardian of other people's affairs. St. Teresa of Avila, for example, says, "Be not curious about matters that do not concern thee; never speak of them, and do not ask about them."

Sticking our fingers through fences can be dangerous. If we want to make sure we keep our fingers intact, we need to keep our hands off other people's lives.

When people don't tell me what they are doing, do I feel annoyed and left out? Do I think I should know everything that's going on? Why?

I MIND MY OWN BUSINESS.

ST. WILLIAM OF TOULOUSE

A.D. 1242

Have you ever been set up? If you have, then you know how little you can do to save yourself. St. William of Toulouse and his companions, William Arnaud, Stephen, Raymund, and nine others were set up—royally. Invited to stay at a castle belonging to Count Raymond VII of Toulouse, they were instead murdered by a band of soldiers waiting there for them.

Being set up, even when it doesn't result in murder, isn't pleasant. At the very least, it makes us angry—as much at ourselves for having been so foolish as at anyone else.

Sometimes, though, there's no one else to blame. We set ourselves up for failure, for disappointment, for discouragement. When we undertake a project without adequate preparation, when we leave an opening for someone with a barbed tongue, when we procrastinate so long we can't fulfill our obligations, then we set ourselves up. In a perverse way, we create situations in which we are bound to fail so that we can't be held accountable for our actions. It may be because we are afraid we can't live up to the standards we assign for ourselves or it may be because we are afraid of success. Whatever the reason, the worst set-ups often come from within.

We can't always prevent others from trying to set us up, but we can keep from setting ourselves up. We can treat ourselves with the same respect we would accord others. More important, however, even when we do set ourselves up, we can always treat it as a learning experience.

Do I set myself up for failure?

STARTING TODAY, THE ONLY THING I WILL SET MYSELF UP
FOR IS SUCCESS.

ST. JOAN OF ARC

1412–1431

At age fourteen, St. Joan of Arc began hearing voices and having visions of St. Michael the Archangel, St. Catherine of Alexandria, and St. Margaret of Antioch. By age sixteen, she was convinced that she was to rescue the city of Orléans from the English and to reestablish the dauphin. Amazingly, she managed to do just that. Eventually she was captured, sold to the British, and burned at the stake as a witch and heretic.

Most of us would probably seek professional help if we started hearing voices urging us to start a war. (At least, we hope we would have the sense to get help.) Yet, sometimes our inner voice—the small still sound in our heart—tells us to right a wrong, even if it means doing battle against mighty forces.

Because the nudge is often so gentle and unobtrusive, it can be easy to ignore. Even Joan tried to ignore her voices, complaining that it would be impossible for her to lead an army since she could neither ride nor fight. While she had a point, the voices told her that God would command her and the army.

When we begin to protest that we cannot possibly fight the armies of bureaucracy and oppression, our inner voice tells us the same thing. We are reminded that when our cause is right, we don't have to fight alone because God will be there with us. That knowledge ought to give us, like Joan, the courage to raise our flag and set forth with confidence.

Do I think it is possible for one person to change the system?
Why or why not?

I DO MY PART TO MAKE THE WORLD A SAFER,
BETTER PLACE.

ST. MECHTILDIS OF EDELSTETTEN

A.D. 1160

Watching the evening news or reading the newspaper can be depressing. Because good news is no news, the media flock to every tragedy, mishap, and horror. A steady diet of such morbid thoughts is bound to make us feel a bit morbid ourselves.

A doctor who worked in a public health clinic in an inner city once said he was beginning to feel like there was nothing good left in the world. Every day he was surrounded by victims of violence, abuse, and drug addiction. Not until he got away from the oppressive situation could he appreciate the beauty and goodness that is still present in the world.

What we see and hear on a regular basis deeply influences the way we think. When St. Mechtildis of Edelstetten was elected the abbess of her convent, she attempted to restore discipline by prohibiting secular visitors with their worldly news from entering the cloister.

Maybe, for a day or two, we should follow St. Mechtildis's orders by banning all television, radio, and newspaper news from our lives. If something *really* important happens, we'll hear about it from friends and neighbors. In the meantime, we can use the time we would normally spend paying attention to *the* world to pay attention to *our* world. We can read a book we've been meaning to, call a friend we haven't talked to in ages. We can take a child for a walk, bake a pie, daydream. We can celebrate the goodness of life, instead of becoming weighted down by its sorrows.

Am I a news junkie?

JUST FOR TODAY, I WILL CONCENTRATE ON THE GOODNESS AND JOY OF LIFE.

ST. JUSTIN

100?–165

Sometimes so-called great thinkers would have us believe that philosophy and religion are antithetical, that once we begin to use our minds for serious thought, we have no choice but to abandon our religious convictions. Conversely, they may imply that if we maintain religious convictions, we cannot pursue philosophical considerations. St. Justin is proof that philosophy and religion can and do coexist quite nicely.

As a young man, Justin searched for truth in various philosophies and religions, primarily the school of Plato. After he converted to Christianity, he became known as the first Christian philosopher.

We humans are sometimes called thinking animals. If our ability to ponder realities beyond that which we can experience through our senses sets us apart from the rest of the animal kingdom, then not only can we use our minds for philosophical ponderings, but we even have an obligation to do so. To do anything less is to reject the gift of reason. When we search for truth, we must have the confidence that its discovery will not destroy our faith.

"Philosophy is the knowledge of that which exists, and a clear understanding of the truth; and happiness is the reward of such knowledge and understanding," St. Justin wrote. If we truly seek happiness here and in the life to come, then we must fearlessly pursue the truth.

How do I feel about accepting things on blind faith? Do I ever feel that examining my religious beliefs is somehow disrespectful to God?

I TAKE THE TIME TO EXAMINE WHAT I BELIEVE AND WHY I BELIEVE IT.

ST. BLANDINA AND THE MARTYRS OF LYONS

A.D. 177

When St. Blandina, a slave, was sentenced to die during the infamous games of the Roman empire, her mistress thought she was too frail to uphold the faith. Yet, Blandina was the last to die of the group of martyrs we remember as the Martyrs of Lyons. Among other tortures, she was wrapped in a net and tossed to a wild bull.

Isn't that often the case? The person we think is the weakest turns out to be the strongest. Somehow, when it counts the most, that person manages to tap amazing reservoirs of strength.

We all have that ability. To reach those deep reserves, however, we need to do one essential thing: surrender. Surrender? In order to become strong? Yes. In one of the great paradoxes of faith, it is when we recognize our weakness that God's limitless strength can work through us.

St. Blandina is said to have repeated the words, "I am a Christian, no wickedness is transacted among us," in order to gain strength to endure her torture. In the same way, we can repeat a favorite prayer—perhaps Julian of Norwich's "All shall be well and all shall be well and all manner of thing shall be well," when we are facing trials we think are beyond our endurance. As we do so, we will learn that with God beside us, all things are indeed possible.

Is there something in my life I don't think I can face alone?

I FACE THE CHALLENGES OF MY LIFE WITH COURAGE BORN OF PRAYER.

ST. CHARLES LWANGA AND COMPANIONS

1885–1887

In 1885 when Joseph Mkasa, the master of the pages in the court of King Mwanga of Buganda, criticized the king both for his immorality and for the murder of the Protestant missionary James Hannington, the king had him killed. He was replaced by another Christian, Charles Lwanga. Several months later, when a page named Mwafu refused to take part in the king's immoral acts, King Mwanga learned that another page, Denis Sebuggwawo, had been giving him secret instruction in Christianity. Denis was sent for and executed. Then the king summoned all the other Christian pages, and when they refused to give up their faith, sentenced them to death. They were tortured, and those who survived were burned alive or beheaded.

The martyrs of Uganda were very young, most in their late teens or early twenties. Yet they showed a maturity beyond their years in their willingness to suffer and die for their faith. In doing so they acted their age. Not their chronological age, of course, but their spiritual age.

All of us are called to act our spiritual age. While our chronological age is dictated by the laws of nature, our spiritual age has no such boundaries. A lot depends on when we began our quest and how much energy we have put into our search. No matter how old we are chronologically, we can continue to mature spiritually until the day we finally enter into eternity.

How old am I spiritually? How old would I like to be this time next year?

I AM GROWING SPIRITUALLY MORE MATURE EVERY DAY.

ST. FRANCIS (ASCANIO)
CARACCIOLO

1563–1608

In 1588, John Augustine Adorno came up with the idea of founding a new religious order of priests. He consulted the dean of Santa Maria Maggiore in Naples and sent a letter to a fellow priest named Ascanio Caracciolo explaining the plan and asking for his assistance. Ascanio was so thrilled with the invitation that he at once agreed to help. The only problem was that he was the wrong Ascanio Caracciolo. The letter had been intended for one of his relatives with the same name. Fortunately for all involved, this Ascanio Caracciolo—who would later take the name Francis in honor of Francis of Assisi—was allowed to participate in the plan. He and Adorno became fast friends and founded the Minor Clerks Regular.

Have you ever had what originally seemed to be a mistake turn out to be a blessing in disguise? You dial the wrong number, but the person on the other end is someone who really needed to talk with you just then. You make a wrong turn, only to learn later that there was an accident on the street you avoided. Such events are examples of divine providence. What seems to be a mistake is really part of God's loving attention to all the details of our lives.

The next time something happens which appears to be a mistake, don't fret. Instead, say a quick prayer of thanksgiving for another example of divine providence at work.

As I look back over my life, can I see where what I thought was a mistake really turned out for the best?

GOD DOESN'T MAKE MISTAKES WITH MY LIFE.

ST. BONIFACE

680?–754

In order to keep in touch with far-flung members, some families have developed a round-robin letter. One person begins by writing a letter and sending it to the first person on a list. As each person gets the packet, he or she adds a letter and sends it along. When it finally returns, the person removes his or her old letter, adds a new one, and sends the robin back on its round.

St. Boniface, who is called the Apostle to Germany, was actually born an Englishman by the name of Winfrid. Because he believed God wanted him to be a missionary, he left the British Isles for Europe. While working abroad, he never lost touch with his beloved England and even wrote a circular letter to all the priests, religious, and laity of England asking for their prayers. Although we don't know exactly how far the letter traveled or how long it was kept in circulation, it's fun to think that Boniface might have started a new tradition in the eighth century.

Maybe you can start a new tradition in your family by sending out your own circular letter. If you don't like to write actual letters, maybe electronic mail might be substituted. Whatever the method, keeping in touch with those we love isn't something we should leave to chance.

Would a round-robin letter work with my family or a group of my friends? Who would I put on the list?

I MAKE IT A POINT TO KEEP IN TOUCH WITH
THOSE I CARE ABOUT.

BLESSED MARY THERESA LEDOCHOWSKA

1863–1922

Although there is no patron saint for those who want to quit smoking, if there were, it might be Blessed Mary Theresa Ledochowska. Blessed Mary was the oldest child of Count Anthony Ledochowska of Austria. A bright and enthusiastic child, she grew up to become a lady-in-waiting at the court of Grand Duke Ferdinand and Grand Duchess Alice. For several years, she combined her glamorous duties with writing against slavery. Finally, in 1891, when her desire to write about the African missions began to usurp more of her time, she asked to be released from court. Reluctantly, the royal family agreed. Blessed Mary wrote in her diary: "Holy Communion offered for the new way of life. Very happy and serene . . . given up smoking."

We don't know if Blessed Mary succeeded in her resolve, but at least she didn't form an anti-smoking league. It can be very difficult to put up with someone who has reformed. Former smokers are among the worst, but any of us who has overcome a bad habit can be equally guilty. A successful dieter is often impatient with those who continue to indulge, and anyone who has discovered the virtues of exercise can be insufferable to the less active.

If we ever feel tempted to preach on the merits of a new-found virtue, let us remember how it felt when we were on the receiving end of the lecture and practice the noble exercise of biting our tongues.

Do I feel the need to lecture others on their bad habits? How do I feel when someone wants to lecture me?

⟨⟨⟨⟨⟩⟩⟩⟩

I WEED MY OWN GARDEN BEFORE I LOOK FOR THE WEEDS IN MY NEIGHBOR'S YARD.

VENERABLE MATT TALBOT

1856–1925

Venerable Matt Talbot was an alcoholic. He came home drunk from his first job at a wine-bottling store at age twelve and spent very little time sober after that. One day, when he was twenty-eight, he found a priest and pledged not to drink for three months. Although he wasn't sure he could hold out, he did, extending his pledge for longer periods until finally he took it for life.

Matt Talbot took care that he was not unduly tempted to break his resolve. To that end, he never carried any money. Matt developed the practice shortly after his conversion, when he had been nearly overcome with desire for a drink. Going into a pub, he tried to buy a drink, but no one would serve him. Finally he left and stayed in a nearby church until it closed.

For the rest of his life, Matt Talbot worked hard, gave most of his money to charity, and spent long hours in prayer and penance. On his way to Mass, he collapsed and died of heart failure. He was sixty-nine. He had kept his pledge for forty-one years.

Breaking free of an addiction is hard work. It requires determination, dedication, and not a small amount of faith.

If you're suffering from an addiction of any kind—whether it's smoking, alcohol, overeating, drugs—the saints are there to help. When temptations grow strong, ask them, especially Venerable Matt Talbot, to pray that you receive the fortitude you need. It's one request the saints can never refuse.

Is there something in my life that is holding me hostage?

MY LIFE IS FREE OF SELF-DESTRUCTIVE TENDENCIES.

BLESSED CECLIA CAESARINI

C. A.D. 1296

One of the lures of Hollywood is the possiblity of seeing a movie star in real life. People are willing to wait for hours near restaurants and clubs known to be celebrity hang-outs on the off-chance that someone famous might just happen along. If their patience is rewarded, they can be assured that for months afterward, friends will ask questions—and for months afterward, the lucky celebrity spotter will be delighted to tell and retell the account.

The venue changes, but not human nature. Many of the details we know about St. Dominic come from Blessed Ceclia Caesarini, who was the prioress of Dominic's convent at St. Sixtus. Even when she was nearly ninety, she could recount precise details of his physical appearance as well as his gentle kindness with the nuns under his direction.

While we may think that eyewitness accounts are limited to celebrity spottings and news events, we are all called to be eyewitnesses; eyewitnesses to the truth.

When we have had a spiritual encounter, whether it is an immediate, undeniable answer to prayer, a meeting with an angel, or a transcendent moment of grace, we are sometimes reluctant to talk about it. We are afraid we will be laughed at, or worse, we may fear that our experience will not seem as miraculous when held up for scrutiny. Such moments, however, are not given to us to hoard. They are given so that we can share the experience with others and help them understand that the entire world is infused with divine favor.

Have I ever had a remarkable spiritual experience? Have I ever told anyone about it?

·⟨⟨⟩⟩·

I HEED THE REMARKABLE IN MY LIFE.

ST. EPHREM OF SYRIA

306?–373

It's hard to imagine a church service without singing. From cathedrals to chapels, music is an integral part of the celebration. More than that, hymns infuse religious teaching into our very being. Take that most popular of all hymns, "Amazing Grace." Few stories of conversion have been told as succinctly, or as enduringly, as the words of the onetime slaver and sea captain, John Newton.

Using hymns as a means to educate and instruct didn't begin in Newton's time. St. Ephrem of Syria, who lived in the fourth century, would take the songs being sung by splinter and heretical groups and rewrite the lyrics to reflect accurate doctrine. In addition, he was one of the first to compose songs for the Church's official worship. He wrote so many hymns that he is sometimes called the Harp of the Holy Spirit.

Over the centuries, many glorious pieces of music have been composed to honor and glorify God. Although they can be enjoyed merely for their aesthetic pleasure, they can also be used as a means to enhance your prayer life. If you have a favorite composition—perhaps Handel's *Messiah* or Mozart's *Requiem*—that is based on a religious theme, why not let it fill the empty places in your soul? As Thomas Campion once said, "Heaven is music . . . "

What kinds of music do I like to listen to? Do I have a favorite kind of music?

I APPRECIATE ALL KINDS OF MUSIC.

BLESSED JOHN DOMINICI

1350–1419

When St. Dominic founded the Dominicans in the thirteenth century, one of its primary purposes was to preach, and in fact its official name is still the Order of Friars Preacher. Given that preaching was an essential part of the vocation, a speech defect would put any candidate at a severe disadvantage. Blessed John Dominici very nearly wasn't allowed to join the Order because of his speech handicap. Even after he was ordained, he wasn't allowed to speak in public. Finally, he prayed to St. Catherine of Siena and his defect disappeared.

Blessed John Dominici *wanted* to be able to speak in public, but most of us would rather not face that challenge. Public speaking often heads the list of people's top 10 greatest fears. Fortunately for most of us, we don't have to speak in public, but that doesn't mean we need not face our fears.

In the novel *Dune*, the duke's son, Paul, is forced to face a test of pain. Before he begins, he reminds himself, "Fear is the mind-killer . . . I will face my fear. I will permit it to pass over me and through me . . . " While the saints might not use those same words, they would probably agree with the sentiment. St. Francis de Sales once said, "Fear is a greater evil than the evil itself." No matter what it is you fear the most, the saints remind us that fear is useless. What is needed is love, for where love resides, fear cannot exist.

What scares me the most? Can I share my fears with anyone?

·⟨░░░░░░░░░░░░░░░░░░░░░░░░░░░░░░░⟩·

I BELIEVE THAT PERFECT LOVE CASTS OUT ALL FEAR.

ST. BARNABAS

FIRST CENTURY

Although not one of the original twelve apostles, St. Barnabas is often called an apostle because of his close association with the leaders of the early Church. For example, he traveled extensively with St. Paul. Originally named Joseph, he was renamed Barnabas by the other apostles, a name that means Son of Encouragement.

What a wonderful name. The word *encourage* means to give hope, and what could be more wonderful than to bring hope to a hopeless world.

The message of the Christian gospel is essentially that of hope. No matter how bleak things look right now, no matter what pain and sorrow we are enduring, St. Paul reminds us, ". . . affliction makes for endurance, and endurance for tested virtue, and tested virtue for hope. And this hope will not leave us disappointed, because the love of God has been poured out in our hearts . . . " (Romans 5:3–5)

Of the three main virtues—faith, hope and love—hope is the one most closely linked with this life. The essence of hope is trust—trust in things unseen and in the love of an unseen God. Once we leave this world, what is hidden will be revealed and thus we will no longer have need of hope. But until that day arrives, hope allows us to say with Robert Browning, "The lark's on the wing;/The snail's on the thorn:/God's in his heaven—/All's right with the world."

When I say, I hope, do I really mean I wish? Do I understand the difference between wishing for and hoping for?

WHEN I AM DISCOURAGED WITH LIFE, I ASK ST. BARNABAS,
THE SON OF ENCOURAGEMENT, TO SEND A
LITTLE HOPE MY WAY.

ST. JOHN OF SAHAGUN

A.D. 1479

William Congreve wrote, "Heaven has no rage like love to hatred turned,/Nor hell a fury like a woman scorned." St. John of Sahagun may have lost his life because of the fury of a scorned woman.

St. John of Sahagun was so fearless in his opposition to sin and evil that the Duke of Alba once sent two men to assassinate him, but the brigands were unable to carry out their task. What may have done St. John in, however, was convincing a prominent man to give up his mistress. The mistress became so furious, it is thought she poisoned the parson.

We all experience the emotion of anger. It's just an emotion, and like every other emotion is, in and of itself, neither good nor bad. It's what we do with our anger that makes it harmful. When we use anger as a weapon or as a justification for hurtful behavior, then anger ceases to be an emotion and becomes a force for evil.

Fury, however, is more than mere anger. Fury is a hurricane in the heart. With little regard for anyone or anything in its path, fury assails the guilty and innocent alike. When its energy is spent, its only legacy is destruction. While we can't control the feeling of anger, we can always choose to control the cold, calculating intensity of fury.

Have I ever been so angry I've lost control? What, if anything, causes me to lose my temper?

I DO NOT ALLOW UNCONTROLLED ANGER TO HAVE ANY PART IN MY LIFE.

ST. ANTHONY OF PADUA

1195-1231

When many Catholics lose something, the first thing they do is pray to St. Anthony. All around the world, people implore his intercession to find everything from lost keys to lost souls.

How a Franciscan priest became a celestial lost-and-found department is uncertain. One legend says that when a friar stole a book, Anthony prayed it would be returned. The sticky-fingered friar was overcome with remorse and brought the book back. Regardless how St. Anthony got associated with the recovery of lost items, he is one of the world's favorite saints.

Anthony was the son of Portuguese nobility. He first joined the Augustinians, but when the relics of Franciscan martyrs were brought through his town, he entered the Franciscan order. Beloved as a preacher and teacher, he was canonized within a year after his death.

Although we usually pray to St. Anthony to help us find things, we can also ask him to help us lose at least one thing. If you are overweight, St. Anthony can sympathize. He was short and chubby, hardly a lean ascetic. Since he knows what it is like to struggle with weight, he might just be a good patron to call on when you begin dieting to fit into a swimming suit or shorts. Who knows? Since most of St. Anthony's time is spent finding things, he might be glad to hear a request to lose something.

What do I need to find (or lose!) right now?

I THINK OF THE SAINTS AS HEAVENLY FRIENDS, READY TO LEND A HELPING HAND IN ALL SITUATIONS.

ST. FRANCIS SOLANO

1549–1610

Words accurately reflect the values of a culture. If anthropologists of the future were to examine American English, they would (rightly!) assume automobiles were essential to twentieth-century life. Just think how many names we use every day to describe the vehicle. We have generic names (car, auto, truck). Descriptive names (four-door, sedan, four-wheeler, 4 by 4, flatbed). Brand names (Ford, Honda, Chevy). Model names (Accord, Lexus, Nova). Finally we even have pet names (check out any vanity plate). All for what is essentially the same thing—a four-wheeled vehicle with an internal combustion engine. Anyone coming to America would have to become fluent in "car-ese" to truly speak the language.

St. Francis Solano, a Franciscan missionary in the waning days of the sixteenth century, was assigned to northern Argentina. A Spaniard by birth, his first duty was to learn the language of the native Argentineans. The man who taught him reported that Padre Solano mastered the language in fourteen days. St. Francis had a compelling motivation: If he wanted to preach, baptize, hear confessions, and teach the people to whom he was sent, he had to be able to talk with them.

One of the greatest gifts we can cultivate is the art of conversation. Knowing how to talk with people entails more than speaking a common language. It means knowing when to listen and when to speak. It means exchanging not just words, but thoughts and feelings. It means being willing to risk friendship.

Whom do I call when I need to talk with someone?

I KNOW THE DIFFERENCE BETWEEN TALKING WITH PEOPLE AND TALKING TO THEM.

ST. GERMAINE OF PIBRAC

1579–1601

Cinderella is one of the most popular of all fairy tales. The story of a poor girl who is mistreated by her stepmother and ends up marrying a prince has been told in many ways, from the Brothers Grimm to Walt Disney.

The life of St. Germaine of Pibrac sounds a bit like Cinderella's. The daughter of a French farmer, Germaine suffered from scrofula, a disease that causes swelling and sores. In addition, her right hand was crippled. Her mother had died when she was an infant and her stepmother loathed her. Consequently, Germaine was forced to live in the stable and eat kitchen scraps.

But that's where the similarity to Cinderella breaks down. No grand ball awaited St. Germaine. Instead, she spent the rest of her short life praying and tending sheep. Worn out by mistreatment and illness, she died when she was only twenty-two.

Although no prince with a glass slipper arrived to rescue St. Germaine, her story has a happy ending. It is said that the night she died two travelers saw a beam of light traveling from heaven to the stable where Germaine lived. Climbing the beam were angels, leading a young girl directly into paradise.

One of the lessons the saints teach is that no matter how sad our beginning, we can always have a happy ending. This life is not the sum total of our existence. As they did for St. Germaine, the angels are waiting to lead us into the company of saints in heaven.

Do I still resent things that happened in my childhood? Isn't it time to let the past go and get on with life?

I WILL NOT LET A BAD BEGINNING RUIN MY CHANCES FOR A HAPPY ENDING.

ST. LUTGARDIS

1182–1246

Do you ever get the feeling you're in the wrong place in life? That you really should have done something different? St. Lutgardis may have had the same thoughts.

She never planned to be a nun. Her family dumped her in a convent when she was twelve because her dowry had been lost in a poor business deal and her parents figured they could never marry her off. St. Lutgardis didn't immediately spring into mystical holiness. She treated the convent as a kind of rooming house and went about her ordinary life. Then one day Jesus appeared to her in a vision and she knew that she was meant to enter the convent, not just live there.

If we wait for a mystical vision to tell us what we are supposed to do, we might wait for a long time. But if we open our eyes to our surroundings, we may discover we are already where we are supposed to be. All that is required is for us to enter wholeheartedly into the life we have been presented. As Blessed Henry Suso said, "Let each look to himself and see what God wants of him and attend to this, leaving all else alone." Once St. Lutgardis attended to her place in the convent, she realized that she had not been placed there by accident; it was where she was meant to be.

Do I ever feel like I'm in the wrong place in life? What do I want to do—change places or change me?

·⟨⟩·

I BELIEVE ALL OF MY LIFE IS UNFOLDING AS IT SHOULD.

ST. TERESA OF PORTUGAL

A.D. 1250

St. Teresa, the daughter of King Sancho I of Portugal, married her cousin, King Alfonso IX of León. After several years of happy married life (and several children), the marriage was declared void because she and Alfonso were too closely related and had not received the proper dispensations. Alfonso went on to marry a woman named Berengaria and Teresa went home to Portugal where she founded a religious community. Years later, Berengaria sought out Teresa to help settle an inheritance quarrel between their respective children. Although Teresa could easily have born a grudge after her shabby treatment, she did not. With her assistance, a peaceful accord was reached.

Holding a grudge is like hiking with a pebble in your boot. Sometimes it slides off to one side, but most of the time, it just makes every step miserable.

The worst part about grudges is the bitterness they create in our souls. Often the person we are holding the grudge against doesn't even know we are upset and angry. We end up wasting extraordinary amounts of time plotting and planning our revenge, only to discover that revenge is never as sweet as we think it's going to be. If you're holding a grudge against someone or something, now is the time to dump the pebble from your shoe. You're guaranteed to feel better and walk easier.

Am I holding a grudge right now? What stops me from letting go?
Does the person I'm angry at even know that I'm upset?

I FORGIVE THOSE WHO HAVE WRONGED ME.

ST. ELIZABETH OF SCHÖNAU

1130?–1164

Many books are the result of collaboration between two authors. The writers bring their own unique styles and insight, creating a finished product that is better than either could have accomplished alone. St. Elizabeth of Schönau and her brother Egbert were partners on at least three books, one of which is entitled *The Book of the Ways of God.* Based on her visions, these works include scenes from the life of Christ as well as exhortations to repentance and penance. Although the works show definite evidence of Egbert's education, without Elizabeth's visions, they never could have been written.

Creative partnerships often allow both parties to do what they do best. One of the most creative collaborations we can form is with God. Forming a partnership with God isn't quite like drawing up a legal contract. After all, it's hardly a meeting between equals. We bring our humble talents, and God provides his limitless power. The most incredible part is that God would want to enter into such a relationship with us. It would seem that God, the creator of the universe, would have little need to do so. Yet, in this world, God has no hands but ours; we are God's instruments. The collaboration we form is the primary way in which God's grace and goodness are spread throughout the world. In a very real sense, our partnership makes God's work on earth possible.

Would I rather work with someone or do it by myself? How do I feel when I have to share responsibility?

I ACCEPT THE CHALLENGE AND JOY OF COLLABORATING WITH GOD.

ST. JULIANA FALCONIERI

1270–1341

Child-development experts often recommend that parents let children suffer natural consequences instead of imposing punishment. Thus, a child who refuses dinner goes to bed hungry.

St. Juliana Falconieri was forced to suffer the natural consequences of her intense mistreatment of her body. Although the original intent of her strict fasts was to honor God with her penance, she ended up unable to digest any food. The consequence was not merely that she couldn't eat; she also couldn't receive Holy Communion. That unforeseen aftermath of her overly stringent penance was one of the deepest sadnesses of her final days.

Many of our prayers for divine aid are more concerned with consequences than with original actions. For instance, we may not be terribly sorry that we hit the snooze alarm three times in a row, but when the flashing red light pulls us to the side because we were speeding in order to get to work on time, our prayer to avoid a ticket is very real.

In situations like that, God often acts like a parent. Rather than stepping in and intervening, God lets us suffer the natural consequences of our behavior. (Of course, like a child who pleads with his parents until they relent, we can always try desperate prayer.)

As we mature, however, we realize that instead of asking God to bail us out of situations of our own making, we are better off asking for the wisdom to see the consequences of our actions while we still have time to make better choices.

Do I ever think God is punishing me when it's really just natural consequences at work?

I DO NOT EXPECT GOD TO BAIL ME OUT EVERY TIME I'M IN A SITUATION OF MY OWN MAKING.

BLESSED OSANNA OF MANTUA

1449–1505

Prophets are without honor in their own countries and saints are often without honor in their own families. Blessed Osanna of Mantua would fall into ecstasies, during which she would be insensible to everything around her. Once she fell into an ecstasy while on horseback and sat there the entire day.

Her family was less than thrilled with her behavior, and her mother told her, "You will be the death of me and bring disgrace on our family. I can't think what is the matter with you or what will be the end of all this." Her father, a practical man, figured she had epilepsy.

While it is entirely possible that her father was right, the fact remains that Blessed Osanna embarrassed those closest to her. They wanted her to act ordinary instead of calling attention to herself by odd behavior.

Often we want our families to be ordinary. We find eccentrics in other families to be quaint and charming, but we want our own relatives to blend in. We cannot control others, no matter how eccentric or unusual they behave. We can suggest changes; we can even encourage changes, but all we control is our own behavior.

The flip side is that sometimes we need to ask ourselves if our behavior is causing embarrassment to our families. If it is, then maybe we ought to consider changing or modifying our actions—not because we have to, but because charity asks us to think of others before we think of ourselves.

Do any of my behaviors embarrass my family or friends?

I MODIFY MY RIGHT TO ACT THE WAY I WANT OUT OF
RESPECT FOR THE RIGHTS OF OTHERS.

ST. ALOYSIUS GONZAGA

1568–1591

Many saints subjected themselves to such intense acts of penance that they seem almost masochistic. St. Aloysius Gonzaga was one such rigorous penitent. He fasted three days a week on bread and water, scourged himself, refused to allow any heat in his quarters, and deprived himself of sleep. As Aloysius had to learn, however, self-imposed penance often is not as difficult as obedience.

After he entered the Jesuit Order, Aloysius had to eat more, spend time relaxing with the other students, and limit the hours he devoted to prayer. Although he was obedient, it couldn't have been easy. Obedience never is. Yet, as Blessed Jan Van Ruysbroeck says, "God loves obedience better than sacrifice."

Sacrifice is often a onetime deal. It may be hard to give up something we love, but once we've given it up, the hardship is over. It's like cleaning out the attic and giving the excess to charity. Once the truck hauls the boxes away, there's no getting them back. Obedience, on the other hand, happens over and over. Every day, day after day, we have to set aside our own desires and do what we are called to do.

What are you being called to do? We don't have to go searching for extraordinary acts or look for stringent disciplines. All we have to do is look around and see what needs to be done . . . and then do it.

What is my chief responsibility right now?

I REALIZE THE SAINTS OFFER DIFFERENT KINDS OF WISDOM
FOR DIFFERENT OCCASIONS. I CHOOSE THAT WISDOM
WHICH IS BEST SUITED TO MY LIFE RIGHT NOW.

ST. THOMAS MORE

1478–1535

St. Thomas More was not only Lord Chancellor of England under Henry VIII, but he was also a lawyer, theologian, philosopher, and author. For all his talents, though, St. Thomas More is best remembered for his integrity.

St. Thomas More's life, and especially his death, is a tribute to his integrity. When he refused to sign the Act of Succession stating that the children of Henry VIII and his second wife, Anne Boleyn, were rightful heirs to the throne, Henry had him imprisoned, tried, and ultimately beheaded. St. Thomas knew when he refused to sign that he would forfeit his life, but maintained, "I die the king's good servant, but God's first." Since St. Thomas More was both a lawyer and a politician, he surely could have figured out a loophole in the law, but his unwillingness to go against his conscience is an extraordinary example of integrity.

In our increasingly self-centered world, honesty and integrity often appear to have little value. Every day we read about robberies, scandals, and lies on a monumental scale. We may begin to wonder if there's any point in trying to be honest any more. St. Thomas More shows us that there is, for integrity is not just something we put on and take off when the desire suits us. Integrity is a virtue for all seasons.

Am I completely honest with myself as well as with others?

I AM WILLING TO MAKE COMPROMISES WHEN MY
CONSCIENCE ALLOWS, BUT I AM NEVER WILLING TO BE
COMPROMISED.

ST. ETHELDREDA

A.D. 679

St. Etheldreda, or St. Audrey as she sometimes known, has the unusual distinction of remaining a virgin although she was married twice. Her first marriage lasted three years, during which time she and her husband lived liked brother and sister. Her second marriage occurred when her family insisted she marry Egfrid, the child-king of Northumbria. Twelve years later, Egfrid wanted more, and Etheldreda wanted to be a nun. Both got their wishes. Because the marriage had never been consummated, Etheldreda was allowed to found a convent and Egfrid was allowed to remarry.

In our society, which places such a premium on sexuality, St. Etheldreda and her husbands are more than a little unusual, to say the least. Yet the theme of self-denial as a way of spiritual growth is common among the saints.

In many ways we have become so accustomed to instant gratification that the idea of putting pleasure off is not something we normally consider. Yet if life is a continual round of parties, celebrations become commonplace.

The saints try to get us to understand that we must have contrasts. A glass of ice-cold lemonade is much more refreshing on a hot summer day than it is in the middle of a blizzard. In order to know what it's like to have a day off, we have to have a day on. The saints tell us the only way to know what it's like to really feast is to fast now and then.

When was the last time I experienced the pleasure of a long-awaited treat? Did waiting make receiving more rewarding?

I HAVE THE DISCIPLINE NEEDED BOTH TO DENY AND TO REWARD MYSELF. (AND I KNOW THE BEST TIME FOR BOTH.)

ST. JOHN THE BAPTIST

FIRST CENTURY

In *The Patty Duke Show* of the early sixties, Patty Duke played identical cousins—an interesting, although impossible occurrence. Cousins do share some of the same gene pool but not enough to be identical. Yet, outside of our brothers and sisters, cousins are our closest kin. In the United States, first cousins are considered too closely related to marry.

Cousins are interesting relatives. We don't have to associate with our cousins as we must with siblings, and, in some cases, we may not even know who our cousins are. If we do have a relationship with them, it allows for some of the same easy-going familiarity that comes from having shared many of the same family functions and traditions without as much of the stress.

John the Baptist and Jesus are traditionally called cousins because their mothers were related. They were born within six months of one another in towns not far apart. Although the Bible doesn't say so, they must have encountered one another at family weddings and funerals. John began his public ministry a few years before Jesus and ended it by saying that he had merely prepared the way for Jesus.

When we are looking for friends and allies, cousins can be one of our best sources. They already know something about us and our history. Given a chance, cousins can often become good friends.

Am I in touch with any of my cousins? Would I like to establish or reestablish ties?

·⟨▬▬▬▬▬▬▬▬▬▬▬▬▬⟩·

I APPRECIATE THE FAMILY CONNECTION OF COUSINS.

ST. WILLIAM OF VERCELLI

1085–1142

A popular saying goes something like, God never shuts a door that a window doesn't open. Often people tell us that when we have suffered a major disappointment. It's supposed to make us look for the window, but before we can do that we have to grieve for the shutting of the door.

St. William of Vercelli made up his mind to go on a pilgrimage to Jerusalem. His good friend St. John of Matera told him that God had other things in mind, but William was not to be deterred. He started out for the Holy Land but was attacked by robbers before he got far. St. William recognized the attack as God's verification of John's advice and returned home.

Having a door shut in our faces, as it did on St. William's cherished desire to make a pilgrimage, is naturally disappointing. When that happens, it's okay to spend a little bit of time grieving your loss and feeling sorry for yourself. But just a *little* time. Certainly not more than twenty-four hours. Then, it's time to start looking for the open window.

For St. William the window came in the form of a mountain. On the side of Monte Vergine he founded what would be the first of several religious communities. The example of St. William gives us confidence to make decisions and start projects, secure in the knowledge that if it's the wrong direction, God will let us know the right one.

Am I ever reluctant to begin something for fear I might make a mistake? What would happen if I did make a mistake?

I LOOK AT "MISTAKES" AS CHANCES TO FIND A WINDOW.

ST. ANTHELM

1107–1178

An elderly lady was once asked which modern invention she appreciated the most. Several suggestions—television, telephone, automobile, airplane—were offered. She shook her head at all of them. Well, maybe electricity or the radio? Again she shook her head. After pondering the point several more minutes, she had her answer: running water.

Most of us take running water for granted. The only time we think about it is when we turn on the faucet and the water *doesn't* come out. One of the greatest accomplishments of the Roman Empire was its vast system of aqueducts. Even today, a steady supply of fresh, clean water can make the difference between disease and health.

St. Anthelm was a great reformer. When he was named bishop of Belley, he corrected abuses among both the clergy and the laity. He extended his work beyond ecclesiastical matters and rebuilt the monastery of Grande Chartreuse after much of it was destroyed by an avalanche. In addition to restoring the buildings, he revamped the farm lands and supplied fresh water through aqueduct systems.

Running water has long been used as a symbol for new life and rebirth. Today, when you wash your hands, take a few minutes to think about the water as it flows over your palms and through your fingers. Offer up a silent prayer that as the water is washing away the dirt and grim from your hands, so too will the heartache and failure of your past life be washed away.

Is some part of my past keeping me from enjoying the present?

I BELIEVE THAT IT'S NEVER TOO LATE TO START OVER.

ST. CYRIL OF ALEXANDRIA

376?–444

When we think of a doctor, we usually think of a medical practitioner, yet the word *doctor* comes from the Latin *docere* (to teach). The Church has designated several men and two women (Teresa of Avila and Catherine of Siena) as Doctors of the Church. This honorary title is given to those select few whose writings have been instrumental in shaping Church teaching.

St. Cyril of Alexandria is on that short list. Born in Alexandria, Egypt, St. Cyril was not a mild-mannered scholar. As archbishop of Alexandria, for instance, he closed churches belonging to splinter sects. Yet despite his harshness, he was an eloquent spokesman for orthodox teaching during the Council of Ephesus. His thoughtful writings on the nature of Christ's birth and divine nature earned him the title Doctor of the Incarnation.

Not everyone who has truth on their side is pleasant to be around. When someone takes a different position than we do or holds a view we can't agree with, we have the responsibility to treat that person with respect and patience. St. Cyril might still have become a saint even if he hadn't learned that lesson, but fortunately for his opponents, he mellowed a bit as he aged. He never gave up defending what he believed to be the truth, but he became more understanding of those who disagreed with him. St. Cyril had to grow old before he grew wise. We don't need to wait that long.

Am I growing wiser or am I just growing older?

WISDOM COMES FROM PATIENCE AND UNDERSTANDING. EVERY DAY I STRIVE TO BE A LITTLE WISER THAN I WAS THE DAY BEFORE.

ST. IRENAEUS

130?–202?

Many religions have been based on the idea that only a select few are privileged to have special knowledge about God, including the secrets of eternal life. In order to gain that knowledge, you have to go through mysterious procedures and rituals designed to make you part of the chosen elite. Once you are accepted, you are sworn never to reveal the secrets to anyone outside the group.

God's love is just the opposite. It's meant to be shared with everyone. "Go and make disciples of all nations," Jesus told his followers. He didn't say, "Go and keep this to yourself."

In the third century, certain groups began to teach that Jesus had kept secrets, that his "real" teaching had been reserved for the twelve apostles. Only a few people were allowed to hear the so-called truth.

St. Irenaeus, the bishop of Lyons, adamantly opposed such an idea. Recognizing the allure of secret information, he wrote several works comparing the so-called hidden knowledge with the teachings of the apostles and scripture. By doing so, he was able to squash the idea that Jesus came only for a few special people.

If people tell you they have secret knowledge about God, don't believe it. No such information is available. Divine truth is free to all who seek it. All you have to do is ask and you shall receive.

Do I ever wonder if there really is such a thing as secret information about God?

I KNOW THAT KNOWLEDGE OF GOD IS MINE WHENEVER I SEEK IT.

ST. PETER

FIRST CENTURY

Do you ever rush off half-cocked? Do you often discover that your foot is lodged firmly in your mouth? Do you make rash statements that you later regret? Are you impetuous, exuberant, and filled with joie de vivre? If so, then you're spiritually related to St. Peter.

Peter was a man who never believed in doing things half-way. He was willing to jump out of boats, walk on water, and declare his unending love for his Lord. He also denied Christ three times, lost his confidence, and nearly drowned. Whatever he did, he did with all his heart and soul. He made mistakes, but he got up, dried himself off, and kept going. Peter was filled with passion; passion for Christ, passion for the gospel, passion for life.

All too often we sip at life as if it were a tepid cup of weak tea. St. Peter tells us that instead of taking tiny little mouthfuls, we need to grab life with both hands and swig it down like an icy cold glass of spring water on the hottest day of summer.

There is a bumper sticker that sums up St. Peter's philosophy: Life is not a dress rehearsal. We can't wait for what we think is opening night to decide we'll go on stage. If we do, we'll discover the play is almost over and the curtain is ready to fall.

Do I enjoy life as much as I could? What am I waiting for?

I TAKE JOY AS MY LIFE MOTTO.

ST. PIERRE TOUSSAINT

1776–1863

Most of us believe in giving credit where credit is due—especially when we're due the credit. Almost nothing rankles as much as someone else taking the honors for something we've done. If that happens, we often feel compelled to set the record straight, to make sure the world knows who was really responsible for the good deed.

St. Pierre Toussaint took the opposite tack. He did everything possible to conceal his extraordinary generosity.

Born in French Haiti, Pierre Toussaint was a slave on the Jean Berand plantation. When unrest threatened the island, Monsieur Berand moved his wife and sisters to New York. Before he returned to Haiti, he apprenticed Pierre to one of the city's most prestigious hairdressers. Things went from bad to worse for the Berands. Jean Berand died of pleurisy, the family plantation was destroyed in a massive slave uprising, and Mrs. Berand's New York investments were lost when the firm collapsed.

For the rest of her life, Marie Berand was supported by St. Pierre, who had become both wealthy and famous as a hairdresser. To all outward appearances, he remained her slave, even serving as a waiter at her parties (parties his money provided!). Finally, when she was dying, Madame Berand granted Pierre his freedom.

St. Pierre did many of the things other saints did. He faithfully attended Mass, gave generously to the poor, nursed the sick, and educated the illiterate. Perhaps the most remarkable thing he did, however, was to allow a proud aristocrat to keep her dignity . . . at the expense of his own.

How important is it to me to save face?

TODAY 1 WILL DO ONE KIND DEED FOR A STRANGER,
KNOWING THAT 1 WILL NEVER BE REPAID.

BLESSED JUNÍPERO SERRA

1713–1784

To read a map of the California coastline is to recite a litany of saints: San Diego, San Juan Capistrano, San Luis Obispo, Santa Clara, Santa Barbara, San Francisco—the twenty-one missions established by the Franciscan friars. Of those twenty-one missions, nine were founded by one man, Blessed Junípero Serra.

Blessed Junípero definitely liked to walk. When he first landed in the New World, he and another friar walked three hundred miles to Mexico City. It was on that journey that he was bitten by something poisonous—some say an insect, others a snake—that left him lame and in pain for the rest of his life. Nevertheless, he covered thousands of miles as he founded the California mission chain. He even walked to the chapel for Communion the night he was dying.

We all know that vigorous exercise is good for our hearts, but only recently have health experts concluded what people like Fr. Serra have known all along—walking is an excellent form of exercise.

Walking does more than just get the blood flowing. It also lifts the cobwebs from our brains and the weariness from our souls. The next time you're feeling sluggish and blah, go for a walk. Stop to appreciate the flowers in a neighbor's yard. Scratch a kitten under the chin. Watch the clouds drift by. Your heart—and your soul—will be glad you did.

Do I enjoy walking by myself or would I rather walk with a companion?

TODAY I WILL APPRECIATE BEING OUTSIDE ON A SUMMER AFTERNOON.

ST. OTTO

A.D. 1139

St. Otto, bishop of Bamberg in the twelfth century, was caught between the proverbial rock and a hard place. As chancellor in the service of Emperor Henry IV, he was required to support the state. But when Henry established an antipope, St. Otto—as a loyal member of the Church—could not approve the appointment. Interestingly, he seems to have kept in the good graces of both the Holy See and the emperor by refusing to support the schism but still upholding other political decisions.

Learning when and how to compromise is a fine art. Compromise doesn't mean caving in, nor does it mean being unyielding. It means giving a little here, while standing firm over there. We've all met people who never learned to compromise. They have to fight every battle as if it were the turning point of the war. While they sometimes get exactly what they want, it's at the expense of their—and our—peace of mind and composure.

One of the insights the saints provide is the wisdom to know that not every issue demands a firm stand. For St. Otto, the question of which Pope was legitimate demanded a resolute position. Other decisions by Henry didn't require the same unyielding stance. Otto was able to keep peace by knowing when to resist and when to relent. When we face similar situations, let us ask for the wisdom to know which position we should take.

*In what areas can I never compromise? Are there areas where
I could be a little less rigid?*

I KNOW WHEN TO HOLD ON AND WHEN TO LET GO.

ST. THOMAS

FIRST CENTURY

Doubt (dowt) n. 1. a feeling of uncertainty about something, an undecided state of mind. 2. a feeling of disbelief. 3. an uncertain state of affairs. (Oxford American Dictionary)

When it comes to spiritual matters, it might be nice to be able to say we've never experienced doubts, but most of us would be lying. It may a fleeting thought or it may be a longer, darker night of the soul, but most of us have at least wondered about the mysteries of the universe, including the existence of God. Even when we think we've got it figured out, we may still experience moments when questions loom larger than answers.

St. Thomas had those same feelings. The only difference is that we can sometimes keep our doubts hidden; St. Thomas's uncertainty has been recorded for all posterity. Not only that, but his very name has become associated with someone who questions everything—a doubting Thomas.

When Jesus appeared to his apostles after the resurrection, Thomas wasn't present. When he heard the news, Thomas refused to believe it unless he could touch Jesus's wounds himself. Eight days later, much to his shock, Jesus appeared and invited him to do just that.

Thomas was able to have his doubts resolved by a personal visit from Jesus. Most of us won't have that same privilege, but through the eyes of faith, we can pass from disbelief to conviction. After all, when Thomas fell on his knees, saying "My Lord and My God," Jesus answered, "Because you have seen me, Thomas, you have believed. Blessed are they that have not seen and have believed."

Do I find it hard to believe?

I HAVE CONFIDENCE THAT AS I SEEK THE TRUTH,
I WILL FIND GOD.

ST. ELIZABETH OF PORTUGAL

1271–1336

There is a saying, a place for everything and everything in its place. St. Elizabeth of Portugal might modify that to read, "A time for everything and everything in its time."

The daughter of the king of Aragon, she married the king of Portugal when she was only twelve. Although he was not a pious man, he never interfered with his wife's devotions. Thus, she got up early and recited numerous prayers before daily Mass. In the afternoons she said Vespers and other set prayers. In between she maintained a schedule that included taking care of her household duties (she did have a castle to run, after all), her royal responsibilities, and her family matters.

Sometimes we think that being tied to a schedule is monotonous and boring. Yet without a schedule of some sort, we're likely to fritter away our time.

Keeping a schedule doesn't mean maintaining a minute-by-minute accounting. It doesn't even mean that we can't make adjustments if something comes along that we hadn't planned on. What keeping a schedule means is that we hem the edges of our lives so that they don't completely unravel. It means we make sure we have enough time for work and for play, for exercise and for rest, for solitude and for company. Keeping a schedule simply means that we bring balance into our days.

If I'm an overscheduler, what can I do to lighten up? If I never plan, how can I arrange to put a little more discipline in my days?

TWENTY-FOUR HOURS IN A DAY IS ENOUGH FOR ME.

ST. ANTHONY ZACCARIA

1502–1539

One of the measures of spiritual growth is how we treat those who mistreat us. When we seek revenge or look for ways to harm our enemies, we have not traveled very far on our spiritual journey. When, however, we are able to look kindly on those who would wish us ill, we know we are well on our way to maturity.

St. Anthony Zaccaria first studied to be a medical doctor, then entered the priesthood. A vigorous preacher, his frank presentation did not endear him to everyone. Although he knew what it was like to be on the receiving end of criticism, St. Anthony wrote, "We should love and feel compassion for those who oppose us, since they harm themselves and do us good. . . ."

One of the most effective defenses against those who mistreat us is to "kill them with kindness." Instead of giving back the same kind of treatment we receive, we can be patient, loving, and understanding.

Such behavior may cause our enemies to reverse their position and cease attacking us. Even if that doesn't happen, our unexpected actions may put them on their guard, wondering what on earth we are up to.

Is there someone in my life who dislikes me,
but whom I can "kill with kindness"?

I KNOW THAT EACH TIME I CHOOSE LOVE OVER HATE,
I GROW SPIRITUALLY.

ST. MARIA GORETTI

1890–1902

It's easy to talk about forgiveness when we don't have anyone to forgive, but what about crimes that are so heinous that every fiber of our being calls out for revenge?

St. Maria Goretti was only eleven when she was attacked by a young man she knew. Several times before the final attack, Alessandro Serenelli had tried to touch her, but she had managed to put him off. This time, however, when his attempted rape failed, he stabbed her fourteen times. During the twenty-four hours it took for her to die, Maria Goretti repeatedly prayed that her attacker would repent.

That alone would be remarkable, but the story doesn't end there. Alessandro was released from prison after twenty-seven years of confinement. During his incarceration, he said Maria appeared to him in a dream, holding a bunch of white lilies. One of his first acts was to go to Maria's mother, who was still living, and ask her forgiveness. Although it is Maria who was canonized, the fact that her mother willingly forgave her daughter's murderer is testimony to her sanctity as well. Both Alessandro and Maria's mother attended her canonization ceremony on June 25, 1950.

Sometimes we think forgiveness is only for those who have committed a wrong. But forgiveness goes both ways. It blesses the one who is forgiven, but it blesses equally the one who forgives. It doesn't take a saint to ask for forgiveness, but it can make one out of the person who gives it.

Have I ever refused to forgive someone? Has anyone ever refused to forgive me?

⟨⟨⟨⟨⟨⟨⟨⟨⟨⟨⟨⟨⟨⟨⟨⟨⟨⟩⟩⟩⟩⟩⟩⟩⟩⟩⟩⟩⟩⟩⟩

STARTING RIGHT NOW, I FORGIVE ALL WHO HAVE HURT ME, LIVING OR DEAD.

BLESSED PIER GIORGIO FRASSATI

1901–1925

Sometimes we think that if we were to really commit ourselves spiritually, we'd have to give up everything we love. After all, nobody ever got canonized for eating all the chocolate they wanted. To paraphrase St. Augustine, we are inclined to pray, make me a saint. But not quite yet.

Blessed Pier Giorgio Frassati was young, handsome, and fond of downhill skiing and cheap cigars. He climbed mountains, sang off-key, and fell in love. He also attended daily Mass and frequently spent all night in prayer. Pope John Paul II called him "the man of the Beatitudes." His friends called him a saint with a cigar. Blessed Pier loved every moment of his short life. (He died of polio when he was only twenty-four.) "It is the certainty of a better life in the hereafter if we work doing good," he said, " and so let's get off to work, staying united, and comforting each other, and urging one another on the way to good."

Blessed Pier might have lived with his eyes fixed on heaven, but his feet were firmly planted on earth (except when he was mountain-climbing). He attended the theater and the opera, although he bought less expensive tickets so he would have money to give to the poor. For the same reason, he rode third class on the trains. He studied at university, was involved in politics, played practical jokes . . . and still was saintly.

Becoming a saint doesn't mean we have to stop doing what we love; it merely means doing everything we love *with* love.

What saints do I find the most attractive?

I BELIEVE LIFE IS TO BE LIVED EVERYDAY.

ROSE HAWTHORNE LATHROP

1851–1926

If the name Hawthorne seems familiar, it should. Rose Hawthorne Lathrop was the daughter of the famous American novelist Nathaniel Hawthorne. Rose, a Unitarian, and her husband, George, became Catholics after nearly twenty years of marriage. Although she always loved him, George's alcoholism finally forced Rose to ask for a legal separation. After George's death, Rose began to work with cancer patients, eventually founding a religious order, the Dominican Servants of Relief for Incurable Cancer.

Unlike many of the saints in this book who practiced severe discipline, Mother Alphonsa, as Rose became known, delighted in indulgences as well as necessities for her cancer patients. She bought a dog for one and a parrot for another. She even spent $150 on a radio, a hefty sum in the early twentieth century.

Although Rose is not yet an official saint, her love and compassion for the poor and sick as well as her understanding of the need for a few "extras" in life makes her worthy of our attention.

We all crave a little indulgence. While the words are sometimes used interchangeably, *indulgence* is different from *luxury*. A luxury is something costly. An indulgence, on the other hand, is merely something pleasurable. Having fresh flowers delivered daily would be a luxury. Having a single perfect red rose is an indulgence.

The saints often warn us against the dangers of becoming too attached to luxuries, but as one of Rose Hawthorne Lathrop's patients pointed out after being cared for and indulged by the sisters, "This is heaven!" Let us not be afraid to bring a little heaven to earth now and then!

Do I allow myself and those around me to enjoy their little indulgences?

TODAY I WILL SURPRISE SOMEONE (MAYBE EVEN ME!) WITH A SPECIAL TREAT.

ST. NICHOLAS PIECK AND COMPANIONS

A.D. 1572

Few topics can create a more heated argument than that of religion. What may start out as a polite discussion can rapidly disintegrate into discord. Many times, religious differences have even led to violence.

In the summer of 1572, St. Nicholas Pieck and eighteen companion priests and religious were hanged. The martyrs of Gorkum, as they are called, died simply because they were Catholics. One of their number, St. Antony Van Willehad, was ninety years old.

Countless pages of history have been stained by the blood of martyrs. No group is above reproach. Non-Christians have killed Christians. Christians have killed non-Christians. Protestants have killed Catholics. Catholics have killed Protestants. All because of a lack of religious tolerance.

Sometimes we get the mistaken notion that to tolerate means to accede. We believe that unless we denounce something vehemently we may be seen as agreeing wholeheartedly. Yet practicing religious tolerance doesn't mean that we have to give up our own faith. It doesn't mean we have to believe that all religions are interchangeable. It doesn't even mean that we have to pretend there are no differences. Religious tolerance means that we treat other people's beliefs with respect, not because we believe they are right or even because we think they are reasonable, but because to do anything less would be uncharitable. A good rule for any discussion, but particularly when it involves religion, is to never say anything about another's beliefs that you wouldn't want said about yours.

Have I ever been discriminated against for my beliefs?

I AM WILLING TO DISCUSS MY CONVICTIONS, AND I LET OTHERS DISCUSS THEIRS.

ST. THEODOSIUS PECHERSKY

A.D. 1074

If you feel stuck in a spiritual rut and don't know quite how to get back on the road, you might need a spiritual director. As the abbot of the Caves of Kiev, St. Theodosius Pechersky invited people of all ages to share their struggles, serving as a spiritual director to all who asked.

Unlike a cult leader, a spiritual director doesn't attempt to take over your life or change your beliefs. A good director merely helps you reflect on the work of the divine in your life. His or her role is to help you sort out the authentic from the sham, the real from the contrived. In many ways, a spiritual director acts like a signpost, pointing the way out of the rut and back to the path.

Where can you find a spiritual director? Although many priests and ministers give spiritual direction, some of the best directors are not ordained. A man or woman of prayer, who has traveled far on his or her own spiritual journey may be your best choice. While no one can tell you exactly where you will find your spiritual director, the words of an old proverb offer the best key. "When the student is ready, the teacher will appear." When you are ready for spiritual direction, have confidence that the right person will be there for you.

Do I know someone who has traveled far on their own spiritual journey? Is it possible he or she could be my spiritual guide?

I KNOW THAT WHEN I AM READY TO STEP INTO THE DARKNESS, I WILL BE HANDED A LIGHT.

ST. BENEDICT

480?–547

The expression, he died with his boots on, originally referred to someone who died unexpectedly (probably from a gunshot wound) who didn't even have to time take off his boots. In time, however, it has come to mean a person who never gives up on life.

St. Benedict built twelve monasteries; one, Monte Cassino, was rebuilt three times. Under his rule, monasteries became sanctuaries of learning and hospitality in the Middle Ages. Without the monasteries to keep the light of learning lit, the Dark Ages would have been dark indeed.

St. Benedict's influence on monastic life was so great that his rule, or plan, for monks became the standard throughout Europe. Even today, many religious orders operate under the Rule of St. Benedict.

True to form, Benedict died with his boots on (more likely his sandals). Although he needed some support from his monks, he was standing in the chapel with his hands raised to heaven when he died.

Many of us fear old age. We worry that we will become a burden to our families and to ourselves. Although life doesn't come with guarantees, the saints encourage us not to worry what might or might not happen. They point out that even when we can no longer work physically, we can still perform spiritual labors, such as forgiving those who have hurt us, praying for others, and comforting the sorrowful.

Have I ever thought of spiritual labor as real work? What kind of spiritual labors am I being called to do today?

NO MATTER WHAT MY PHYSICAL CONDITION, I CAN PUMP UP MY SPIRITUAL MUSCLES.

ST. JOHN GAULBERT

A.D. 1073

Which is harder to do: eat one salted peanut (but only one!) or not eat any at all?

For a lot of us, it's easier to push the whole bowl aside than to take a single nibble. Better not be tempted, we say. But did you know that when you do just take a taste and leave the rest, you aren't being tempted; you're exercising the virtue of temperance?

Temperance got a bad name when it was linked with Prohibition. From then on, its real meaning was overshadowed. Temperance, however, has as much to do with salted peanuts, shopping sprees, and reckless driving as it does with drinking.

Temperance simply means moderation. It means striking a balance between extremes. It means eating a few peanuts instead of the whole bowl; buying the things you need, not everything that strikes your fancy; obeying the speed limit, even when the road is straight and there are no highway patrol in sight.

St. John Gaulbert, the founder of an offshoot branch of Benedictine monks, recognized the need to balance lenience with harshness. He understood that both extremes can lead to sin. In short, he knew that spiritual safety lies in temperance.

When we act temperately, we listen to the wisdom within that tells us when we are overdoing. We pay attention to the nudges that warn us when we are trying to do too much (or too little). We heed the divine counsel that says we need to find a middle ground for our sanity . . . and the sanity of everyone around us.

Am I inclined to go overboard on things?

BY PRACTICING TEMPERANCE, I FIND THE PROPER
BALANCES FOR MY LIFE.

ST. HENRY II

972–1024

In 1021, when St. Henry II, emperor of the Holy Roman Empire, was returning from a conflict with the Greeks, he stopped off at the Monte Cassino, the abbey founded by St. Benedict. While there he fell ill. The story goes that Benedict cured him by his prayers. Whether it was prayer alone or the medicinal herbs the monasteries of the Middle Ages were famous for that cured Henry, we can't be sure, but we can be sure that prayer makes a difference in illnesses.

Scientific studies have shown that, although prayer does not bring about healing in each and every case, it can have a profound effect on recovery. In some cases, it can even bring about a total cure.

Miraculous healings cannot be fully explained. If they could, they would no longer be miracles. There always remains an element of doubt: perhaps the cancer would have gone into remission on its own, maybe the tumor wasn't malignant after all. Trying to analyze a miraculous cure doesn't make it any more or less miraculous. All it does is create an atmosphere of question and distrust. Instead, when a miracle occurs, our first response should be one of profound thanks. It doesn't matter how the cure happened—from natural processes or divine intervention. The point is that it did happen and that alone should give us sufficient reason to rejoice.

Have I ever experienced a cure that could be called miraculous?
When I am sick, do I pray for recovery?

I BELIEVE IN MIRACLES.

BLESSED KATERI TEKAWITHA

1656–1680

Do you sometimes feel out of step with the world? Do you find yourself moving in directions that leave your family and friends shaking their heads?

Writer and naturalist Henry David Thoreau once wrote that if we do not keep pace with our companions, perhaps it is because we hear a different drummer.

For Blessed Kateri Tekawitha, daughter of a Mohawk chief and an Algonquin mother in pre-Revolutionary America, the drumbeat was indeed different. Although marriage was the only viable option for a girl of her tribe, she defied convention by converting to Christianity and dedicating her entire life to God. Because of her unorthodox lifestyle—she spent her days in prayer, charity and penance—her life was often in danger. She wrote, "The state of helpless poverty that may befall me if I do not marry does not frighten me. All I need is a little food and a few pieces of clothing."

All too often, we let other's criticism get in the way of our personal growth. Instead of becoming the person we are truly meant to be, we let tradition and convention dictate our life choices. Kateri Tekawitha shows us that to be truly free, we sometimes have to let go of everyone else's expectations and, as Thoreau said, "step to the music which [we] hear, however measured or far away."

Do I let others choose my direction for me? What do I really want to be when I grow up?

I AM BECOMING THE PERSON I'VE ALWAYS WANTED TO BE.

ST. BONAVENTURE

1221–1274

Ever notice how most rich and famous people tend to marry other rich and famous people? A lot of reasons are postulated, among them that it's easier for someone who is already famous to put up with the pressures of celebrity life.

Often the real reason is overlooked: people tend to fall in love with the people they associate with. As Mark Twain wryly put it, "familiarity breeds." Since rich and famous folk tend to hang out with other rich and famous folk, it's only natural that their lives would intertwine.

The same is true of saints. Not only do they tend to associate with each other, they also tend to influence each other. St. Bonaventure knew two of the greatest saints in the world: St. Francis of Assisi and St. Thomas Aquinas. When he was a young boy, St. Francis cured him of a serious illness. Then, while he was studying at the University of Paris, he became friends with Thomas Aquinas. The two received their degrees of doctor of theology at the same time. Since we know they were friends, we can assume that the two great saints often talked and shared their faith. They became spiritual friends as well as social companions.

Talking about faith with a spiritual friend can be a great comfort. Our friends can strengthen us in times of trial and encourage us in times of doubt. They can brighten our lives and make the path to spiritual maturity easier to walk.

Do I have a spiritual friend? What qualities would I want a spiritual friend to possess?

I GIVE THANKS TO ALL WHO HAVE HELPED ME COME TO A GREATER UNDERSTANDING OF MYSELF AND MY WORTH.

BLESSED IGNATIUS AZEVEDO AND COMPANIONS

1528–1570

One of the most popular rides in the Disney theme parks is the Pirates of the Caribbean. The buccaneers are presented as rather jovial, despite their pillaging and burning of the town. Real pirates, on the other hand, were brigands who brought terror to everyone they encountered.

In 1570, Blessed Ignatius Azevedo, a Jesuit priest, and forty companions boarded the *Santiago,* a merchant ship sailing to the Canary Islands. As they headed across the Atlantic, Jacques Sourie, a French pirate, began to chase them. He caught up with the *Santiago* on the way to Las Palmas and boarded her. Although the passengers and crew tried to fight, they were no match for the pirates. The crew he spared, but Sourie butchered the forty Jesuits.

Although we don't need to dwell on it, we can't overlook the fact that real evil exists in the world. We may try to dress it up and turn it into a theme park ride, but under the pretense lurks a darker reality. Like street smarts, we need spiritual smarts. We need to keep our eyes open so that we are not caught unaware by evil. The captain of the *Santiago* foolishly tried to outrun the pirate ship. It would have been far better if he had planned his route so that it would have not been in the pirates' path. Likewise, we are far better off avoiding the entrapment of evil than we are trying to fight it on its own terms.

Have I ever tempted fate by placing myself in a situation of unnecessary danger?

⸻

I AVOID THOSE PLACES AND SITUATIONS IN WHICH MY SPIRITUAL WELL‑BEING MAY BE ENDANGERED.

BLESSED CESLAUS OF POLAND

1180–1242

In a world that seems to have gone crazy, individual life appears to have grown less valuable. We constantly hear about senseless murders, massive genocide, and pointless wars. When we hear about so much violence, it is all too easy to become desensitized to the pain of others. It is all too easy to begin to put abstract principles above human life and insulate ourselves from other people's suffering with lofty words about humanitarianism.

For Dr. Albert Schweitzer, one of the world's greatest humanitarians, such action would be anathema. "Humanitarianism," he says, "consists in never sacrificing a human being to a purpose."

Blessed Ceslaus of Poland came to Rome to witness the consecration of his uncle St. Hyacinth as bishop of Cracow. While there, he was inspired by St. Dominic and returned to Poland as a missionary. The rest of his life was spent in sweeping deeds of preaching and teaching. His greatest deeds, however, involve individuals. Among other things, he became famous for curing the sick and maimed.

How easy it is to become so caught up in saving the forest, we forget to appreciate the individual trees. The Gospel of Matthew says that not even a single sparrow can fall to the ground without God knowing it. If God keeps track of sparrows, how much more so must each of us be valued?

Do I let God show me that I am valuable? How do I show others they are valued by God?

TODAY I WILL TREAT MYSELF AS A BELOVED CHILD OF MY HEAVENLY FATHER.

ST. BRUNO

A.D. 1123

Nobody's perfect. Not even the saints. St. Bruno, one of the greatest Scripture scholars of his time, made at least one serious error. He maintained that a priest who committed simony—buying and selling spiritual gifts—could not validly administer the sacraments. In other words, he incorrectly believed that a priest who sold a church office could not celebrate Mass or administer baptism. While selling church offices is wrong, such action doesn't invalidate a man's ordination. St. Bruno's error should encourage all of us. Making a mistake is just that—a mistake.

No one likes to be wrong, but all of us are sometimes. Occasionally our mistake is serious, with long-range consequences, but most of the time it has only momentary consequences. It may be inconvenient; it may be embarrassing, but it isn't the end of the world and we shouldn't treat it as such.

When we recognize that we've made an error, we can and should try to rectify it, but when correction is impossible, the best course is simply to admit it and go on. Berating yourself, condemning yourself, and tearing yourself down won't change the mistake, but it will change you. It will erode your self-confidence and make it more likely that you'll make an error in the future.

When you discover you're in error, give yourself a break. Give yourself permission to rejoin the mistake-prone human race.

Am I a perfectionist? Am I harder on myself for my mistakes than I am on others for theirs?

I KNOW IT ISN'T A CAPITAL OFFENSE TO BE WRONG.

ST. MACRINA

330?–379

There is an old saying that behind every great man stands a good woman. Apparently it was true in St. Macrina's family. The oldest of ten children, she helped educate her siblings, including St. Gregory of Nyssa, Basil the Great, and St. Peter of Sebastea. While her brothers achieved fame, Macrina lived quietly with her mother and other women on an estate in Pontus. It may appear that Macrina got short shrift, since Gregory himself credited his sister with having taught him humility and the love of Scripture, but as Milton points out, "They also serve who only stand and wait."

Most of us don't like to stand and wait. It's no fun to be stuck at the bus stop of life while everyone else seems to be riding in a stretch limo. What's worse, if we do catch the bus, it sometimes feels like we have to get off at just another bus stop, while the people in the limo head on to a great party.

If this were all there were to life, then St. Macrina was foolish not to grab some of the credit from her brothers—and we would be equally foolish not to highjack a limo for our own use. But the saints remind us that we aren't eternally waiting; we're waiting for eternity. There's a big difference between the two. We aren't just standing around until we dissolve into nothingness. Even when it feels like we are going nowhere fast, we really are coming a little bit closer to that moment when we join the heavenly party that never ends.

Do I find it hard to wait? What am I currently waiting for?

I REALIZE THAT I DON'T HAVE TO BE DOING SOMETHING IN ORDER TO BECOME SOMEONE.

STS. JUSTA AND RUFINA

A.D. 304?

One of the ways pottery manufacturers make a profit is through mass production. Hour after hour, day after day, their factories turn out thousands and thousands of cups and plates, all exactly the same. While mass production means that you can replace any item you might break with one that looks identical, it also means that all individuality is lost. Two pieces of hand-thrown pottery seldom look alike. While they may be made of the same clay and have the same glaze, each one is just a little bit different. Before the invention of modern assembly lines, all pottery, even that which was produced in quantity, was made by hand.

Sts. Justa and Rufina were Christian women who sold pottery in fourth-century Spain. Because they valued their earthenware, they would not allow it to be sold for use in pagan sacrifices. As a result, all of their pottery was broken and they themselves were executed.

Each of us is as individual as a piece of hand-thrown pottery. Even identical twins, who are as close to being exactly the same as human beings can ever get, have their own distinctive fingerprints and personalities. You are unique. There never has been and there never will be another person just like you, with your talents and abilities, your dreams, your hopes, your gifts. You are a one-of-a-kind creation of the divine potter. Treasure yourself.

Do you let others treat you as if you were "mass produced"?
Do you ever treat yourself as if you were a factory reject?

I KNOW THAT I HAVE BEEN LOVINGLY AND CAREFULLY CREATED.

ST. LAWRENCE OF BRINDISI

1559–1619

Have you ever asked for directions and heard something like: Well, you go down Pioneer until you get to Murphy's store and then you turn left on Park and go until you get to the next light . . . no, make that the second light and turn right. The next line is invariably, you can't miss it.

Yeah, right. It's almost a sure bet you'll end up lost. Or asking for directions again.

If we have this much difficulty understanding one another when we speak the same language, no wonder people who speak different languages have trouble communicating.

St. Lawrence of Brindisi was one of those extraordinary people who are gifted with a facility for learning languages. In addition to Italian, he spoke Greek, German, Bohemian, Spanish, French, Latin, and Hebrew. His Hebrew was so good that some people thought he was a Jew who had converted to Christianity. Because of his ability with languages, St. Lawrence became an effective communicator throughout much of Europe.

Communication isn't merely a matter of spoken words. Our body language often speaks volumes. Someone who says I love you but whose arms are tightly folded and lips pursed is giving two different messages. What we say with our bodies often determines how people treat us. If you find that people aren't treating you the way you want, check to see if your body language is communicating more than your words.

What does my body language tell others about me and my intentions?

· ⟨⟨⟨⟨⟨⟨⟨⟨⟨⟨⟩⟩⟩⟩⟩⟩⟩⟩⟩⟩ ·

I PAY ATTENTION TO THE BODY SIGNALS I SEND OUT TO
OTHER PEOPLE.

ST. MARY MAGDALENE

FIRST CENTURY

For centuries, Mary Magdalene has been identified with the sinful woman who anointed Jesus's feet with perfume at the house of Simon, the Pharisee. What's more, since the sinful woman is often thought to have been a prostitute, Mary gets stuck with that label also. Yet there's no evidence that the Mary who lived in the town of Magdala and from whom Jesus cast out seven devils had anything to do with the woman "who was a sinner." Mary Magdalene was more likely to have been mentally ill or demonically possessed than she was to have been immoral.

Poor Mary is the victim of untruth in labeling. Over the centuries, more careful reading of Scripture has allowed us to know the truth about Mary Magdalene. She is now seen for what she really was, not what she was imagined to be.

We need to do the same for ourselves. We need to see ourselves for what we really are, not what someone else imagines us to be. Often we allow others to give us labels that may or may not be appropriate. One way to find out if you've been mislabeled is to listen for the words *always* and *never*. If the people around you tend to say, 'you always . . . ' or 'you never . . . ' you can be certain that untrue labeling is at work. Instead of accepting such mislabels without question, take the time to politely yet firmly point out that saying 'you never' and 'you always' are never true and are always a mistake!

How would I describe myself? Is it the same way others would describe me?

THE ONLY LABELS I APPLY TO MYSELF OR TO OTHERS ARE THE KIND WITH ADHESIVE ON THE BACK.

ST. BIRGITTA OF SWEDEN

1303?–1373

If you were stranded on a desert island, what three things would you take with you? Although answers vary greatly, most people would take a book of one kind or another.

Books were so important to St. Birgitta of Sweden that they were exempt from the restrictions of poverty. The founder of a religious community that admitted both men and women (albeit in separate enclosures), she maintained the strict rule that at yearend all excess income had to be given to the poor. The one exception was that every nun and monk could have as many books as she or he wanted.

Books are the great escape. As Emily Dickinson says, "There is no frigate like a book, To take us lands away."

St. Birgitta undoubtedly caught a frigate of a book now and again. Not only did she have a monastery to run, she had children to worry about. Prior to entering religious life, she had been happily married for twenty-eight years. She and her husband, Ulf, had eight children, one of whom became a saint (Catherine of Sweden), several of whom must have given her headaches. One daughter married a man Birgitta called the Brigand and while in Naples her favorite son took up with Queen Joanna I, despite the fact that her third husband was living in Spain and his wife was living in Sweden.

No wonder Birgitta told her religious they could have all the books they wanted. If they were reading, they couldn't get into trouble!

What book would I take with me to a desert island? Why would I choose it?

·⟨░░░░░░░░░░░░░░░░░░░░░░░░░⟩·

TODAY I GIVE THANKS FOR ALL WHO WERE INVOLVED IN THE MAKING OF THE BOOKS THAT HAVE CHANGED MY LIFE.

ST. CHRISTINA THE ASTONISHING

1150–1224

There are some saints who, if they lived in the twentieth century, would probably be declared insane. If the accounts of her life contain any accuracy, St. Christina the Astonishing would be one of them. She is supposed to have loathed the smell of her fellow humans, to have clung to windmills as they carried her round and round, and to have prayed either while balancing on a hurdle or while curled up like a ball, not to mention climbing in ovens and jumping in rivers. It's safe to assume that she would not have made it through the modern canonization process.

While we might not find much about Christina to emulate, we can in her friend, Louis, Count of Looz. Louis is said to have always treated her with kindness and respect. Maybe it's Louis who should have been declared a saint instead of Christina.

Sometimes we don't treat the mentally handicapped, the insane, or the poor with as much respect as we could. When we encounter a disheveled, ragged streetperson (Christina dressed in rags and lived by begging) do we avert our eyes and walk a little faster so as to avoid any contact? Or do we swallow our fear and distaste and see if there is anything we can do to help? Even at those times when offering assistance isn't wise or safe, we don't have to go out of our way to be rude or cold. We can still be respectful, remembering that "there but by the grace of God go I."

How tolerant am I of people who are mentally handicapped or insane? Do I ever blame the poor for being poor?

I SHARE MY BLESSINGS WITH THOSE WHO ARE LESS FORTUNATE.

ST. JAMES THE GREATER

FIRST CENTURY

St. James the Greater was the first of the apostles to die, be-headed by King Herod Agrippa I. Ironically, although he was killed in Jerusalem, tradition says his body was moved to Spain, where his shrine at Compostela became one of the greatest pilgrimage desti-nations of the Middle Ages. Moreover, even though he was never anywhere remotely near the British Isles, hundreds of churches in England are dedicated to him. Finally, he is the patron saint of both Guatemala and Nicaragua. Pretty good for someone who never left the Holy Land.

If someone had told St. James how influential he would become, he probably would not have believed it. We often don't believe we have any influence either. We refuse to believe that one lone person can make any difference. Yet we can. Recently, in a metropolitan area with a population of more than 200,000, a proposal to build a new library was defeated by only ten votes. All those people who stayed home, believing the measure would pass and their vote wasn't needed, were undoubtedly shocked. Everyone who voted against the proposal could think with satisfaction that perhaps it was their ballot that made the difference.

Mother Teresa of Calcutta was once asked how she could keep working for the poor when there were so many of them and only one of her. She said she hadn't been called to be successful; she had been called to be faithful. We aren't called to be successful either, but we are called to do our part. When we do that, we may be much more influential than we think we are.

Am I a registered voter? Do I vote regularly?

I TAKE MY RESPONSIBILITIES TO MY CITY, STATE, AND COUNTRY SERIOUSLY.

BLESSED TITUS BRANDSMA

1881–1942

Father Titus Brandsma was a journalist and author. As the spiritual adviser to the Dutch Catholic journalists, he declared that Catholic publications could not print Nazi propaganda ads and still remain Catholic. It was because of his proclamation that he was arrested and imprisoned at the infamous concentration camp at Dachau.

The nurse who killed him testified to his last days. She had been raised a Catholic but had fallen away from her faith. As he prepared for death, Father Titus gave her his rosary. She said she had forgotten the prayers, but he told her she could still say the last words, "Pray for us sinners." On July 26, 1942, the nurse injected Father Titus with poison and he died within minutes. After the war, she not only returned to the Church, but she also spoke out on behalf of Father Titus's holiness.

Sometimes the stories of the martyrs seem so ancient and remote, they almost appear to be myths. Then we read about someone like Blessed Titus Brandsma and we realize that the age of martyrs has not yet passed.

Father Titus knew when he made his declaration against the Nazis that he would be arrested. He also knew that an arrest would probably mean death. He was willing to take the risk because his conscience would not let him cooperate with evil. He could not let his silence make him a contributor to a cause he knew was wrong. Can we say the same thing?

Do I pay attention when my conscience warns me of injustice or immorality?

I LISTEN TO MY CONSCIENCE AND TAKE CARE THAT I DO NOT DULL IT BY INATTENTION OR NEGLECT.

ST. PANTALEON

A.D. 303?

St. Pantaleon was not only one of the first Christians, he was also the personal physician to Emperor Galerius. Naturally he was deeply involved in court life, to the extent that he even lost his Christian faith for a time.

When we are very involved in our activities, it's easy to put our spiritual life on hold. Maybe we don't have time to go to church this weekend, but next week we will. Or perhaps we are so busy with friends, we really can't find time for prayer and meditation, but we will soon. All too easily we become so wrapped up in so-called urgent matters that we forget what is really important.

Of all the seasons, summer tempts us the most away from God. Kids are out of school and routines are altered by vacations, three-day weekends and long, lazy afternoons. What might have seemed critical in January somehow dissipates in the July sunshine.

Fortunately, even when we take a vacation from God, God doesn't take a vacation from us. When we are ready to return, God is always ready to welcome us back. Like the Father in the story of the Prodigal Son, God watches the road every day, waiting for our appearance. When we come into sight, God is there with outstretched arms, rejoicing at our safe return.

This summer, even when our lives overflow with activity, let us not stray so far that we cannot find our way safely home.

When do I find it hardest to pray?

I KNOW GOD ALWAYS WAITS FOR MY RETURN.

ST. SAMSON

C. A.D. 565

One of life's more embarrassing moments happens when you think you're invited to something, but you aren't. Perhaps friends are getting together and you assume you've been included. When you ask what you can bring, everyone shuffles nervously until finally someone speaks up and tells you that you aren't invited. Maybe it's said tactfully and maybe it isn't, but the upshot is you're embarrassed. The others, if they have a modicum of sense, are embarrassed too.

St. Samson, bishop of Dol, ought to be patron of such embarrassing situations. After he was consecrated, he set out to Cornwall to visit a monastery. You would think that monks, who traditionally maintain high standards of hospitality, would at least let Samson rest awhile, but no, they sent out one of the members to tell the bishop it wasn't convenient for him to stay there. Most of us would probably have told the monks what they could do with their monastery, but Samson was a saint (literally!), so he merely continued on his way. Eventually he must have had a happier reception since he founded at least two churches in Cornwall.

In kindergartens and grade schools, the teachers sometimes make a rule that you can't hand out invitations in class unless you invite everyone to the party. It's a good rule, even when you're grown up. As Edwin Markham wrote, "He drew a circle that shut me out. . . . But Love and I had the wit to win: We drew a circle that took him in!"

Have I ever been deliberately excluded from something? Have I ever deliberately excluded anyone without a good reason?

I AM WILLING TO INCLUDE ALL DIFFERENT KINDS OF PEOPLE IN MY LIFE.

ST. MARTHA

FIRST CENTURY

Here is a quick quiz: Are you more inclined to remember your mistakes than your successes? When you've accomplished a major task, do you immediately go on to the next thing rather than sitting back and enjoying the fruits of your labor? Do you try to do more than can realistically be expected of any one person and then berate yourself if you can't get it all done?

If you answered yes to any of the above, you're probably a perfectionist.

Such people are wonderful at heading committees and giving parties. Everything will be done, well, perfectly. The only problem is that perfectionists often are perfectly miserable and they make everyone around them perfectly miserable as well. Nothing ever quite lives up to their standards. Because they can see the way life *could* be, they often think that's the way it *should* be.

St. Martha was a perfectionist. When Jesus came to her house, she wanted to be the perfect hostess, so while her sister was listening to Jesus teach, Martha was setting the table and fixing the dinner. Then, like most perfectionists, Martha got irritated. Here she was making everything wonderful and no one was helping her. When she complained to Jesus, he pointed out that she was so busy, she didn't have time for the important things in life. While Jesus appreciated her cooking, he would have appreciated her company more.

If you know you're a perfectionist, for one day try letting go and letting someone else help.

Do I treat life like a giant To Do list? Am I frequently disappointed when things aren't quite up to my standards?

·〰〰〰〰〰〰·

"GOOD ENOUGH" IS SOMETIMES GOOD ENOUGH.

ST. PETER CHRYSOLOGUS

C. A.D. 450

The next time you attend a lecture or sit in a meeting, see if you can judge people's B.Q.s—Boredom Quotients. Those with a short B.Q. will start fidgeting after about ten to fifteen minutes. Those with an average B.Q. will begin squirming after about a half hour, and even those with a high B.Q. will get restless after an hour of sitting still. That's why good teachers give students occasional breaks. They know if they don't, they'll lose their students' attention.

St. Peter Chrysologus took the Boredom Quotient into account when he wrote his homilies. An exceptional preacher, he often based his sermons on Biblical passages. What makes St. Peter's homilies so unique is not only their brilliance, but also their brevity. All 170 of the homilies we still have are very short. He kept them brief because he didn't want to lose the attention of his listeners.

"Brevity is the soul of wit," Shakespeare wrote. It's also the soul of good teaching. If you can't say what you need to quickly and succinctly, it's a sure sign that you haven't given the idea enough thought. Being brief doesn't mean being superficial. Often the most profound ideas can be expressed in just a few words. St. Peter Chrysologus's discourses, although very short, were erudite enough to have him declared a Doctor of the Church. In fact, his last name isn't a last name at all; it's a title meaning "golden word." When we have the opportunity to speak and teach, may our words also be golden.

What is my Boredom Quotient? Do I get impatient when people talk too much?

I DO NOT FILL MY MIND WITH EMPTY THOUGHTS OR MY MOUTH WITH EMPTY WORDS.

ST. IGNATIUS OF LOYOLA

1491–1556

St. Ignatius of Loyola originally planned to be a soldier, but when a French cannonball shattered his leg, his military career abruptly ended. Incidentally, his leg was originally so badly set that it had to be rebroken and reset—without the benefit of anesthetics. While St. Ignatius is the patron of soldiers, he would also be a good patron for returning students since he was in his mid-thirties when he went back to school and didn't graduate until he was forty-three.

Going back to school today isn't the oddity it was in Ignatius's time; people who didn't have a chance to go to college when they were young or who had to leave before they graduated are returning in droves.

Older students have many advantages over younger ones. Because they want to be in school, they tend to work harder and to apply themselves more diligently. They are serious about their studies because they are serious about themselves.

If you want to go back to school, what's stopping you? A man once said that he always wanted to be a teacher, but if he went back to school, he would be in his fifties before he graduated. How old will you be if you don't go back? he was asked.

If St. Ignatius could attend classes with students half his age, then still go on to found the Jesuits, one of the greatest religious orders in the world, there's still time for you to be whatever you want to be.

If I were in school right now, what subjects would I like to study?

·⸺⸺⸺⸺⸺⸺·

I'M NEVER TOO OLD TO LEARN.

ST. ALPHONSUS LIGUORI

1696–1787

Just as St. Francis de Sales pointed out a difference between having poison and being poisoned, so there's a difference between being a prude and exercising prudence. Being a prude won't earn you any brownie points—not even among the saints. The problem with prudes is that they often take offense at relatively insignificant things. What's more, because they are offended, they want everyone else to be offended too. Exercising prudence, on the other hand, means applying foresight and good judgment.

St. Alphonsus de Liguori, the founder of the Redemptorist Order, was prudent, but he wasn't a prude. Because he loved the music played in the theaters of his native Naples, he longed to attend the performances. Along with the music, however, the theaters often provided "licentious tableaux." Obviously this presented a problem, but St. Alphonsus was a master of prudence. He bought a ticket for the farthest back of the theater and then, when the curtain went up, he took off his glasses. Since he was well-known to be extremely near-sighted, he could appreciate the music and not give scandal to those who might see him.

We too need to be careful not to give scandal. Like St. Alphonsus, we may enjoy certain harmless activities that the prudes of life might find offensive. While we don't need to stop doing the things we enjoy so long as they are not morally damaging, we do need to remember to exercise prudence while we are doing them.

Am I careful when I'm with people who might be easily offended?
Do I maintain my own standards without imposing
them on others?

I AM CAREFUL NOT TO GIVE OFFENSE INADVERTENTLY BY
THE THINGS I SAY OR DO.

BLESSED JANE OF AZA

1140–1202

Most saints did *something* to be remembered. They founded religious orders or were noted for their extreme charity or were missionaries. Only a handful have achieved sainthood just by living ordinary, unspectacular lives. St. Thérèse of Lisieux is one. Blessed Jane of Aza is another.

We know very little about her, except that she was the wife of Felix of Calaruega and the mother of three sons. It is precisely in those unremarkable facts that her claim to sainthood lies, for all three of her sons became priests, the youngest of whom, St. Dominic, founded the Domincans.

Sometimes you hear that So-and-So is a bad influence. Blessed Jane proves there is such a thing as a good influence. It's more than likely that her sons were inspired by her faith and devotion.

The world has plenty of bad influences. What we need now are a few good influences. Blessed Jane's life shows that you don't have to do anything spectacular to be a good influence. No matter where we are or what we are doing, whether in our homes, our places of work, or even the stores we frequent, we can all be good influences. Going about our daily business might not make us official saints, but we can never know for sure! After all, as she was picking up around the castle and telling her sons to put their swords away, Blessed Jane probably never thought she would become a saint either.

Do I ever think of myself as a good influence? Who has had the greatest influence on my life?

⋅ ⟨══════════════════════⟩ ⋅

I REALIZE THAT DEVOTION TO DUTY IS AS SURE A PATH TO
HEAVEN AS ARE DEEDS OF GLORY.

LYDIA

FIRST CENTURY

Being the first to do something is one sure way to get your name in the record book. The first person to circumnavigate the globe. The first person to run a three-minute mile. The first person to reach the South Pole. Lydia holds a first, too. Her household was the first in Europe to convert to Christianity and be baptized.

Lydia was a purple merchant. That might not mean much to us today, but in the first century, it meant she was a very wealthy woman. Because purple dye was painstakingly extracted from a certain shellfish, only the elite could afford to have clothing dyed that color. A merchant who sold the extremely costly dye was wealthy by any measure.

Wealth is often cited as one of the major stumbling blocks to spiritual growth. We are warned that "It's easier for a camel to go through the eye of a needle than for a rich man to enter the Kingdom of Heaven." That doesn't mean, however, that being poor makes you an automatic shoo-in. A poor person who hoards a few possessions is no better than a wealthy person who hoards many. There's no indication that Lydia gave up her business after she converted to Christianity. But there is a good deal of evidence she used her fortune wisely. She understood that the real value of wealth lies in how you use it, not in how much you have.

Do I worry about money? Do I realize that I will always have enough—once I stop worrying?

⬩⟨⟨⟨⟨⟨⟨⟨⟨⟨⟨⟨⟨⟨⟨⟨⟨⟨⟨⟨⟨⟨⟨⟨⟨⟨⟨⟨⟨⟨⟨⟨⟨⟨⟨⟨⟨⟨⟩⬩

¶ I USE MY MONETARY RESOURCES WISELY AND GENEROUSLY.

ST. JOHN MARIE VIANNEY

1786–1859

Do you ever get the feeling you don't really belong in this world? That you really belong in a different time or place? While some religious traditions accept the idea of reincarnation, Christians and Christian saints do not. But the saints would acknowledge the feeling of estrangement is real.

"Our home is—Heaven," says St. John Marie Vianney, more commonly known as the Curé of Ars. "On earth we are like travelers staying at a hotel. When one is away, one is always thinking of home."

One indication that our real home is not this earth is the innate sense of justice and fairness all of us are born with. Even the smallest children can be heard to say, that's not fair, when someone cheats. How do we know what's fair unless we have some instinctive knowledge of a place where everything is fair, where justice reigns and where death and suffering are no more?

Each of us is born with a compass in our soul pointing not to magnetic north, but to heaven. Like a celestial homing device, it's always with us, reminding us we are indeed merely travelers on earth and that our real home, with its welcoming surroundings, awaits us at the end of our voyage.

Where do I feel the most peaceful? If I could be anywhere right now, where would I be?

I ACCEPT THE REALITY THAT ALTHOUGH I LIVE ON EARTH,
I AM REALLY A CITIZEN OF HEAVEN.

BLESSED MARY MACKILLOP

1842–1909

When Blessed Mary MacKillop founded the Sisters of St. Joseph to provide a Catholic education to children in Australia, she naturally figured her sisters would ride horseback throughout the vast country. The bishop, on the other hand, wasn't quite so keen on having young women riding alone. Sister Mary realized that new ideas require new procedures. She undoubtedly would have agreed with St. Madeleine Sophie Barat, who said, "Times change and to keep up with them, we must modify our methods."

Sometimes we cling to our old methods without really considering why we are clinging to them. A story is told of a family who always cut the end off the roast before putting it in the oven. One day, one of the daughters asked her mother why. The mother shook her head and said, because my mother always did. The daughter went to her grandmother, asked the same question and got the same reply. So the daughter visited her great-grandmother and asked why she cut the end off the roast. Because it wouldn't fit in the pan if I didn't, was the reply.

Often we are like the family who dutifully cut off the ends of the roast or the bishop who was aghast at the thought of sisters on horseback. We do things the way they have always been done without stopping to consider if the time has come for a change.

What am I unwilling to change? Would my life be easier or more productive if I let go of some of my staid ways?

I AM WILLING TO TRY NEW THINGS AND NEW APPROACHES.

ST. HORMISDAS

A.D. 523

Other than the fact that he was a widower when he was elected pope and his son, St. Silverius, also became pope, we don't know too much about St. Hormisdas. We do know that he hated quarrels, since he rebuked some African monks for their squabbling.

Some people like to stir up trouble. It's almost as if they look for ways to be disagreeable and contentious. Then, when trouble happens, they're the first to say, I told you so. Such people are harbingers of self-fulfilling prophesy.

Often we create our own self-fulfilling prophecies. When we use negatives like I can't or I never, we mentally set up situations in which we expect to fail. Then, when we do flounder, we too can complain, I told you so.

Self-fulfilling prophecies don't have to be negative. We can create our own positive prophecies. One technique to help make good things become a reality is through creative visualization. By closing your eyes and imagining the best, instead of the worst, you program your mental computer to expect the best. This kind of visualization is used by athletes before a major competition, surgeons before a tricky operation, and actors before going on stage. While it's not magic, and it can't guarantee a positive result, it does create an atmosphere in which you're more likely to look for positives than negatives. That alone is a big step in the right direction.

Do I expect the best or the worst out of life? Do I usually get what I expect?

I DO NOT LET MYSELF DWELL ON NEGATIVE POSSIBILITIES.

ST. SIXTUS II

A.D. 258

The catacombs of Rome have been the inspiration for many lurid tales. The idea of secret chambers where early Christians gathered to avoid the Romans has sparked the imagination of many a novelist. While the catacombs were used by the Christians as places of private worship, they were primarily burial chambers. The authorities always knew of their existence; in fact, while Pope Sixtus II was celebrating Mass there one day, imperial soldiers suddenly appeared and beheaded him.

About this time of year, although summer is in full bloom, when the light slants just right, an ever-so-faint tinge of yellow can be seen in the green of the trees and a whisper of winter drifts through the open window. The summer must end; it is the way of all life.

The early Christians used the catacombs for their greatest celebrations. There, amid the bodies of their dead, they rejoiced in the promise of eternal life. In one of the great paradoxes of faith, we all must die before we can have eternal life.

It's not only our bodies that must die. We must die to the attachments and strings that keep us earthbound. We must let go of our selfish desires and our concern for material possessions. We must let go of everything so our empty hands can be filled with eternity. When we learn to do that, then rejoicing in life amid the dead in the catacombs doesn't seem quite so strange.

Do I ever hold onto things so tightly that I squeeze the life out of them . . . and me?

. ⟨━━━━━━━━━━━━━━━━━━━━━━━━⟩ .

I WORK ON DETACHING MYSELF FROM MY POSSESSIONS
SINCE I REALIZE I CAN'T TAKE THEM WITH ME ANYWAY.

ST. DOMINIC

1170–1221

The first half of the thirteenth century saw the rise of one of the most popular saints of all times—a man whose free spirit has captured hearts all over the world. That man was, of course, St. Francis of Assisi. During the same time period, another man was founding another religious order whose members would have an equally profound effect throughout the world. That man was St. Dominic.

Sometimes we get the mistaken notion religion is sort of a one-size-fits-all commodity. St. Dominic and St. Francis show that even when two individuals are called to the same work, they shape it according to their unique personalities and worldviews. Francis became the beggar who beguiled the world; Dominic became the preacher who taught it.

When we see someone with a wealth of spiritual knowledge, we may feel like we either have to catch up or give up. Had St. Dominic been able to foresee the immense popularity of St. Francis, he might easily have decided to give up—fortunately, he did not.

Similiarly, we need to view those who do the same things we do not as our competitors, but as our companions. Legend has it that when Dominic met Francis he said, "If we hold together, no earthly power can withstand us." Ever since the days of their founders, the Dominicans and Franciscans have offered Mass in each other's churches as a sign of unity in a common goal.

Do I feel threatened when someone has the same idea I have? Do I automatically assume they will be more successful than I will be?

I DO MY BEST AND DON'T COMPARE MYSELF WITH OTHERS.

BLESSED TERESA BENEDICTA OF THE CROSS

1891–1942

Chances are, you've never used in real life many of the courses you took in school. You took them because you had to, but once that part of your life was done, you closed the books and never looked back.

Sister Teresa Benedicta of the Cross, a brilliant scholar who earned a doctorate in philosophy by age twenty-five, taught and lectured throughout Germany. At age forty-three, she closed the books of academia to enter a Carmelite cloister. She might have disappeared from public notice if Hitler had not begun his Jewish pogrom. Since Sr. Teresa was of Jewish descent, she was arrested and sent to various concentration camps, eventually dying on August 9, 1942, in the infamous gas chambers of Auschwitz.

Saints come in all shapes and sizes, all types of personalities, all degrees of intelligence. Some, like Blessed Teresa were college graduates; others could barely read and write. The saints remind us that each of us, no matter what our level of education, has an equal chance at holiness. God does not grade us by our test scores or our degrees. Instead, God's report card lists such subjects as Love, Patience, Charity, Fortitude. And, unlike school where we must either pass or fail, God rewards all of our efforts. Where God is concerned, we don't have to succeed; all we have to do is try.

What area of my life would I like to improve today?

I KNOW I DON'T HAVE TO EARN GOD'S LOVE. IT IS ALWAYS FREELY GIVEN TO ME.

ST. LAWRENCE

A.D. 258

When saints are designated as patrons of certain fields or work, sometimes the connection is obvious. Joseph of Arimathea, for instance, who lent Jesus his grave, is the patron of cemetery keepers. Sometimes the connection is a bit strained; for example, the Archangel Gabriel, who announced to Mary that she would be the mother of Jesus, is the patron of telecommunications. Sometimes the connection can be downright odd. St. Lawrence, for instance, is the patron of Rome, the poor, and cooks.

Rome is a fairly logical subject for St. Lawrence. A deacon under Pope Sixtus II, he lived in Rome. His association with the poor is also logical. Legend has it that when the prefect of Rome demanded that Lawrence surrender the Church's wealth, Lawrence collected the blind, the lame, the widowed, the orphaned, and the leprous and presented them, saying, "These are the treasure of the Church."

But cooks? The only possible reason to connect St. Lawrence with cooks borders on the bizarre: he was martyred for his faith by being roasted over hot coals.

While it seems more than a bit distasteful to think of praying to St. Lawrence while fixing dinner, the church has long held him in highest regard. His day is designated a feast. In the calendar of the saints, a solemnity is the highest honor. Only Joseph, Peter, Paul, John the Baptist, and Mary, the Mother of Jesus, are accorded that respect. The next highest is feast, and St. Lawrence shares that category with the apostles and Stephen, and only a handful of others.

What would I present as my greatest treasure?

I WILL LEARN MORE ABOUT THE LIFE OF THE SAINT WHO IS THE PATRON OF MY VOCATION OR AVOCATION.

ST. CLARE

1193–1253

Often we want a quick fix to problems without realizing that much of our spiritual growth comes not from finding quick and easy answers to life's difficulties, but from making a commitment and seeing it through to its natural conclusion.

When St. Clare was eighteen, she heard St. Francis of Assisi preach and made a commitment to lead the same kind of poverty-based life he did. One night, in secret, she met Francis and his monks at his chapel, where he cut off her hair and gave her a rough woolen habit. When her family learned what she had done, they tried to remove her forcibly from the convent where Francis had placed her. But Clare's determination to go through with her decision was firm. She refused to leave. Eventually her family relented, and her mother and sister joined her.

When we make a commitment to a cause, an ideal, or a person, let us strive to have as much determination and perseverance as did St. Clare. Let us make sure we do all we can to make it work before we look for a way out. Let us work at honoring the obligations we have, even when we no longer find them pleasurable. Most of all, let us ask for the wisdom to make the right commitments in the first place.

Do I keep the promises I make to myself and to others? If I have broken a promise, can I make amends?

WHEN I GIVE MY WORD, I WILL DO WHAT I SAY I WILL DO.

VENERABLE MOTHER MARIA MAGDALENA BENTIVOGLIO

1834–1905

If you want to be a saint, you have to love all the trials and crosses life presents you. But you don't have to like them.

In 1875, Venerable Mother Maria Magdalena Bentivoglio came to the United States to found the first Poor Clares in the United States. Although she was an exemplary nun, Mother Maria confessed that she sometimes wanted to toss out her prayer book and that she hated the plain convent food. Nonetheless, she accepted the difficulties of each day. When asked how she had so much patience while undergoing a particularly stressful ordeal, she replied, "All my life I have asked God for crosses and now that He has sent them, why should I not be glad?"

Mother Maria obviously had the patience of a saint, but what's more, she tried the patience of a saint! St. Madeleine Sophie Barat was a friend of Maria's family and, as a young girl, Mother Maria traveled with her. During one trip she teased and tormented St. Madeleine unmercifully. One night they had to share a single bed and Mother Maria said, "And so I slept with a saint, and I kicked the saint."

Sometimes we think we should have more patience, but we may not realize that when we ask for patience, we will be given opportunities to *try* our patience. Rather than asking for new trials and difficulties, let us, like Mother Maria, love the ones that come our way, even if we don't like them.

Am I patient or impatient? How is my sense of humor when my patience is sorely tested?

I ACCEPT THE DIFFICULTIES I MUST FACE AS PART OF MY NECESSARY GROWTH.

ST. BENILDUS

1805–1862

Do you sometimes feel you just can't stand another minute of the same old thing?

If so, St. Benildus knows exactly how you feel. A member of the Christian Brothers, St. Benildus taught school and lived the ordinary life of a religious brother for forty years. At times he became so frustrated by his students he said, "I imagine the angels themselves, if they came down as schoolmasters, would find it hard to control their anger." But control his he did, in addition to developing what were for his time revolutionary teaching techniques that included positive reinforcement instead of punishment to motivate students.

Throughout his long career, St. Benildus did nothing spectacular, but he did everything for the love of God. Because of St. Benildus's dedication to duty, Pope Pius XI called him the Saint of the Daily Grind.

Sometimes daily life is so . . . daily. We do the same things over and over until we think we could scream. Nothing different ever seems to happen. We begin to think about getting out, running away, doing something exciting.

St. Benildus shows us it isn't the monumental highlights that make a saint. It's daily life. The sacrifices we make for our loved ones, the discipline we exercise in doing our jobs, even when we don't feel like it—these are the actions that transform our souls. These are the actions that can change ordinary life from a daily grind into a heavenly experience.

At the end of each day, can I say that I have truly done my best and tried my hardest?

·⟨▰▰▰▰▰▰▰▰▰▰▰▰▰▰▰⟩·

I LOOK FOR WAYS TO TRANSFORM EVERY DAY INTO A
POSITIVE EXPERIENCE.

ST. MAXIMILIAN MARY KOLBE

1894–1941

Hemingway defined courage as "grace under pressure." But courage is more than that. Courage is the ability to rise above pain and fear. Courage is the ability to tap into divine wellsprings in situations where our human nature trembles.

As the Nazi commandant at Auschwitz arbitrarily selected ten prisoners to die because another prisoner had escaped, one of the victims began to wail and beseech for mercy.

"I would like to take that man's place," said Number 16670. The commandant agreed and Fr. Maximilian Kolbe stepped into the line-up. In the "block of death," the prisoners were so desperate for food and water, they drank their own urine. When the guards finally came to remove the bodies, Fr. Kolbe was still alive, still praising God. In an act of severe mercy, the guards hastened his death with an injection of carbolic acid.

Fr. Kolbe was undoubtedly fearful when he offered his life for another, but his courage and faith triumphed over his fear.

Who of us does not know what it is like to be afraid? Who of us does not doubt our capacity for bravery? Only when we allow the wellsprings of God's own courage to fill our hearts can we face our greatest fears. Only in overcoming what we fear the most can we begin to live.

What am I afraid of? How can I go beyond my fears to tap into God's divine courage?

I KNOW THAT WITH GOD'S HELP I WILL FIND NEW SOURCES OF COURAGE IN MY LIFE.

BLESSED MARIA OF JESUS CRUCIFIED

1846–1878

If you could be a vegetable, what would you be? Blessed Maria of Jesus Crucified wanted to be an onion or a potato "because they grow unnoticed and do good things."

Maria Baouardy was born in Galilee in the mid-1800s. The only one of thirteen children to survive childhood, she moved to Egypt with her aunt when both her parents died. She entered religious life at age nineteen. Although her path was filled with a number of false starts, she ended up becoming a Carmelite nun and founding a Carmel in Bethlehem.

Among other things, Blessed Maria was gifted with the ability to "envision." She was able to envision building not only a monastery in Bethlehem, but also a second monastery on the forgotten site of Emmaus mentioned in the Gospels. Although she strove to be as unnoticed as an onion or a potato, her ability to direct building projects as well as her deep spirituality made her loved by her fellow nuns.

"Envision-ation," a cross between imagination—the ability to form a picture in your mind—and envisioning—the capability to see what does not yet exist—is truly a gift from God. Children are graced with this ability almost without effort, but as adults we sometimes let it wither from lack of use and the weight of practical matters.

When you feel the whisper of envision-ation telling you that things could be different and you could make a difference, don't just push it aside. It may be one of the saints trying to wake up the child still living inside each one of us.

What am I envisioning right now?

I KNOW I CAN MAKE A DIFFERENCE.

ST. STEPHEN OF HUNGARY

975–1038

As we approach the year 2000, speculation about the fate of the planet is bound to increase. Despite the fact that time and dates are purely human inventions (no one woke up one morning saying, "Why, it must be the year 0!"), we attribute an almost mystical quality to the calendar turning from 1999 to 2000. Some people see it as the frontier of the future, while others assume Christ will return and the world will end on that date.

Millenarianism, with its fears about Armageddon and the end times, has happened before—when calendars flipped from the 999s to the 1000s. In those days, as now, people looked for signs from heaven. For the people of Hungary, the crowning of St. Stephen on Christmas Day 1001 as the first king of Hungary must have heralded great promises. A man with a deep love for the Church and a commitment to serving the poor, Stephen is the patron of his native Hungary. Unfortunately, when his son was killed in a hunting accident, the succession to the throne was blurred, and violent family disputes arose.

When everyone around us is being swept up in speculation over the future, we can sometimes forget that no one, not even the saints and angels, know when the world will end. It could end tomorrow. Or in the year 2000. Or not for another 10,000 years. Because we can't know when it will happen, we must live each day as if it were our last, for only when we appreciate the fragility of life can we rejoice in its glory.

Do I let people with predictions of doom upset my peace of mind?

I WILL TAKE CARE OF TODAY AND LET THE FUTURE TAKE CARE OF ITSELF.

ST. ROCH

A.D. 1378

St. Roch is one of those saints whose lives are so shrouded in legend it's impossible to sort fact from fiction. All we know for sure is that he nursed the sick during an outbreak of the plague. One story says he also miraculously cured cows; hence he is recognized as the patron of cattle.

Cattle are about the only animals to have their own patron saint, although animals in general are under the patronage of St. Anthony the Abbot (not St. Francis of Assisi as is commonly thought). Maybe cattle are singled out for patronage because they are specifically mentioned in Genesis: "God made all kinds of wild animals, all kinds of cattle, and all kinds of creeping things of the earth." (Genesis 1:25)

For too long in our history, we've viewed animals as resources. In recent years, however, we have come to realize that we and the animals are co-inhabitants of the same fragile space. When we disturb their balance, we also disturb our own.

The spotted owl of the Pacific Northwest has been accused of being the destroyer of the logging industry and heralded as the savior of the wilderness. In truth, it is neither. The spotted owl and all other creatures are merely part of the ongoing, larger ecosystem begun when the world was created. What is important for us to remember is not only are we are part of that system, but when it was created, "God saw how good it was." (Genesis 1: 25) It's up to us to help make sure it stays that way.

Am I doing my part to help keep the world safe for all life?

·⟨▬▬▬▬▬▬▬▬▬▬▬▬▬▬▬▬▬▬▬⟩·

I THANK GOD FOR THE GOODNESS OF ALL CREATION,
ESPECIALLY THE ANIMALS.

ST. HELEN

A.D. 303

St. Helen's spiritual fame rests on the fact that she is believed to have discovered the cross of Jesus, but she could be the patroness of first wives who were divorced by their husbands to marry more attractive women.

The daughter of an inn-keeper, Helen married the Roman general Constantius Chlorus. After she bore him a son who would become Constantine the Great, he divorced her and married Theodora, stepdaughter of Emperor Maximian.

Although some bad things seem to happen just because evil exists in the world, many more unfair and unfortunate things happen because someone somewhere didn't pay attention to the prickings of conscience. Constantius Chlorus had to have known that it wasn't right to abandon Helen, even if he did have the chance to marry Maximian's stepdaughter. Likewise, many of the bad things that happen to us are the result of someone who either ignores the impulse to do good or gives in to the temptation to do bad. For instance, you come out of a store and find the right side of your car smashed in. The person who hit you had a choice: leave a note with his or her name and insurance company or hightail it out of there before being caught, in which case you'll be stuck with a large repair bill.

We have the responsibility to pay attention when our consciences nag us. When we know what we should do but fail to do it, we may be creating unnecessary hardship in someone else's life.

Is there someone I should forgive for having treated me unfairly?

·⟨⟨▰▰▰▰▰▰▰▰▰▰▰▰▰▰▰▰▰▰▰▰▰▰▰⟩⟩·

I PAY ATTENTION TO THINGS I DO . . . AND THE THINGS
I DON'T DO.

ST. JOHN EUDES

1601–1680

St. John Eudes was the eldest child of a French farming couple. Although they wanted him to marry, St. John joined the Oratorians and was ordained at age twenty-four. For the next several years, he worked as a parish missionary. Then, because he felt drawn to found seminaries, he left his community and founded a new one called the Eudists (Congregation of Jesus and Mary). He failed to obtain papal approval, however, because of his lack of prudence and tact.

Some people make extra work for themselves. If there's an easy, expeditious way of doing things or a more difficult, stressful way, they seem to tend toward the rockier road.

St. John Eudes appears to be one of those people. Yet, despite his lack of planning and tact, St. John Eudes brought the love of God (as well as material help, such as housing) to the lowest echelons of society—the prostitutes, the plague victims, the unwanted. When his plan for the Eudists didn't work out as he hoped, he founded another community—the Sisters of Charity of the Refuge, specifically to help prostitutes who wanted to change their lives.

St. John may have made more work for himself at times, but his heart was always in the right place. Sometimes we make more work for ourselves through lack of planning, improper preparation, and inadequate resources. When we catch ourselves in those situations, we need to stop, reevaluate, and see if perhaps one of the reasons we aren't making any progress is because we are heading in the wrong direction.

Do I ever make things more difficult than they have to be?

I HAVE ENOUGH TO DO WITHOUT MAKING MORE WORK FOR MYSELF.

ST. BERNARD OF CLAIRVAUX

1090–1153

When St. Bernard of Clairvaux joined the monastery founded by St. Stephen Harding, strict silence was the rule. Yet, despite being cloistered, Bernard was constantly consulted, both in person and by mail. In frustration, he said, "And where, I ask you, is the leisure, where the quiet of silence when one is thinking, composing and writing? . . . How can the mind be quiet when composing a letter and a turmoil of expressions are clamoring and every sort of phrase and diversity of senses are jostling one another? . . . Do you tell me there is any quiet in all this? Can you call this silence, even if the lips are not moving?"

Often when we try to write something important, we experience the same clamoring and jostling that St. Bernard speaks about. We recall our good suit is missing a button and the cat needs more food and we haven't watered the flowerbeds. The more we try to push the thoughts aside, the more insistent they become. Such distractions occur not only when we try to write, but whenever we have to exercise mental discipline. When reading a challenging book or learning a new skill we are often lured astray by our own mental maneuvering. When that happens, our best recourse is to let the unwanted thoughts flow through our mind but not disturb our peace of mind. But as St. Bernard pointed out more than eight hundred years ago, that's much easier said than done.

Am I easily distracted? How do I react to mental interruptions?

﹒⟨═════════════════⟩﹒

I ASK THE SAINTS FOR HELP IN LEARNING HOW TO FOCUS
AND CONCENTRATE.

ST. PIUS X

1835–1914

What do you think of when you hear the word *routine?* Dull, boring, and repetitious? That's certainly one meaning, but routine can also mean prepared and disciplined, such as a finely choreographed dance routine. It can also mean regular, like the routine involved in getting ready for bed. And sometimes it can mean all three!

St. Pius X, who is best remembered for encouraging frequent Holy Communion and for lowering the age of First Communion to about seven years old, also encouraged routine reading of the Scriptures. In fact, he urged daily reading of the Bible as part of his motto, "Renew all things in Christ." To promote more regular reading of Scripture, he set up a commission to revise and correct the official text of the Bible used by the Church in addition to establishing the Biblical Institute for scriptural studies.

Getting in the habit of reading uplifting spiritual works such as the Bible requires preparation, discipline, and regularity. First we have to prepare our minds and our hearts. Second, we have to be disciplined. It's all too easy to put off exercise in all forms, and spiritual reading is definitely mental exercise. Finally, we must be regular. If we try a hit-and-miss approach, our learning will also be hit and miss. In short, we have to establish a *routine* if we want to make any concrete spiritual progress.

Do I have any kind of a routine for regular spiritual reading? What spiritually uplifting books would I like to read over the next year?

I MAKE TIME EACH DAY TO READ SOMETHING THAT STRENGTHENS MY FAITH AND RENEWS MY SPIRIT.

BLESSED ISIDORE BAKANJA

1885–1909

If Blessed Isidore Bakanja had cursed the man who had him beaten to death with an elephant hide strip studded with nails, it would have been understandable. Instead, even as he lay dying of the massive infection resulting from his untreated wounds, he said, "Certainly I shall pray for him. When I am in heaven, I shall pray for him very much."

Blessed Isidore was a member of the Boangi tribe in what was then the Belgian Congo. A convert to Christianity, he was whipped for refusing to remove his scapular. Although the beating took place in February, he lingered for nearly six months, suffering intense pain from the open, festering wounds covering his back. When medical treatment was finally sought, it was too little too late.

When someone hurts us, we want revenge, not a chance to practice forgiveness. Yet, to put a new twist on an old saying, time wounds all heels. Everyone gets their comeuppance sooner or later. If it doesn't happen in this lifetime, it will in the next. That's one of the immutable laws of the universe. No good deed goes unrewarded and no evil deed goes unpunished. When we understand that we don't have to be judge, jury, and executioner for all who hurt us, we are free to leave vengeance to the Lord. It might not come in the way we would like and it probably won't come in the time frame we would choose, but it *will* come.

> *Have I ever plotted revenge on someone? Was the outcome as sweet as I had hoped or was it a disappointment?*

I DO NOT WASTE MY TIME OR ENERGY TRYING TO HURT THOSE WHO HURT ME.

ST. ROSE OF LIMA

1586–1617

The first canonized saint of the Americas, St. Rose of Lima wanted to enter a convent, but her parents wanted her to marry. After years of struggle, a compromise was reached when Rose joined the Third Order of St. Dominic and wore the white habit and black veil of a nun, but lived at home.

Making peace with our parents is one of the fundamental tasks of growing up. Few of us reach adulthood without experiencing some conflict with our parents. Learning to separate and establish our own identity and self-worth is our part of the equation. Learning to let go and allow children to become their own persons is our parents' part.

As Hodding Carter says, "There are only two lasting bequests we can hope to give our children. One of these is roots; the other, wings." Both roots and wings are essential if we are to become whole, healthy, integrated human beings who relate to our parents as adults. Even if our parents aren't alive, we can still make peace with them by forgiving them for the hurts, real and imagined, they caused us and by asking them to forgive us for the hurts, real and imagined, we caused them.

St. Rose's parents didn't always understand why their beautiful daughter rejected all suggestion of marriage. St. Rose didn't understand why her parents couldn't accept her total dedication to God. But to both their credit, they finally let Rose keep her roots in the backyard while her wings carried her to heaven.

Have I made peace with my parents? Are there still unresolved areas of conflict I could work on?

⟨⟨⟨⟨⟨⟨⟩⟩⟩⟩⟩⟩

I REALIZE MY PARENTS WEREN'T PERFECT, BUT THEN I
REALIZE I'M NOT PERFECT EITHER.

ST. JOAN ANTIDA THOURET

1765–1826

It's saintly to be modest about your accomplishments, but too much modesty can be as great a failing as too little. When St. Joan Antida Thouret was asked by the novice mistress at the convent she was joining what she could do, St. Joan said, "Nothing." The novice mistress replied, "You are always saying that you can do nothing; you must say that you can do everything, for you do well everything which is given to you."

Because she was a saint, Joan Antida Thouret probably was being honest when she claimed no special skills, but sometimes when we fail to give ourselves credit, it isn't because we think we deserve no praise; it's because we're secretly fishing for compliments. While there's nothing wrong with wanting to hear that we've done a good job, angling so we can appear humble while still being praised is deceptive. It's far better to honestly accept the original praise with a simple and sincere thank you than to practice false modesty under the guise of self-deprecation.

Although we need to give ourselves credit for our abilities, we also need to recognize our failings. When we take a negative view of our skills and abilities, we destroy our sense of self-esteem. We can also be guilty of overestimation. If we are constantly bragging, we are in danger of becoming self-centered and selfish. The saints remind us to do our jobs to the best of our abilities and to let the compliments and the criticism fall as they may.

Which is easier for me to accept—compliments or criticism?

I ACKNOWLEDGE MY ABILITIES, BUT I NEITHER BRAG ABOUT NOR BELITTLE THEM.

ST. LOUIS

1214–1270

If you had to choose one word to describe King Louis IX of France it might be "just." During his reign he forbade usury, began a system of trial with witnesses instead of battles to determine the verdict, and instituted written court records. Once when three children were hanged by a count for hunting rabbits on his land, King Louis ordered ordinary judges to try him, not his fellow nobility. The judges condemned the count to death. King Louis, who was as compassionate as he was just, commuted the sentence to an enormous fine, which caused the count to lose most of his landholdings. The king then gave the wealth to charity.

Although justice and judging both can be traced back to the Latin word for law, they have quite different meanings. Justice is derived from the Latin *justitia* meaning upright, while judging comes from the Latin words *jus* (law) and *dicere* (to say). When you are judging, you are literally "saying the law." There is no room for mercy or mitigating circumstances. When you exercise justice, you make correct decisions, based not on the letter of the law but on its spirit.

King Louis was known for his justice, not his judgment. Even when judgment could demand the harshest retaliation, such as the death of the count, justice may allow for mercy. Like King Louis, we need to learn when judgment is called for . . . and when justice should prevail.

What one word would I use to describe myself? What word would others choose?

I KNOW I CAN ALWAYS TRUST IN DIVINE JUSTICE TEMPERED WITH MERCY.

ST. ELIZABETH BICHIER DES AGES

1773–1838

Building sandcastles is sometimes used as a metaphor for wasting time. After all, no matter how much energy and care you put into the construction, it will all be swept away on the next tide. Other than amusing children, sandcastles don't serve any useful purpose, or do they?

Believe it or not, building sandcastles may be one of the most important things any one of us can do in life. Sandcastles can't be marketed or sold. They can't be saved. All you can do with a sandcastle is savor the moment. Isn't that what we are all called to do: savor the moment? This moment, this slice of reality is all we have. We can remember the past fondly and anticpate the future eagerly, but the only time we can enjoy is the here and now.

What's more, sandcastles are built out of the substances we have at hand. We don't plan a sandcastle. We let it evolve, by adding a little more sand here, a gull feather there, a shell on the top. Similiarly, the best parts of our lives are often those we don't try to control, but merely allow to unfold as they ought. Finally, sandcastles are just plain fun, and we all could use a little more fun in our lives.

So what does all this have to do with St. Elizabeth Bichier des Ages, the foundress of the Sisters of St. Andrew? It's simple: her favorite game as a child was building sandcastles.

Do I feel like I always need to be productive?

·⟨░░░░░░░░░░░░░░░░░░░░░░░░░░░░░░░⟩·

I DON'T ALWAYS HAVE TO HAVE A REASON FOR WHAT I'M
DOING. SOMETIMES I CAN JUST HAVE FUN.

ST. MONICA

332–387

> He drew a circle that shut me out
> Heretic, rebel, a thing to flout
> But Love and I had the wit to win
> We drew a circle that took him in.

Edwin Markham's poem "Outwitted" could easily describe the relationship between St. Monica and her son St. Augustine. Although Augustine was raised a Christian, he was never baptized. As a young man, he lived with his mistress, who bore him a son, but much to his mother's dismay he had no interest in marriage.

Over the years, she prayed, fasted, cajoled, pleaded, and begged her son to change his ways. She was so insistent that her spiritual director finally told her, "Surely the son of so many tears will not perish."

As one might expect, Augustine didn't take kindly to his mother's nagging. Once when he was sailing for Rome from his home in North Africa, he lied about the time of departure and left without his mother's knowing. He underestimated Monica, however. She caught another ship and followed him. In fact, she dogged Augustine until he finally was converted. No matter how many circles he drew to shut her out, she was just as quick to draw another wider circle of love that took him back in.

Are my circles inclusive or exclusive? Is there someone I should be
including, but because he or she has excluded me,
I'm shutting them out?

ıT'S TRUE! LOVE AND ı DO HAVE THE WIT TO WIN.

ST. AUGUSTINE

354-430

Have you ever had a dream in which you solved all your problems? In your dream you kept saying to yourself, now I understand! Now it all makes sense. You may have even rousted yourself enough to scribble a few notes in the dark to be sure to remember all the details. Then, when you wake up in the morning, it's all gone. Your notes are gibberish, the babbling of a dream-drunk soul. All you have left is the haunting feeling you once knew the secrets of life.

St. Augustine, arguably one of the greatest influences on early Church teaching, had something similar to say about fathoming the mysteries of God. "If you have understood," he wrote, "then what you have understood is not God."

We can know God, we can love God, but we can never fully understand God. In the Book of Job, Job longed to comprehend God's actions. Finally, out of the whirlwind came the answer. Only it wasn't an answer at all: "Where were you when I laid the foundation of the earth? . . . Who set its measurements, since you know? . . . Or who laid its cornerstone when the morning stars sang together. . . ?" (Job 38: 4–7) Although God's response to Job was nothing more than questions, Job finally understood. God cannot be reduced to a series of pat responses. We want answers, but God wants to talk about the Pleiades and the wild horses and storehouses of the hail. We want a road map, but God hands us a musical score instead.

Do I get frustrated when I can't make sense of life?

I AM WILLING TO ACCEPT THE FACT THAT NOT ALL MY
QUESTIONS WILL BE ANSWERED.

MOTHER TERESA OF CALCUTTA

B. AUGUST 27, 1910

When Agnes Gonxha Bejaxhiu entered the order of the Sisters of Our Lady of Loreto, she thought she was going to be a teacher. She was, for eighteen years, until she received "a call within a call" to leave the safety of her convent and to work with the poor and dying in the slums of Calcutta. Little did the former teacher know she was just beginning her life work. A work that would introduce her to the world as Mother Teresa.

When the insight came to change her life, Mother Teresa had the courage and wisdom to obey, even though it meant turning her comfortable and settled world upside down. While few of us will receive as dramatic a call for change as Mother Teresa did, we are all sent divine messages every day. These messages ask us to shake up our settled routines and look for new ways to bring love and caring into the lives of the people around us.

Sometimes the call comes as a clarion herald, other times it is a whisper on the wind. But when we are truly listening, we will always hear and recognize God's voice urging us to make life-nourishing changes.

What response do I make when I get a divine nudge? How do I react when God asks me to expand the boundaries of my comfort zone?

TODAY I WILL LISTEN FOR GOD'S CALL, KNOWING THAT GOD WILL NEVER ASK FOR MORE THAN I AM CAPABLE OF GIVING.

ST. PAMMACHIUS

A.D. 410

St. Pammachius and St. Jerome were, if not exactly friends, at least good acquaintances since Pammachius was married to the daughter of one of Jerome's closest friends. The differences between the two were striking. St. Pammachius was a Roman senator and presumably a happily married man. St. Jerome was an ascetic celibate. St. Pammachius built a hospice where he personally tended the pilgrims who came to Rome. St. Jerome was a hermit who lived in a cave. St. Pammachius was forthright. St. Jerome was bad-tempered and overbearing.

The two men couldn't have been more different, yet they both became saints. Of all the lessons the saints offer, one of the greatest is their variety. The more we know about them, the more we realize that variety is the soul of sanctity.

We all need a little variety in life. Tomorrow instead of doing the same old thing, shake up the ordinary. Have a cup of tea instead of coffee. Take a different route to work. Tune to a rock station if you normally listen to country.

Once you get out of your usual patterns and habits, you'll discover a whole world you never even knew existed. People you never would have seen if you didn't travel a different route. Songs you never would have heard if you hadn't switched stations. Tastes, smells, and sights you've never experienced. So today, "saint" up your life with a little variety.

If I could have an adventure today, what would I do? Where would I go? Who would I share it with?

I WILL NOT ALLOW MYSELF TO BECOME SO COMFORTABLE THAT I BECOME COMPLACENT.

ST. AIDAN

A.D. 651

What do you do when you receive a gift you don't like? If you're like most of us, you tuck it in a drawer until a respectable length of time has gone by and then you give it to charity.

St. Aidan did the same thing, only he immediately gave away the gifts the king and his friends bestowed on him. A native of Ireland, Aidan was more interested in helping the poor than in flattering nobles.

The gifts we receive in life—both material and spiritual—are like a stream flowing through our lives. We are given good things for our use, but like a free-flowing stream, we must let them pass through our lives when we are finished with them.

All too often, however, we try to dam up the stream. We want to keep the good things in our own private pond. The problem with turning streams into ponds is that they drown all the life around them. At first the banks just climb a little higher, but eventually they start to lap at the roots of the trees and creep over the tops of the bushes. Soon, what was a little stream is a swollen lake submerging everything for miles around. What's more, the little stream has disappeared. It no longer flows out and even the inlet becomes hidden under the ever-climbing water. Not until we break open the dams of selfishness and greed can the water start flowing again—back into our lives and the lives of others.

Am I willing to freely share the gifts I have been freely given?

TODAY I WILL GIVE AWAY SOMETHING I ONCE TREASURED
BUT NO LONGER USE.

BLESSED BEATRICE DA SILVA

1424–1490

Have you ever been caught in a situation beyond your control? Blessed Beatrice da Silva was. A vivacious girl in the court of Princess Isabel of Portugal, she was once thrown in prison for three days because of a false rumor.

Sometimes we find ourselves thrown in figurative prisons because of situations we think are beyond our control—a bad marriage, addiction, a dead-end job. When we look around, we see only bars and barricades. We feel trapped in our prisons, chained by hopelessness and anger. One natural reaction is to become dejected and depressed. Another is to take stock of the situation and decide to grasp the first opportunity to make some changes. That's what Blessed Beatrice did. Once she got out of prison, she left the court and ultimately founded the Congregation of the Immaculate Conception of the Blessed Virgin Mary.

It isn't easy to make radical changes, especially when they involve other people. But sometimes the only way out is through. Blessed Beatrice had been raised in the court. It couldn't have been easy to leave her friends and family behind, but she realized that as difficult as leaving might be, staying would be even more difficult.

Each of us faces situations where every option is painful. In times like those we have only one viable recourse: to ask for the wisdom to make the right choice and then do the best with the information we have.

Do I feel trapped right now? What have I done to make the changes I need to make?

I REFUSE TO ACCEPT THE LIMITATIONS OTHERS PLACE ON ME.

BLESSED ANDREW GRASSET DE ST. SAUVEUR

1758–1792

Most of the time when we think of missionaries or martyrs, we think of someone going from an older established country to a younger, less developed one. Blessed Andrew Grasset de St. Sauveur was born in Montreal, Canada, but he died a martyr's death in Paris during the French Revolution. His father had served as secretary to the governor of New France, but the family had returned to France where Blessed Andrew was ordained to the priesthood. The unrest in France increased until on September 2, 1792, a mob invaded a Carmelite monastery that had been turned into a prison where Blessed Andrew, 187 other priests, and 3 bishops were being held. When the prisoners refused to swear allegiance to a schismatic church that did not recognize the Pope, all were killed.

Blessed Andrew couldn't have suspected when he left Montreal as a child that he would one day become embroiled in a political upheaval forcing him to choose between the government and his faith. And yet, that's what happened. When we embark on a new direction we often don't suspect what choices we will have to face. All we can do is trust that if we have made our earlier decision in good faith and good conscience, then no matter what happens, all is unfolding as it should.

Have I ever had to choose between my political and my spiritual allegiance? When I have to make a choice between being politically correct and spiritually correct, what do I do?

·⟨⟩·

I CHOOSE THE RIGHT PATH, NOT THE PATH OF LEAST RESISTANCE.

ST. GREGORY THE GREAT

540?–604

St. Gregory the Great was a keen observer of human nature. Who doesn't recognize the truth in the saying, "Those who stumble on plain ground should shrink from approaching a precipice"? Or the clarity of reminding people that it is easier to give up possessions than to change your heart, for "to renounce what one has is a minor thing, but to renounce what one is, that is asking a lot."

Recently, Gregory's name has become popularly known again with the release of a best-selling recording of Spanish monks singing Gregorian chant. Ironically although we know that St. Gregory reformed the liturgy of the Church during his reign as pope, we aren't sure how much of the reformation of the music bearing his name he is actually responsible for.

Nevertheless, Gregorian chant has made something of a comeback after being relegated to obscure monasteries for several hundred years. The renewed appeal of this centuries-old music has baffled industry experts. (But it hasn't prevented them from making a profit off of it!) What is it about chant that can attract even a modern audience raised on rock and roll?

The answer may lie in the chant itself. Gregorian chant is a form of sacred singing that can be traced back to ancient Jewish synagogue music. When correctly performed, it is sung without accompaniment. Gregorian chant isn't the only kind of chant (Ambrosian is another, for instance), but it is the best known. Once you've heard chant, you'll never forget it. And you'll either love it or hate it.

Do I ever reject something just because it's old?

I'M WILLING TO LOOK TO THE PAST FOR NEW IDEAS.

ST. ROSE OF VITERBO

1235–1252

St. Rose of Viterbo must never have heard the saying, children should be seen but not heard. At age twelve, she began publicly speaking out against the excommunicated Emperor Frederick, who had taken over her hometown of Viterbo. She was so insistent in her haranguing that she managed to get her whole family banished. When Frederick finally died, they returned and Rose tried to enter the convent of St. Mary of the Roses but was turned down. She continued to live at home until her death at about age seventeen.

If you have ever been around children for any length of time, you know kids say exactly what's on their minds. Although we, as adults, know sometimes a little tact is necessary, saying what we mean and meaning what we say is a good rule to adopt. When we are forthright in our speech, we are less likely to be misinterpreted. Of course, we never have license to be rude, but we can be honest. When we are asked for our opinion, we can give it. When we see a wrong, we can point it out. Conversely, when we encounter something positive, we have an equal obligation to extend our praise and gratitude.

St. Rose was outraged when Frederick II tried to conquer the papal states. Although she had a right (and perhaps even an obligation) to speak up, she was unwise to endanger her family. Her example is both an encouragement to point out injustices when we see them and a warning to be careful how we do so.

Am I as honest in my speech as I am in my actions?

I SAY WHAT I MEAN AND I MEAN WHAT I SAY.

ST. LAURENCE GIUSTINIANI

1381–1455

Lately, instead of giving actual gifts, many people are sending checks. The reasons cited are that it's easier and that the recipient can pick out the exact gift he or she wants. While it is easier and you *can* pick out exactly what you want, something vital is lost when gift giving is reduced to a monetary exchange.

No matter what anyone says, seeing a check with your name on it isn't the same as opening a gift chosen with you in mind. Even if the gift isn't something you particularly like, the fact that someone took the time and energy to select it for you imbues it with meaning. Even if you cash the check and buy something you want, it becomes a gift you give yourself, not a gift that was given to you. And, of course, money has a way of getting eaten up by the necessities of life. If you're short on funds, a gift check is more likely to go for the rent than it is for a bouquet of flowers, no matter what the giver might have intended.

St. Laurence Giustiniani understood the significance of giving actual goods, not just money. He willingly gave food and clothing to all who asked but was reluctant to hand out money because he knew cash has a way of evaporating into the wrong things.

Giving real presents may be more work, but it's also more in the spirit of real gift giving.

How do I feel when I get a gift I know was chosen just for me?

I GIVE GIFTS OUT OF LOVE, NOT OUT OF OBLIGATION.

BLESSED BARTOLO LONGO

1841–1926

The story of the Ugly Duckling has almost universal appeal. We know what it's like to feel unattractive and out of place. Most of us secretly harbor the idea maybe we will turn out to be a swan after all.

Blessed Bartolo Longo wanted to establish devotion to the rosary in the valley where the ancient city of Pompeii had existed. All of his attempts to interest the inhabitants failed. He then had the idea of bringing a picture of Our Lady of the Rosary to the area, but the only image he could find was a mess. It didn't help much that the only way he could get it shipped was on a wagon of manure.

Blessed Bartolo's friend (and later his wife) Countess Marianna de Fusco thought the picture was so ugly that she said, "It must have been painted purposely to destroy devotion to Our Lady." Yet, after it had been restored, it became the focus of numerous pilgrimages and the center of a major shrine to Our Lady of the Rosary.

What in your life feels wrinkled and shabby? What is making you feel unattractive and unwanted? Blessed Bartolo (and the Ugly Duckling) looked beyond the outside to the potential of the inside. No matter how you are feeling right now, you have enormous potential. Blessed Bartolo's example teaches us that with faith, optimism—and a little hard work—all things can be made like new.

Is it difficult for me to see my own self-worth? Am I insecure when it comes to evaluating my own potential?

STARTING TODAY, I WILL LOOK AT THOSE THINGS THAT MAKE ME FEEL LIKE AN UGLY DUCKLING AND BEGIN TO CHANGE THEM.

ST. CLOUD

524?–560

St. Cloud or Clodoald was a descendant of King Clovis. Raised by his grandmother Clotilda, he saw both his brothers murdered in a plot to take over the kingdom. He alone escaped, becoming a hermit and spending the rest of his life in seclusion.

In a nutshell, that's the life story of St. Cloud. But there must be more to it. There always is. In obituaries, people's lives are reduced to a list of facts. A whole lifetime reduced to a paragraph. What's missing in obituaries—and in the few facts we know about St. Cloud—is personality, those distinctive qualities that make us who we are.

Virtually every living creature has its own personality. Certainly we can see it in our pets, but people who spend time with wild animals, including turtles, fish, and reptiles, report they too exhibit their own unique qualities. It's as if personality is hardwired into every creature ever created—including humans.

While we don't have total control over the facets of our personalities, we do have control over some of the traits we exhibit. For instance, if we are solemn by nature, we don't have to act moody and brood all the time. We can cultivate our most appealing qualities and weed out those that are less appealing. Then, when our life story is written, there may be more to report than just the bare facts of our existence.

How would I describe my personality? What do I like best about myself? What do I like least?

·⟪≈≈≈≈≈≈≈≈≈≈≈≈≈≈≈≈≈⟫·

TODAY I WILL GIVE THANKS FOR ALL THOSE THINGS THAT MAKE ME WHO I AM.

ST. ADRIAN

C. A.D. 306

The earliest lives of the saints say St. Adrian, an officer in the Roman army, was so moved by the patience of the Christians whom he persecuted that he himself converted to Christianity and was martyred. After his death, his relics were taken first to Constantinople, then to Rome, and finally to Flanders.

Relics are one of the more interesting aspects of the saints. By definition, a first-class relic is a part of a saint's body, such as a bone chip; a second-class relic is something belonging to the saint, such as clothing; and a third-class relic is something that has been touched either to the saint or to his or her tomb.

When described so methodically, relics sound a bit morbid, but, in fact, most of us keep relics of our loved ones. It's just that we don't call them relics. Do you have your grandmother's ring? Then you own a second-class relic. Do you keep a flower from your sister's wedding bouquet? Then you're treasuring a third-class relic. If someone you loved was cremated and you have the urn, you may even have a first-class relic.

Our relics help us remember our loved ones even after they have died. They are a way to remind us of our connection here on earth and to encourage us in the hope of our reunion in heaven. It's exactly the same way with relics of the saints. They help us recall our hope that one day, we, too, will meet face to face.

What relics do I treasure?

·⟨⟨▬▬▬▬▬▬▬▬▬▬▬▬▬▬⟩⟩·

TODAY I WILL LOOK AT SOMETHING THAT BELONGED TO
SOMEONE I LOVE AND REMEMBER THE PERSON IN PRAYER.

ST. PETER CLAVER

1581–1654

When it comes to learning something new, showing beats telling every time. Take cooking. Hearing a lecture on making soufflés just isn't the same as being in the kitchen having someone show you what the mixture is supposed to look like.

Show, don't tell could have been the life motto of St. Peter Claver. Born in Spain, he studied under the Jesuits and asked to be sent to the West Indies. Instead he ended up at Cartegena in present-day Columbia, one of the major centers for the New World slave trade. There he worked unceasingly ministering to newly arrived slaves from Angola and the Congo who were bound for the markets. While it is estimated that he baptized more than three hundred thousand slaves during his forty years of work, he knew that words alone weren't sufficient. "We must speak to them with our hands, before we try to speak to them with our lips," he said. To that end, he provided food, medicine, and clothing before he ever began to teach the gospel.

St. Peter Claver exemplifies the old saying, actions speak louder than words. We can talk endlessly about God and holiness and spiritual progress, but if we don't practice what we preach, no one will listen. St. James said it best, "What use is it if . . . one of you says . . . 'Go in peace, be warmed and be filled,' and yet do not give them what is necessary for their body, what use is that?" (James 2:16)

What have I done today to help someone less fortunate?

¶ LET MY ACTIONS SPEAK LOUDER THAN MY WORDS.

ST. NICHOLAS OF TOLENTINO

1245–1305

This St. Nicholas isn't the St. Nicholas associated with Santa Claus. This St. Nicholas was the son of a childless couple who had prayed to the *other* St. Nicholas for a son. This St. Nicholas entered the Augustinian friars and spent the rest of his life preaching and ministering to the people of Tolentino, where he lived for thirty years.

One of the many things he did was preach in the streets. Since things were different then, he wasn't met with the derision he would probably encounter today, but was, in fact, a great success. He used a method that was suitable for his times; if he had lived today, undoubtedly he would have used a method of communication more suitable to today's technology.

Being able to communicate is essential in today's fast-paced society. One of the reasons St. Nicholas was so successful was because he had direct contact with the people he wanted to reach. Sometimes, under the guise of being efficient, we use modern techniques to become more isolated. We hide behind computer screens and voice mail and never actually get out and talk with others. But when we use technology as a way to avoid contact, we lose sight of one of the fundamental realities of life: we need other people. If we want to have deep, meaningful relationships, we have to have real-life contact, not just the appearance of intimacy via technology. We need human contact to stay human.

Do I ever use technology as a way to avoid intimacy?

⟨━━━━━━━━━━━━━━━━━━━━⟩

I TAKE TIME TO BE WITH MY FRIENDS IN ACTUAL REALITY.

ST. PAPHNUTIUS

A.D. 350?

Among the tortures St. Paphnutius suffered under the persecutions of the Emperor Maximinus was being blinded in one eye. Despite the handicap, he became known for his defense of the faith and was a prominent figure in the Nicaean Council of 325.

Losing one's physical sight is a tragedy, but losing one's spiritual sight is even worse. When we are spiritually blind, we cannot see the truth, even when it is presented to us. Specifically, when we are spiritually blind, we cannot see the truth about ourselves. We may exaggerate our faults, or we may overemphasize our virtues. Both parts of the vision are essential. While it's important to emphasize our good qualities, the saints point out that it is equally important to acknowledge our not-so-sterling qualities.

This time of year, as the leaves are changing color and the circle of the seasons draws to a close, let us take a mental inventory of our lives. Let us look at those things we have accomplished, but let us not forget to examine our flaws. Let us take a courageous look at those times when we haven't lived up to our potential. Let us acknowledge both our vices and virtues, vowing to eliminate the former and cultivate the latter.

If I had to list my best qualities, what would be first? What is one thing I would like to change about myself?

⟨⟨⟨⟨⟨⟨⟨⟨⟨⟩⟩⟩⟩⟩⟩⟩⟩⟩

ALONG WITH ROBERT BURNS I ASK, "O WAD SOME POW'R THE GIFTIE GIE US, TO SEE OURSELS AS OTHERS SEE US!"

ST. GUY OF ANDERLECHT

A.D. 1012

Every day thousands and thousands of dollars are spent on lottery tickets. When the jackpot reaches mind-boggling proportions, millions may be spent. No matter that the odds against winning are astronomical; the idea that perhaps a particular series of numbers will bring wealth is enough to keep the lottery business booming.

Most of us wouldn't turn down a chance to get rich quick. Neither did St. Guy of Anderlecht. The sacristan of the church of our Lady at Laeken near Brussels in the eleventh century, he invested all his savings in a shipping prospect. The ship sank and with it all of St. Guy's investment. Since he had given up his job as a sacristan, he was left penniless and jobless.

It's fun to think what we would do if we were suddenly wealthy, but as St. Guy's example shows us, it's foolish to spend more than we can afford to lose. While few saints would get jobs as financial consultants (most would be prone to giving everything away), they do know something about investing—investing in eternity.

If we want to be truly wealthy, we need to build up treasures that will last. The wealth the saints urge us to seek consists of the virtues of goodness, peace, kindness, patience, self-control, faithfulness, gentleness, and love. When we invest in these ventures, we can be sure that our ships will not only always arrive in port, but also will be laden to overflowing with profits.

Do I spend more time thinking about my financial future or my spiritual future?

∙⟨𝖆𝖆𝖆𝖆𝖆𝖆𝖆𝖆𝖆𝖆𝖆𝖆𝖆𝖆⟩∙

I WOULD RATHER INVEST IN ETERNAL TREASURES THAN IN EARTHLY WEALTH.

ST. JOHN CHRYSOSTOM

347–407

There's nothing like the pricking of a guilty conscience to make a person take offense. When your conscience is bothering you, suddenly every remark seems to be addressed directly to you.

Empress Eudoxia must have had a guilty conscience because when St. John Chrysostom preached against vanity and extravagance among women of the court and made comparisons with the infamous Jezebel, she (and a number of other people) assumed he was speaking about her. Like many people with a guilty conscience, Eudoxia figured the easiest way to get rid of the pricking was to get rid of the person with the needle. She arranged to have St. John Chrysostom banished; he died while on his journey to the Black Sea.

What do you do when your conscience bothers you? Do you try to ignore it or do you pay attention? Sometimes we think the only purpose of a conscience is to make us feel guilty, but in reality, a conscience is your inner guide, directing you away from danger and toward safety. It's a little like the warning lights on the dash of your car. When the gas gets low or the oil pressure drops, a light comes on to alert you. In the same way, your conscience tries to alert you when you are making choices that aren't in your best interest. It tries to warn you when you move in directions harmful to your spiritual growth and development, so you can stop in time to make a better and more productive choice.

Is my conscience pricking me right now?

I PAY ATTENTION WHEN I SEE A SPIRITUAL YELLOW LIGHT.

ST. NOTBURGA

C. A.D. 1313

At certain restaurants in New York or Los Angeles, you may be waited on by an aspiring actor or actress. If they're lucky—and you have a good memory—someday you might even be able to say you had your salad served by an Academy Award winner. Count Henry of Rattenberg could go one further. He was served by a saint.

St. Notburga was the count's kitchen servant. One of her acts of charity was to take the leftovers and give them to the poor. The count's wife insisted she feed the swine instead. Notburga obeyed— for a time—then figured the poor needed the leftovers more than the pigs. When the countess discovered her orders had been ignored, she fired Notburga. However, the story has a happy ending (at least for Notburga). The countess died, the count remarried and rehired Notburga. He also allowed her to resume feeding the poor.

We never know where we will encounter a saint. Simply put, a saint is someone who is now in heaven. The major difference between a saint with a capital "St" and everyone else in heaven is that the former have been officially recognized by the church. But that doesn't mean the person who waits on your table isn't a saint. It just means he or she isn't in heaven yet.

If I knew someone was a saint, would I treat that person any differently than I do now?

· ⟨░░░░░░░░░░░░░░░░░░░░░░░░⟩ ·

I TREAT EVERYONE AS IF THEY WERE A SAINT-IN-WAITING.

ST. CATHERINE OF GENOA

1447–1510

It isn't fair, but beautiful people get preferential treatment. When teachers are shown pictures of students along with a list of grades, they attribute the better grades to the more attractive students. In job interviews, more attractive applicants score higher than do more ordinary-looking ones.

St. Catherine of Genoa was a beauty of the fifteenth century. She was also intelligent, sensible, and religious. Definitely the kind of person you love to hate. Sometimes we become envious of people like St. Catherine who seem to have it all. We see only their physical perfection and their sterling qualities, and we assume they and their lives are perfect. We compare their bounty with our lack and begin to feel great surges of jealousy and envy.

Envy is one of the most destructive of all sins. Not for naught is it one of the so-called seven deadly sins. Envy is a cancer in the soul. It eats away at our peace while at the same time desiring ill for the other person. It wants what we cannot have, but more than that, it doesn't want anyone else to have it either.

The only way to overcome envy is to realize that nothing . . . and no one . . . is perfect, not even a saint. Although she possessed many virtues, Catherine is said to have lacked both humor and wit. Moreover, her husband was an unfaithful spendthrift with a temper. When we realize that the qualities we envy come in a boxed set with other features we wouldn't want, it's easier to be satisfied with what we have.

When I feel envious, is it of physical attributes like beauty or intangibles like intelligence?

I WOULDN'T TRADE PLACES WITH ANYONE.

ST. CORNELIUS

A.D. 253

During the time of the Roman persecutions, some early Christians renounced their faith. Many of us, facing the choice between the lions and an oath to the emperor, would do the same. However, when the persecutions finally ended, some who had abandoned the church wanted to return.

Certain officials believed that everyone who denied the faith was out of luck. Once out, always out, they held. Others felt that those who left should be allowed back but only after strenuous penance. Still others believed that everyone should be welcomed back no questions asked.

St. Cornelius was pope during this period of great controversy. Things finally got so heated that he convened a synod, which determined that those who had jumped ship, so to speak, could be let back on board through the usual means of the sacrament of penance.

In one sense, St. Cornelius is the saint of second chances. Because we all make mistakes, we all need a second chance sometime in our lives. We blow it big time and there's nothing for us to do but say we're sorry and ask for forgiveness. While our fellow human beings might not always be so willing, God is always ready to welcome us back. The only thing that can separate us from the love of God is our own stubbornness and refusal to ask for forgiveness.

Have I ever done something that I thought was so bad that God could never forgive me? Have I asked for forgiveness?

TODAY I WILL TELL GOD THAT I AM SORRY FOR ALL THE THINGS I DID THAT I SHOULD NOT HAVE DONE AS WELL AS FOR ALL THE THINGS I DID NOT DO THAT I SHOULD HAVE DONE.

ST. HILDEGARD OF BINGEN

1098–1179

St. Hildegard of Bingen was one of the great mystics of the Middle Ages. Her writings inspired even such influential saints as Bernard of Clairvaux. She also built a new monastery for her growing community of nuns (with running water), corresponded with the pope, advised not only laity but also priests, wrote numerous letters, composed hymns and sacred plays, and still had time to write down the gist of twenty-six of her symbolic visions dealing with relations between God and humanity. Oh yes, she also traveled extensively through Germany.

St. Hildegard was obviously creative, energetic, and very busy. Busy-ness might have been a virtue for St. Hildegard, but it's almost a vice today. We are so accustomed to layering our life with activities that we may feel we have to do at least two things at the same time to be accomplishing anything.

Today, take a break from the busy-ness of life. Toss out all the shoulds, musts, have-tos; along with them, toss out the guilt that says you aren't doing enough. You are accomplishing exactly what you need to accomplish. If you don't get done everything you planned, maybe you planned too much. Just for today, do less rather than more. Life is too short to be wasted in busy-ness.

*Do I try to do too much in too little time? Do I feel guilty when
I'm not busy?*

TODAY I WILL DO AT LEAST ONE THING THAT I ENJOY
WITHOUT FEELING LIKE I SHOULD BE DOING SOMETHING
MORE CONSTRUCTIVE WITH MY TIME.

ST. JUAN MACÍAS

1585–1645

When we are lonely, we need to remember we are never alone. Mary, all the saints, and all the angels are always with us. For St. Juan Macías, a Dominican brother, the saints were real companions indeed. As a small child tending sheep in his native Spain, he was said to have been visited often by St. John the Evangelist, as well as Mary and the Christ child.

When we get to know the saints, we soon learn they can be our companions also. While we may not actually see them (and, to be honest, we may not want to *actually* ever see a saint), we can feel their presence in our hearts and minds. When we have questions or concerns, we can turn to them as we would to any other friends.

The saints won't enter our lives without an invitation. They wait for us. If we never get to know the saints, it's probably because we haven't taken the initiative to get to know them.

Isn't that often the case? We know someone, but because of fear of rejection or insecurity, we don't take the initiative to reach out. We figure they wouldn't be interested or they would think we are being pushy, so we don't make that phone call or issue that invitation. When you deny yourself the chance to reach out, who is really the loser?

Do I find it easy or hard to take the first steps in a friendship?

TODAY I WILL MAKE A NEW FRIEND (MAYBE EVEN AMONG THE SAINTS).

ST. EMILY DE RODAT

1787–1852

One piece of saintly advice is to take up our crosses every day. What does that mean? Are we supposed to look for ways to suffer?

Some of the saints did deliberately seek out suffering. They punished themselves with cruel penances, sometimes even breaking their health in the process. Such extraordinary means aren't necessary, though. Most of us have enough crosses to bear without going out and looking for additional ones. In fact, the most difficult crosses are usually little things.

St. Emily de Rodat, the foundress of the Congregation of the Holy Family of Villefranche, suffered from ringing in the ears, growths in the nose, and cancer of the eye. None of her ailments was fatal, but all were difficult to bear. Near the end of her life, she left the administration of her convents to her successor, saying that she had nothing left to do but suffer.

When we have to put up with discomfort and ill health, one of two things can happen. Either we become irritable and crabby, a pain to ourselves and everyone around us. Or we can take up our cross and use our discomfort as a way to grow spiritually. When we do the latter, we use our crosses as a testing ground for such virtues as patience and peace of mind. Putting up with ringing in the ears may not seem as glamorous as becoming a martyr, but sometimes it can be just as difficult.

Is there some cross I can take up right now?

·⟨⟨⟨⟨⟩⟩⟩⟩·

I ACCEPT THE SUFFERING THAT COMES MY WAY AS PART OF
MY SPIRITUAL TRAINING.

ST. ANDREW KIM TAEGON AND COMPANIONS

1839–1846 AND 1862–1867

The canonization ceremony of St. Andrew Kim and his 102 fellow Koreans was the first canonization ceremony to take place outside Rome in more than seven hundred years. The martyrs were representative of the more than ten thousand Christians killed in Korea for their Christian faith. St. Andrew Kim, the first native Korean priest, was beheaded in 1846. Not until 1882, however, did religious persecution formally end in Korea.

The freedom to choose our religious beliefs without coercion is part of our divine birthright. Through the gift of free will, God allows each of us to make our own choices. Sometimes we make decisions leading us away from God and sometimes we make choices leading us closer, but the right to choose is always ours.

Making choices can sometimes be difficult. We all appreciate a selection, but you can have too much of a good thing. For instance, you go to buy a shirt and are faced with literally rack after rack of selections. Color. Fabric. Price. Style. The possibilities seem so limitless, you may be tempted not to even try to sort them out.

The same may seem true of religion. If you are in the process of trying to make a decision, don't be swayed by fine rhetoric or fancy buildings. Instead, ask God for the grace and wisdom to recognize the truth when you see it. Then ask for the courage to act.

Do I find it difficult or easy to make choices?

.⟨══════════════════════════⟩.

I MAKE MY OWN CHOICES, BUT I DO NOT FORCE THEM ON ANYONE ELSE.

ST. MATTHEW

FIRST CENTURY

Nobody likes taxes. Looking at our first paycheck, we may bemoan that the government gets more than we do. While that's not quite true, it often does feel like the government takes more than its fair share of our income.

In first-century Palestine, sometimes the government—or more precisely the government tax collector—did take more than his fair share. Anything the tax collector could extort over and above the listed taxes was his to keep. How much do you want to bet that under such a system an honest tax collector must have been as rare as a flying penguin?

St. Matthew was one of those despised tax collectors. Then he met Jesus and everything changed. Jesus said, "Follow me," and Matthew did. He left his job, his wealth, and his friends. Tradition says the tax collector became a saint by dying a martyr's death in Ethiopia.

Few things in life are as inevitable as taxes. As the saying goes, the only sure things are death and taxes. But taxes aren't limited to the funds we pay the government to keep itself running. Sometimes we levy heavy taxes on ourselves. When we make ourselves keep paying and paying for some mistake, when we expect perfection, when we are unwilling to forgive our failures, we pay a higher tax for being human than anyone, even God, expects. We all have a price to pay for being human, but we don't have to become self-extortionists, expecting more of ourselves than we can possible pay.

Am I harder on myself than I need to be?

IF I'M BEING TOO HARSH, I WILL LIGHTEN UP ON MYSELF.

ST. THOMAS OF VILLANOVA

1488–1555

Do you ever get the feeling your life has happened more or less by accident? St. Thomas of Villanova, archbishop of Valencia in the sixteenth century, became archbishop totally by accident. Through a clerical error, St. Thomas's name, instead of another religious's, was put on the nomination list.

Sometimes it feels like we are the victims of some kind of celestial clerical error. Only when we look back at our life do we realize we are in exactly the place we were meant to be all along. As archbishop, St. Thomas performed many acts of charity, not the least of which was seeing that no poor girl married without a dowry. For all those girls he helped, St. Thomas was definitely in the right place at the right time.

If you find yourself somewhere you never expected to be, before you complain, take a look around. Is there someone who needs your help whom you might not have noticed if you were someplace else?

When the emperor (who had the right to name archbishops in those days) discovered an error had been made in nominating St. Thomas, he let it stand, saying it must have happened by a "particular providence of God." St. Thomas wasn't thrilled with the turn of events, but he acquiesced and became a stellar prelate. We don't have to be thrilled when life places us where we don't want to be, but we can, like St. Thomas, always bring good out of a bad situation.

Where did I think I would be at this point in my life?

I WILL DO GOOD NO MATTER WHERE I AM.

ST. ADAMNAN

624?–704

Have you ever watched one of those real-life adventure shows on television? Perhaps someone is scaling a sheer cliff and, through the camera's eye, you get to accompany them inch by inch up the precipice. Or maybe a diver is surrounded by great white sharks and again, thanks to the camera, you get to be inches away from those deadly jaws.

While you marvel at the bravery of the person performing the feat, what about the person doing the filming? In order for you to share the adventure, a camera operator has to be dangling off the face of the cliff or tempting the sharks down in the deep right along with the adventurer. Since we don't see the camera operators, we tend to forget their presence. Without them, however, we would never share any of those adventures.

St. Adamnan was a camera operator, so to speak. His relative and fellow monk, St. Columba, was famous by the time Adamnan entered the monastery of Iona. He wrote "Life of St. Columba," one of the earliest and most complete lives of a saint written in the Middle Ages, and recorded the story of Bishop Arculf's pilgrimage to Jerusalem—even though the farthest Adamnan ever got from his native Ireland was a couple of quick trips to England.

What is your role in life? Are you the adventurer or are you the camera operator? Fortunately, both have important contributions to make in the world. The key is, as Mother Teresa says, "not what we are doing or how much we are doing, but rather how much love we are putting in the doing of that work entrusted to us."

Am I content with my role? Would I like to change it—or me?

I ASK PROTECTION FOR ALL WHO MUST RISK THEIR LIVES TODAY.

ST. GERARD

A.D. 1046

St. Gerard, the first bishop of Csanad, was tutor to St. Stephen of Hungary's son Emeric. After Stephen's death, St. Gerard no longer had royal protection. He was martyred near the Danube by some of Stephen's former enemies.

Among Gerard's virtues was the care with which he performed all sacred ceremonies. One of the reasons he was so fastidious was his belief that we need the aid of our senses in order to increase our devotion. In other words, he understood the tremendous influence our surroundings exert on our state of mind.

St. Gerard apparently knew innately what research has come to prove. It's not by accident that hospitals are decorated in soft, soothing colors or preschools are painted in bright, primary colors. It isn't just happenstance that trees and flowers are often planted along busy city streets. And it isn't just by chance that we feel the most comfortable when we are surrounded by our own familiar treasures.

The intimate spaces where we live, work, eat, sleep, and play are all part of our environment. We don't have to accept any old environment, though. If the space we are living and working in doesn't meet our needs, we can take positive steps to create a more suitable atmosphere. Right now, take a look around. What are your surroundings saying about you? How are they making you feel? If they aren't meeting your needs, then you have the right to change them.

Do the colors and objects in my environment reflect my own personality and needs? When people comes into my home or office do they get a sense of who I am?

I CHOOSE THE OBJECTS IN MY ENVIRONMENT WITH CARE.

STS. COSMAS AND DAMIEN

A.D. 303?

Some saints have been venerated for nearly the entire history of Christianity, despite the fact that virtually nothing is known about them. Cosmas and Damien are two such mysterious heroes of the faith. All we know for sure is that their names are recorded in the Eucharistic Prayer of the Mass. Legend, however, holds they were twin brothers who practiced medicine in Syria. Competent physicians, they were called the moneyless ones because they didn't charge for their services. Perhaps that miracle alone is enough to keep them remembered for more than sixteen hundred years.

If you have a particular talent or trade, do you ever give it away or do you always expect to be paid for your services? Sometimes we lose sight of the fact that we have been given our talents and abilities not to store up earthly treasures, but for the good of all humanity.

But I worked hard for what I have, you may object, and feel that you deserve to be paid for your work. That's true and nobody, not even the saints, would say you *have* to give away anything. But giving isn't an obligation; it's a way to say thank you for all you have. As the gospel of Matthew says, "Freely you received, freely give." (Matthew 10:8) When we give, we not only bless others, but we also acknowledge the fact that we have been blessed.

How do I react when someone asks me for free advice or
free services?

SOMETIME SOON WHEN I'M ASKED TO DO SOMETHING I
NORMALLY WOULD BE PAID FOR, I WILL DO IT FOR FREE.

ST. THÉRÈSE COUDERC

1805–1885

St. Thérèse Couderc's motto might have been, if you can't say something nice, then don't say anything at all. Heaven knows she had sufficient reason to speak up. Not only was she isolated from the community of nuns she had founded, because of false allegations about her health and abilities, but she was also forced to do the community's hardest manual labor for thirteen years. During that time, she never responded to her accusers but instead did what was asked with patience and forbearance. At the end of her life, her endurance was rewarded when she was restored to the community and publicly recognized as its founder.

Some people have never learned to keep their mouths shut. Their brains seem to be directly attached to their tongues. They blurt out whatever pops into their heads with little or no regard for the consequences. Learning to govern our tongues may be one of the most difficult lessons any of us has to learn. Our tongues get us into more trouble than does any other part of our bodies. "However large [ships] are . . . they are directed by very small rudders on whatever course the steersman's impulse may select. The tongue is something like that. It is a small member, yet it makes great pretensions," says James. If we can learn to keep our mouth shut when our words would be hurtful or harmful, we will have gone a long way toward learning the self-control and self-discipline we all desire to have.

Do I have a hard time controlling my tongue? Do I ever use my tongue as a weapon?

JUST FOR TODAY, I WILL FOLLOW THE EXAMPLE OF ST. THÉRÈSE COUDERC AND NOT SAY ANYTHING UNLESS IT IS POSITIVE.

ST. VINCENT DE PAUL

1580–1660

One of the best things we can say of our friends is that they know our faults but love us anyway. St. Vincent de Paul, for whom the St. Vincent de Paul Society is named, had friends in all strata of society, from galley slaves to King Louis XIII. Yet, by nature, he was, to put it bluntly, a grump. He says it was only because of his intense prayer life and deep commitment to his faith that he was able to overcome his natural tendencies to harshness and anger. Apparently he was successful since he was well loved in his lifetime and was named the patron saint of charitable works by Pope Leo XIII.

Although grumpiness may be part of your natural tendencies, more often it's the result of self-neglect and overwork. When we don't take the time to recharge our emotional and spiritual batteries, we become irritable and short-tempered. Things we might shrug off if our defenses were stronger suddenly become personal affronts. We take offense where none is intended, and we snap at those we care about the most.

If you find everyone and everything is making you crabby, don't start making demands to shape up or ship out! Rather, ask yourself some hard questions. Are you getting sufficient rest and exercise? Are you working too long and too hard without a break? Are you eating correctly? If you are honest with yourself, you'll probably discover where the real problem lies.

When I'm crabby, do I blame others or do I look to see if I could be at fault?

I MAY NOT BE ABLE TO CONTROL MY FEELINGS, BUT I CAN CONTROL MY ACTIONS.

ST. WENCESLAUS OF BOHEMIA

907?–929

Good King Wenceslaus looked out, on the feast of Stephen.
When the snow lay round about, cold and crisp and even.

Most of us have sung that Christmas carol for years without realizing it was written about a real king and a real saint.

St. Wenceslaus of Bohemia was one of two sons of the king and queen of Bohemia. When his father was killed in battle, his saintly grandmother Ludmilla took over his education, while his non-Christian mother ruled. In order to prevent her helping Wenceslaus come to the throne, his mother had Ludmilla strangled. Nonetheless, others came to his assistance and he became king at the age of fifteen. During his short reign (only seven years), he was well known for his works of mercy and charity. Hence the famous Christmas carol about his taking flesh and wine and pine logs to yonder peasant on St. Stephen's day, December 26.

When he had a son, his brother Boleslaus, who had always resented him and now saw all hopes of becoming king lost to the heir apparent, invited Wenceslaus to a banquet on the feast of Sts. Cosmas and Damien. The next day, as Wenceslaus was heading to Mass, his brother attacked him. Boleslaus's friends joined the fray and killed Wenceslaus at the chapel door. He died asking God to forgive his brother.

When I think of the saints as actual personages in history, does that change the way I feel about them?

TODAY I WILL SAY A PRAYER FOR ALL LOCAL, STATE, AND
NATIONAL OFFICIALS.

ST. MICHAEL, ST. GABRIEL, AND
ST. RAPHAEL

What's the difference between saints and angels? You could list several, including the fact that angels are pure spirits while saints are flesh-and-blood creatures. But then there are Michael, Gabriel, and Raphael, three angels honored both as angels and as saints.

The word *angel* comes from the Greek meaning "messenger," and indeed most accounts of angels in sacred writings portray them as messengers. Angels accompanied Moses as he parted the Red Sea, and visited Daniel in the lion's den. They also announced Christ's birth to the shepherds and encouraged Jesus in the Garden of Gethsemane before his death. They are expected to come at the end of time to separate the wicked from the just.

A good deal of what we believe about angels comes from the writings of St. Thomas Aquinas, who is called the Angelic Doctor. Among other things, Aquinas says each angel is "its own order in the universe, far greater than a star." In other words, angels are a bit like snowflakes; no two are alike.

Whatever we know—or don't know—about angels may be best summarized by Aquinas: "Almost instinctively, we want to know more about them, not only because they can do so much for or against us but because they are all so very close to us and our living . . . We are not nearly so alone as we imagine, whatever the hour or place."

What appeals to me most about the angels?

·⟨▬▬▬▬▬▬▬▬▬▬▬▬▬▬▬⟩·

I ASK THE ANGELS TO BRING ME THE MESSAGES GOD WANTS
ME TO HAVE TODAY.

ST. JEROME

342? – 420

St. Jerome has the reputation of being bad tempered, which, indeed, he was. Best known for his translation of the Bible, he was the prototypical ascetic. He fasted for weeks, prayed incessantly, and constantly berated himself for his failings. He was equally harsh in his advice for raising a virtuous daughter, saying she should learn to make her own clothes (but never fine ones) and suggesting her entire day be spent in reading, prayer, and work. "If you are solicitous your daughter should not be bit by a viper, how much more that she be not hurt by the poison of all the earth," he writes.

St. Jerome is not a warm, kind person. Prickly and unpleasant, his rhetoric and style sound overly rigid and didactic to most modern ears. As far as saints go, he is a bad-tempered porcupine stuck in a bunny hutch. Yet he is honored as a saint, and therein lies his lesson. If St. Jerome can make it to heaven in spite of his faults, we can too.

Heaven is not populated by perfect people; it's filled with ordinary people who tried their best to love God and serve humanity. Granted, some did a better job of it than others. Although St. Jerome was not the most pleasant of persons, imagine what he might have been like if he hadn't been trying to change.

When we feel discouraged or disheartened by our failure to overcome bad habits, let us remember the reward of heaven comes not from our success, but from our struggle.

What bad habits am I working on right now?

· ⟨⟨⟨≈≈≈≈≈≈≈≈≈≈≈≈≈≈≈≈≈≈≈≈≈≈≈≈≈≈≈≈≈≈⟩⟩⟩ ·

EVEN WHEN I AM ONLY TRYING, I AM ALWAYS TRYING MY
BEST.

ST. THÉRÈSE OF LISIEUX

1873–1897

Imagine the scene. You're seated in a dimly lit chapel. Candles flicker on the altar and the soft murmur of voices praying the rosary surround you. In the quiet you resolve to focus completely on the prayers. You lift up your heart and . . . immediately fall asleep. If you can identify with the picture, so can St. Thérèse of Lisieux, better known as the Little Flower.

St. Thérèse entered a Carmelite monastery at age fifteen, after begging Pope Leo XIII to give her permission. She lived the quiet, unassuming life of a cloistered nun until her death at age twenty-four from tuberculosis. It was only after her death that her extraordinary holiness was revealed.

Although St. Thérèse was a saint, she was also very human. She loved the Virgin Mary but disliked praying the rosary. She was a great mystic but hated retreats. She is a model of holiness but often fell asleep during community prayer.

Sometimes when we pray or meditate, especially at night, we, too, fall asleep. While we may feel embarrassed or cross with ourselves when that happens, St. Thérèse said that since parents love their children when they are awake or asleep, so too God loves us even if we fall asleep while praying.

One charming idea says that if we can't finish our prayers, we don't have to worry. Our guardian angel will finish them for us. Even if that isn't the case, no prayer is truly unfinished, for prayer is an ongoing conversation with God. If we take a little break now and then, it's okay. God will be waiting when we wake up.

When do I find it easiest to pray?

I BELIEVE GOD LOVES ME ALL THE TIME, AWAKE OR ASLEEP.

ST. LÉGER

616?–678

St. Léger was a French bishop of the seventh century. As part of his episcopal duties, he not only preached and taught ordinary folks, but he also reformed many of the clergy who had become lax in their responsibilities. He said that if monks were doing what they were supposed to do, their prayers would preserve the world from many disasters.

While he was speaking to clerics, his words also apply to us. If each of us were doing no more and no less than what we were supposed to, the world would be in much better shape. The problem is we sometimes become so overwhelmed we don't know where to start. Whether we're dealing with global issues or sorting out personal ones, the process is exactly the same. We can't try to solve the whole thing at once. We've got to take it one step at a time.

What can you do right now? Not tomorrow, because tomorrow never comes. Not when you are better prepared, because you may always feel inadequate. But right now!

"What you are doing, I may not be able to do . . . What I am doing you may not be able to do . . . But all of us together are doing something beautiful for God." Mother Teresa's words hold the key. If we each do what we can right now, together we will be able to accomplish all that needs to be done.

What issue concerns me the most at this moment? What one thing can I do to help?

I DO WHAT I CAN, NO MORE AND NO LESS.

ST. THOMAS CANTELUPE

1218?–1282

Do you ever find yourself wishing you could get along better with your family members? About this time of year magazines start showing cheerful family gatherings where everyone is delighted to be together. No one is arguing; everyone is having a simply splendid time. But in your own family, you know it won't be like that. Someone will be on the outs; feelings will get hurt, and if memories are made, they won't necessary be happy ones.

If you aren't as close to your family as you might like, St. Thomas Cantelupe probably understands. He had four brothers and three sisters, none of whom he seemed to have liked very much, although he did live for a time with one of his brothers in Paris.

Since we can't actually get rid of our blood relatives (tempting as it might be at times), we often have to make an effort to be friends. But sometimes that isn't possible. While we must always be as pleasant and as kind as possible to our blood relatives, we don't have to spend all of our time with them.

Nonetheless, we all need family. If your blood relatives can't or won't be the kind of family you need, consider creating ties and traditions with friends. You can celebrate holidays, birthdays, and important occasions with friends as well as family. In fact, sometimes close friends can be better family than family!

Who is my family?

⊹ ⎯⎯⎯⎯⎯⎯⎯⎯⎯⎯⎯⎯⎯⎯⎯⎯⎯⎯⎯ ⊹

I ACCEPT THE REALITY OF MY FAMILY, EVEN IF IT ISN'T THE WAY I WOULD LIKE IT TO BE.

ST. FRANCIS OF ASSISI

1181?–1226

If there is one saint who needs no introduction, it would have to be St. Francis of Assisi. The story of young Francesco Bernadone, who gave up his family's wealth to become a poor preacher, has been made into countless books, plays, and movies. The order he founded—the Franciscans—has spread over the entire world.

Francis was one of the most unique personalities the world has ever known. A free spirit, Francis has captured the hearts and imaginations of Christians and non-Christians alike for more than seven hundred years.

St. Francis saw the face of God in everything. In his famous Canticle of the Sun, composed while he was suffering great pain prior to his death, he gave thanks for all of creation, especially for Sister Death, for whom he was anxiously waiting.

Praised by You, my Lord, with all your creatures, especially Sir
   Brother Sun, who is the day and through whom you give us
   light and he is beautiful and radiant with great splendor . . .
Praised by You, my Lord, through Sister Moon and the stars,
   in heaven you formed them clear and precious and chaste.
Praised be You, my Lord, through Brother Fire, through whom
   You light the night and he is beautiful and playful and robust
   and strong . . .
Praised be You, my Lord, through our Sister Bodily Death, from
   whom no [one] can escape. . . .

Do I live in such a way that I am ready to die?

WHEN MY TIME TO DIE COMES, I WILL NOT BE AFRAID, FOR
I KNOW I WILL BE ENTERING THE COMPANY OF THE SAINTS.

BLESSED RAYMOND OF CAPUA

1330–1399

What would a saint confess? Blessed Raymond of Capua would know since he was the confessor to St. Catherine of Siena, one of the greatest mystics of all times.

When Catherine first saw him celebrating Mass, she was delighted and informed him he was to be her confessor (the priest to whom she would regularly and frequently tell her sins). Blessed Raymond was less enthusiastic, although in time he came to appreciate Catherine's intelligence and mission to restore the papacy.

Confession is good for the soul, even the souls of saints. Although we can always talk to God directly, telling another human being what we have done wrong and expressing our sorrow is an important step both in forgiving ourselves and in being assured of God's forgiveness. It is, for instance, a fundamental step in 12-step recovery programs.

For Catholics, the sacrament of confession is the logical place to make those revelations since the priest is bound by the seal of confession. Even courts of law uphold the right of a priest to keep the seal of secrecy.

Why would a saint like St. Catherine of Siena want to go to confession regularly? What could she be doing that was so wrong?

It probably wasn't so much what she had done as what she wanted to become. Confession does more than assure us our sins are forgiven; it also helps us become more aware of our weaknesses and tendencies. After all, it is only when we are aware of errors that we can begin to make corrections.

What needs correction in my life? Is there anyone I need to make amends to?

I AM SORRY FOR ALL THE SINS OF MY PAST LIFE.

BLESSED MARIE ROSE DUROCHER

1814–1849

Herbert Spencer said, "Education has for its object the formation of character." Blessed Marie Rose Durocher, the foundress of the Sisters of the Holy Names of Jesus and Mary, would agree. She urged her sisters to pray, "Give me the spirit you want [the children] to have."

As a young woman in French Canada, Marie Rose Durocher taught children in her parish, but eventually, albeit after much struggle, she began a girls' boarding school. Today the Holy Name Sisters teach and work throughout the world.

Interestingly, without the Holy Name Sisters, private schools might not exist in America. In 1925, the U.S. Supreme Court heard a case entitled *Pierce* vs. *the Society of Sisters of the Holy Names of Jesus and Mary*. In what is more commonly called the Oregon School case, the justices declared unconstitutional a state law mandating public school education, stating "The child is not the mere creature of the state; those who nurture him and direct his destiny have the right coupled with the high duty, to recognize and prepare him for additional obligation." With the Supreme Court decision, the freedom of parents to chose their children's education was guaranteed throughout the United States.

Sometimes when we are in school we view education more as an obligation than a privilege, but education can change the future. If you desire to further your education, there's no better time than the present to begin.

Is there something I've always wanted to learn how to do?

·⟨⟨⟩⟩·

I AM ALWAYS LEARNING, EVEN WHEN I'M NOT IN SCHOOL.

BLESSED GIANNA BERETTA MOLLA, M.D.

1922–1962

Gianna Beretta was a thoroughly modern woman. Born in October 1922, she loved sports, including skiing and mountain climbing. She rode a motorcycle, read fashion magazines, and wore red nail polish. After she graduated from medical school, she married Pietro Molla and set up her medical practice. They had a son in 1956 and two daughters in 1957 and 1959. Then in 1961, when she discovered she was pregnant, she also learned she had a tumor of the uterus. Dr. Molla demanded her baby not be killed during the operation. Although the tumor was removed and her baby saved, Dr. Molla was not so certain about her own future. Her premonition came true when, after her healthy daughter Gianna Emmanuela Molla was born, Dr. Molla died of peritonitis. At her beatification on April 24, 1994, her husband and children, including daughter Dr. Gianna Emmanuela Molla were present.

Saints have lived in all times and all places. Blessed Gianna Beretta Molla is one of the most contemporary. Unlike so many of the ancient saints, she didn't found a religious community or live like a hermit or go through extremes of self-mortification and penance. Instead she lived a perfectly ordinary life as a wife, mother, and pediatrician . . . with one exception. She strove to "live the Will of God every moment and to live it with joy."

When we think we don't have the right stuff to become saints, we only need to look at Blessed Gianna Molla with her red nail polish, high-fashion clothing, busy medical practice, and young family.

Do I ever think of myself as becoming a saint?

I REALIZE BECOMING A SAINT DOESN'T MEAN BECOMING SANCTIMONIOUS.

ST. THAIS

A.D. 348?

St. Thais was a wealthy prostitute who lived in fourth-century Egypt. When she reformed, she gathered all the presents her clients had given her and burned them in the street. An early account of her life says, "To have kept any of those presents would have been not to cut off all dangerous occasions which might again revive her passions and call back former temptations."

Often, when we make a radical change in our lives, we, too, have to get rid of everything that would tempt us. One of the reasons we fail in our good resolutions is because we overestimate our ability to withstand temptation. We may have a great deal of willpower, but there's no reason we have to try ourselves to the nth degree. If, for instance, we give up smoking, we shouldn't keep a couple of packs of cigarettes lying around the house. Or if we go on a diet, we shouldn't stock up on chocolate chip cookies the day before.

If you are trying to change a bad habit or reform some aspect of your life, make it easier on yourself. Purge your life of those things that would tempt you back into old, unhealthy, or unsafe behaviors.

Often, though, it isn't things but people who draw us back. If you're serious about making a change in your life and the people you associate with aren't, you may have to sever your ties with them—maybe temporarily, maybe permanently. Making those kinds of changes is never easy, but it's sometimes necessary.

How good am I at resisting temptation?

I DON'T ALLOW MYSELF TO BE TEMPTED BEYOND MY ENDURANCE.

ST. LOUIS BERTRAND

1526–1581

St. Louis Bertrand was not only related to St. Vincent Ferrer and baptized in the same baptismal font (albeit 175 years later), but he also joined the same religious order—the Dominicans. Once while he was working as a missionary in Colombia, he was attacked by an armed man. It's said that when he made the sign of the cross over the gun, it was transformed into a crucifix.

While we can't change guns into crosses, we can follow St. Louis's advice to young missionaries. He taught that prayer must always precede all other actions, including preaching and teaching. In contrast, we often use prayer as a last-ditch effort. When situations are desperate and we feel trapped, then we are likely to begin praying. It's almost as if we turn to prayer when we have nothing left to lose, instead of, as St. Louis suggests, making prayer our first recourse.

Prayer can and does change our lives. We can ask God's help in both large and small matters, and, more often than not, the answer will be yes. One way of taking an objective look at how prayer affects your life is to keep a prayer journal. For the next week or so, jot down everything you ask for in prayer. You may feel silly writing down things like 'help me find a parking place,' but note them anyway. Then mark down whatever answer you receive: yes, no, or not answered yet. At the end of the week, take a look at your journal. You will undoubtedly be surprised at the results.

Do I really believe my prayers are answered?

⸱⸨═══════════════════════⸩⸱

¶ USE PRAYER AS MY FIRST RECOURSE, INSTEAD OF MY LAST.

ST. FRANCIS BORGIA

1510–1572

We've all heard of families having a black sheep, but St. Francis Borgia was the white sheep of his clan. A member of the notorious Borgia family, he was the grandnephew of the infamous Lucrezia Borgia, who was, in turn, the daughter of the immoral Pope Alexander VI. Despite (or perhaps because of) his relatives, St. Francis Borgia was a man of great holiness. Even as viceroy of Catalonia, he spent as much time as he could in prayer without neglecting either his work or his family. After his wife's death, he longed to enter the Jesuits but waited until his eight children were old enough to do without him before turning his titles and estate over to his son.

One of the more interesting facts about St. Francis Borgia is that he is said to have had a semicircle cut from his dining room table to accommodate his excessive girth.

If we don't fit society's current model for bodies, we can take heart from St. Francis Borgia. Even as a saint-in-the-making, he didn't quite fit the mold. Although he became thinner after his ordination, he never was a lean ascetic.

Those who try to convince us that perfecting our outsides will automatically perfect our insides have it backward. St. Francis Borgia didn't become thinner until he focused on his spiritual development, not on his diet. When we focus on our spiritual growth, then we, too, become more aware of how the choices we make physically can also affect us spiritually.

Do I spend more time worrying about how I look or how I act?

1 TAKE CARE OF MY BODY AND MY SOUL.

ST. MARY SOLEDAD

1826–1887

When we read the lives of the saints, we may get the idea they were all brave and stalwart. St. Mary Soledad wasn't. The foundress of a nursing order, she was terrified of dead bodies. Although she learned to quell her fears later in life, she always assured her sisters such fears were quite natural.

While our intellect tells us dead bodies can't harm us, our imagination and emotions whisper a different story. It's the same with many fears. Even when we are grown up, some of the apprehensions we had as children linger in the back of our intellect. For instance, although few would admit it, many adults feel uncomfortable sleeping with an arm or leg dangling over the edge of the bed, even though we all *know* there aren't any monsters lurking in the dark.

We may think of bravery as performing great and wondrous deeds or displaying extraordinary courage in the face of danger, but often the bravest deeds are done in ordinary life situations. Raising children to be mature, independent adults requires a great deal of courage. Staying with a spouse who is chronically ill or dying takes enormous courage. Being loving and respectful in situations where you are not loved or respected can be an act of highest courage. St. Mary Soledad's example helps us understand that we don't have to look for places to be brave; we just have to be brave in the places where we are.

What do I fear the most?

I WILL NOT LET MY FEARS AND APPREHENSIONS RULE MY LIFE.

ST. WILFRID

634–709

Some people seem to live quiet, uneventful lives, while others are constantly embroiled in controversy. St. Wilfrid is one of the latter. Sometimes the mess was of his own causing—as in the case of King Egfrith and his wife Etheldreda. For ten years, Etheldreda refused to consummate the marriage and St. Wilfrid took her side, helping her escape to a convent. Needless to say, the king was not particularly pleased and took his revenge by having Wilfrid's diocese subdivided. Other times, the uproar didn't seem to be Wilfrid's fault—as when King Egfrith's successor had him banished for obscure reasons.

Regardless of what caused the controversy, Wilfrid lived his entire life in a state of flux. Can you identify with Wilfrid? Many of us can. Our lives seem to be like those birthday candles that keep reigniting after you blow them out. We just seem to get things under control when little fires break out again . . . and again . . . and again.

When the fires of controversy result from our own doing—as did Wilfrid's when he helped the queen—we don't have much room to complain. But when the controversy isn't the result of something we've done, but something done to us, then we have the right to demand restitution.

When the archbishop of Canterbury ordered Wilfrid to give up his seat as bishop and move to an abbey, Wilfrid had had enough and appealed to Rome. After much wrangling (by now the story of Wilfrid's life), he was allowed to keep his position but had to live in the abbey. Wilfrid didn't win his last controversy, but didn't lose it either.

Do I ever intentionally or inadvertently create controversy?

I SEEK PEACE IN ALL SITUATIONS.

BLESSED AGOSTINA PIETRANTONI

1864–1894

Are you so angry you can hardly see straight? Do you have something you just have to get off your chest? Then write a letter. Vent all your spleen. Express all your frustration. Say everything you ever wanted the other person to hear. Then, when you're through, instead of mailing the letter, tear it up! You'll have had the satisfaction of saying what you want, but you won't have hurt anyone's feelings or caused any rift in a relationship.

Blessed Agostina Pietrantoni worked in the tubercular ward of the Hospital of Santo Spirito in Rome. When the patients, many of whom came directly from prison, would frustrate her, she would write letters to the Blessed Virgin and "mail" them behind a picture just outside the ward.

At times it isn't safe or prudent to share all our feelings with another person. But ignoring our feelings isn't healthy either. We need a way to express our feelings, especially negative ones, without creating damage to our relationships. That's where unmailed letters can be therapeutic. In a letter you can say all the things you would never dare express out loud. You can be as flamboyant and as dramatic as you want. Just don't mail the letter. (And don't leave it behind a picture where someone can find it after you die!)

Have I ever said something in anger I later regretted?

I EXPRESS MY FEELINGS IN NONHARMFUL WAYS.

BLESSED MARIE POUSSEPIN

1653–1744

Blessed Marie Poussepin came from a family of stocking makers. After the death of her father, she revolutionized the family business by not only giving up silk in favor of wool (which was more profitable), but also by introducing the use of a loom in place of knitting needles.

It's hard to tell what her family thought, but her innovations created an economic boom for her village. More than likely she was esteemed for her economic reform as much as for her deep spiritual life.

An unwillingness to try new things is one of the first signs of mental stagnation. You certainly don't have to reject everything from the past, but you also don't need to hold onto old ways so firmly that you leave no room for new ones to take root. After all, if you try something new and it doesn't work, there's no reason you can't go back to the old ways. You'll never know if the new way is better if you don't try.

Blessed Marie Poussepin showed a willingness to accept innovation. As St. Madeleine Sophie Barat once said, "It shows weakness of mind to hold too much to the beaten track through fear of innovations. Times change and to keep up with them, we must modify our methods." Blessed Marie Poussepin obviously would agree.

Do I distrust changes? How willing am I to try new things?

WHEN SOMETHING NEW COMES ALONG, I'M WILLING TO GIVE IT THE BENEFIT OF THE DOUBT.

ST. TERESA OF AVILA

1515–1582

One day St. Teresa of Avila and some of her sisters were attempting to cross a storm-swollen stream in a small cart. Their donkey balked, and St. Teresa ended up drenched to the skin and covered with mud. Looking to heaven, she said, "God, if this is the way you treat your friends, no wonder you have so few of them!"

For St. Teresa, God wasn't a remote, distant entity but an everyday friend. She felt comfortable talking with God about every aspect of her life, including stubborn donkeys. This doesn't mean she wasn't reverent or respectful. St. Teresa is also the author of two of the greatest mystical treatises of all times—"The Interior Castle" and "The Way of Perfection." In addition, she was one of only two woman to be named doctors of the Church for their profound insight and wisdom. (Catherine of Siena is the other.) What St. Teresa knew, and what we all must try to learn, is that God can't be removed from the everyday occurrences of our lives.

God isn't like good china, to be brought out for special occasions and then carefully packed away the rest of the time. When we save our china for special occasions, pretty soon we never use it because no occasion is quite special enough. The same is true of God. If we only talk to God on formal occasions, soon we won't talk with God at all. Instead, we need to bring God into all aspects of our lives, like stoneware used on the table for every meal.

Do I keep God and religion in their Sunday places?

I BELIEVE GOD IS WITH ME AT ALL TIMES AND IN ALL PLACES.

ST. HEDWIG

1174–1243

While many saints gave up all their earthly possessions to seek a heavenly inheritance, St. Hedwig didn't. The wife of King Henry I of Silesia in Poland, she enjoyed being queen. Not only did she help govern the country, she also used her wealth to serve the poor. When Henry died, St. Hedwig lived with a group of nuns, but she didn't surrender her wealth. Instead, she continued to use her fortune as she saw best on behalf of the poor.

Learning to control our finances is an essential part of maturity. When we were children, our parents took care of all the financial arrangements, but as adults, the responsibility becomes ours. All too often, we find ourselves in debt because we confuse our wants with our needs. We begin to believe we can buy happiness, but happiness is only found in relationships—particularly in our relationship with God.

If you are feeling restless and unfulfilled, don't run up your credit cards trying to fill the empty places in your soul. Instead, use your financial resources to take care of your needs and then ask God to help you discover what's missing from your life. It may be friendship. It may be intellectual stimulation. It may be love. Whatever it is, however, two things are certain: first, you won't find it in any mall and second, only after you ask can God help make it a reality in your life.

What do I need to do to make certain I am being fiscally responsible?

I AM RESPONSIBLE IN ALL ASPECTS OF MY LIFE, INCLUDING MY FINANCES.

ST. IGNATIUS OF ANTIOCH

C. A.D. 107

We might not have known much about St. Ignatius of Antioch if he hadn't been literally carted off to Rome. The bishop of Antioch, he was condemned to death by Emperor Trajan. Since famous Christians always drew big crowds in the public games, he was hauled to Rome in a cart. One might think that on his long journey St. Ignatius would have felt sorry for himself or looked for a way to escape, but instead he used the time to defend the beliefs that got him condemned in the first place. As he traveled, he wrote seven letters, which are still in existence, encouraging and exhorting other Christians not to lose their faith despite persecution.

Sometimes when we are in poor health or growing older, we may feel like we are being sent off to die like St. Ignatius. St. Ignatius shows us that even when our bodies are being held by forces outside our control, our minds and spirits can never be enslaved. We can continue to seek spiritual truth, and even when things are bleakest, we can still be serene, knowing God is always with us.

While he undoubtedly would have preferred not to have been eaten by the lions, St. Ignatius was willing to accept his fate graciously, even asking the Christians at Rome not to risk their lives to save his.

Is it difficult for me to be thankful when things are out of my control?

I STRIVE FOR SERENITY IN ALL SITUATIONS.

ST. LUKE

FIRST CENTURY

St. Luke could just as easily be called Dr. Luke since St. Paul refers to him as our beloved physician. The author of the gospel of Luke and the Acts of the Apostles, Luke accompanied Paul on many of his missionary journeys. After Paul was beheaded, Luke disappears from history, although tradition says he died an old man in Boeotia.

In his gospel, Luke always shows interest in the medical details of Jesus's cures. He is the one, for instance, who reports on the cure of Peter's mother-in-law and gives accounts of the paralyzed man who was let down through the roof, the man with the withered hand, and the woman who had been hemorrhaging for twelve years. He even criticizes his own profession when he says the woman who had been bleeding was "incurable at any doctor's hands."

Any good physician will tell you medicine is as much art as it is science. For physicians to be effective, they not only have to know anatomy and diseases, they also have to understand the human heart. The best doctors look at their patients not just as sick bodies, but as hurting people. They treat not only the disease but also the individual.

No matter what our profession, we must never forget that people are more important than business processes or bottom lines. God loves each of us as if we were the only person alive. We, in turn, must strive to love the image of God in every person we encounter.

What qualities do I look for in a medical caretaker?

·⟨⟩·

I GIVE THANKS FOR ALL WHO ARE IN THE MEDICAL
PROFESSION.

ST. ISAAC JOGUES

1607–1646

We sometimes have selective vision when we look at the past. We remember times not necessarily as they were, but as the good old days. We glamorize simpler and more primitive lifestyles and we idealize the people who lived in them. We tend to think people were nobler and more upright than they are today. Some of us even assume that the farther one gets from civilization, the closer one gets to idyllic harmony with all living creatures. But the fact is, no time or place has a copyright on cruelty and barbarism, especially when it comes to harming fellow human beings.

The missionary adventurer St. Isaac Jogues was brutally tortured by the Iroquois Indians. Among other things, several of his fingers were cut, chewed, or burned off. When an epidemic broke out, the indigenous people blamed St. Isaac Jogues. As he entered an Indian longhouse for a supposed peace banquet, they hit him with a tomahawk and beheaded him. Although some might argue that St. Isaac Jogues should not have been attempting to convert the Native Americans from their traditional beliefs, his missionary activity actions did not justify the cruelty he experienced.

When we feel ourselves drawn to a romanticized picture of the past, let us remember the French saying that the more things change, the more they stay the same. The venue might be different, the techniques might have altered, but the inherent capacity for both good and evil inherent in each of us has not changed.

Do I ever think that life was easier in the past?

ㆍ⦅≈≈≈≈≈≈≈≈≈≈≈≈≈≈≈≈≈≈≈≈≈⦆ㆍ

I REALIZE THAT THE CHOICE BETWEEN GOOD AND EVIL IS ALWAYS MINE.

ST. BERTILLA BOSCARDIN

1888–1922

When children are growing up, they are often asked what they want to be when they grow up. One answer that is probably rarely, if ever, given is, a saint.

Do you want to be a saint? Most of us have never seriously considered the question, but St. Bertilla Boscardin did. When she entered the convent, she told the novice master, "I'm a poor thing, a goose. Teach me. I want to become a saint." She never lost sight of her goal, even while working as a nursing sister on the front lines of World War I. While her friends and family said all along she was a saint, she was officially recognized as one in 1961.

St. Bertilla set sainthood as her goal. What's your goal? To paraphrase the song from *South Pacific,* if you don't have a goal, how you gonna have a goal come true?

Without a goal, we're like sailboats with broken masts. We can't hoist a sail even when our lives depend on it, so we flop and flounder in the seas of life, sometimes coming dangerously close to capsizing even in the mildest weather. We have no capacity to weather the storms that will come sooner or later. Having a goal doesn't guarantee success any more than having a mast guarantees a safe voyage, but it does dramatically increase the odds in your favor.

What goals have I accomplished in my life? What do I still want to achieve? What steps am I taking to make those goals a reality?

TODAY I WILL TAKE TIME TO EVALUATE THE GOALS IN MY LIFE, KEEPING THOSE WITH MEANING AND LETTING GO OF THOSE THAT NO LONGER SERVE MY NEEDS.

BLESSED AGNES GALAND

1602–1634

One way to tell the difference between an optimist and a pessimist is to hold up a half-glass of water. To the optimist, the glass is half-full. To the pessimist, it's half-empty.

Blessed Agnes Galand was a French Dominican nun in the seventeenth century. At the time, France was suffering from a definite lack of vocations to the priesthood. Although the situation hardly warranted optimism, Blessed Agnes devoted much time and energy to praying for a priest whom she believed was destined to open seminaries in France. When he was called to Paris, she knew her optimism (and prayer) had been rewarded.

Sometimes we don't get what we want because we expend more energy focusing on the negative than on the positive. If we aren't getting what we want out of life, we have to be honest with ourselves. Are we always expecting the worse? Constantly focusing on the negative is nothing more than a bad habit . . . and bad habits can be broken.

If we wish to restore the optimism that is part of our natural inheritance, we need to banish all negative thinking. When you catch yourself saying the "not" words—I can't, I won't, I haven't, I don't—immediately replace them with the positive—I can, I will, I have, I do!

By nature, am I an optimist or a pessimist?

I AM TEACHING MYSELF TO LOOK ON THE BRIGHT SIDE OF ALL SITUATIONS.

ST. PHILIP OF HERACLEA

A.D. 304

During the Communist domination of Eastern Europe, most churches were boarded up or turned into public state buildings. No religious services were held and for all outward purposes, the faith had died. But when the walls collapsed (literally and figuratively), it was discovered that faith had remained alive and vibrant, even though the places of worship had been destroyed.

When his church doors were sealed during the Roman persecution of the Christians by Emperor Diocletian, St. Philip of Heraclea held his services outside. "Do you imagine that God dwells within walls, and not rather in the hearts of men?" he said.

At times we act like we'd prefer God to dwell within walls. Then instead of springing into our lives when we least expect it, God would be serious and proper; more god-like, so to speak.

If we were assigning job descriptions, we'd give God the big tasks—like keeping gravity in working order and overseeing major events, like war and famine. But God isn't bound by our narrow ideas of what God should be or do. Instead, God is as interested in sparrows and flowers and your sniffles as in cosmic affairs. It's not that God doesn't care about the big things; it's just that all things—big and small—are equally important.

Since we're limited to doing one thing at a time, it's difficult to understand how God can do all things at once, but that's the essential mystery of the divine. If we don't understand, it is because we are not meant to. God is God after all.

Am I ever guilty of thinking I could do a better job of being God than God?

I ACCEPT THE MYSTERY OF GOD.

ST. JOHN CAPISTRANO

1386–1456

Many a saint has converted in prison; St. John Capistrano is one. A lawyer and governor in fifteenth-century Italy, he was captured during a squabble between two provinces and spent a goodly length of time in prison. When he finally got out, he joined the Franciscan Order. For the rest of his life he worked zealously on behalf of both the people he served and his religious order.

An organization in Brussels named after St. John Capistrano has as its motto, Initiative, Organization, Activity. These three words are an accurate description of the life of St. John Capistrano, but they are also a good description of what our lives should be like.

Of the three virtues, perhaps the most difficult is organization. Most of us can get started and most of us can keep busy, but learning to organize can be difficult. Some people have an innate ability to be organized. They know instinctively how to put things back after they use them, to pick up as they go along, and to prioritize their time. Others are not so blessed; the "organizedly-challenged" often spend as much time looking for the necessary tools as they do working on a task.

If you fall into the latter category, you aren't doomed to remain in organizational Hades. If you want to learn to become more orderly, read one of the many good books on the topic or take a class. Of course, you can also ask St. John Capistrano to lend you a hand. Just be ready for a flurry of initiative, organization, and activity.

What parts of my life are the most organized? Which parts are the least organized?

I AM AWARE OF THE NEED FOR ORGANIZATION IN MY LIFE.

ST. ANTHONY MARY CLARET

1807–1870

Do you find yourself with too much to do and not enough time to do it all? One solution is to spend more time in prayer. About now you may be saying, "More time in prayer! I don't have enough time as it is!" The truth is the time you spend in prayer is never lost; it will always be returned to you—and then some. It's the Prayer Principle.

St. Anthony Mary Claret, the founder of the Claretian Order and the archbishop of Cuba, was very busy. He not only wrote more than 140 books, preached more than 25,000 sermons, confirmed more than 100,000 people, he also served as confessor to Queen Isabella II of Spain for eight years. On top of all that, he built a science laboratory, a natural history museum, and schools of music and education. Despite his heavy workload, he is said to have always had his rosary in his hand.

Perhaps St. Anthony Mary Claret learned the prayer principle as a young man in his father's weaving business. He encouraged the workers to pray the rosary and to attend daily Mass. He did not cut their pay during the time they were praying, and soon the shop was prospering.

The prayer principle isn't something you can read about. It's something you've got to experience. The next time you're feeling overwhelmed by all the things you must accomplish, take a few minutes and ask God and the saints for their help. After all, you have very little to lose and everything to gain.

How often do I pray during the day?

I REST SECURE IN THE KNOWLEDGE THAT PRAYER IS NEVER A WASTE OF TIME.

ST. GAUDENTIUS

C. A.D. 410

St. Gaudentius probably could identify with Emily Dickinson's words "Of God we ask one favor, That we may be forgotten. . . ." Educated under the bishop of Brescia, he made a pilgrimage to Jerusalem, partly for spiritual benefit and partly because he hoped to be forgotten at home. He had no such luck, however. When he got back to Brescia, he learned that the bishop had died and that he was chosen as the successor.

Celebrities often complain about loss of privacy being the price of fame, but fame also has other pitfalls. One of most insidious is the belief that fame in and of itself justifies special treatment.

It's understandable why such a belief would arise. Famous people get to go places and do things ordinary folk only dream about. And because wealth often accompanies fame, the famous are often spared the messiness of life. Regardless of whether Marie Antoinette actually said "Let them eat cake" when she was informed the poor had no bread, her comment stands as an example of the blindness often accompanying fame and fortune.

We don't have to be famous to be blind to the less fortunate. Fame only aggravates a natural tendency. Every day we are presented with chances to practice acts of kindness and generosity. And every day, countless acts go undone because we fail to see the need for them. We aren't being selfish on purpose. It's just that we're often so preoccupied with our own desires, we forget to look around and see the needs of others.

What is preventing me from being more generous with my time and resources?

I KNOW THERE ARE NONE SO BLIND AS THOSE WHO WILL NOT SEE.

ST. CEDD

A.D. 664

If St. Cedd had been familiar with lemons when the king of Deira gave him a piece of land for a new monastery, he probably would have figured that's what he'd been given. Located in a remote area of Yorkshire, the land was hardly an ideal spot to start a monastery. But St. Cedd spent forty days in fasting and prayer, consecrating the land—and subsequent monastery—to God. In the end, the lemon became known as the monastery of Laestingaeu.

The lemons of life aren't major crises. They're merely the nasty zingers we all encounter: insurance companies that lose your claim, laundries that ruin your blouse, milk that spoils before the expiration date. The worst thing about lemons is they tempt us to become angry and spiteful—at the wrong person. For instance, we may want to shout at the store clerk, but it isn't her fault the milk is sour. It may be the fault of the processor or the dairy, or perhaps it isn't even anyone's fault. It just is. That's the way with life's lemons. They make us want to blame someone, but there's no one to blame.

The only sane way to deal with lemons is the "saintly" way—consecrate them like St. Cedd consecrated his less-than-desirable land. When we consecrate something we turn it over to God; we let God transform it into something holy. Our ruined blouse isn't suddenly going to be turned into a sacred icon, but God can help us use our frustration and annoyance to grow in patience and peace.

Do I let the little things of life get to me?

WHEN LIFE HANDS ME A LEMON, I MAKE LEMONADE.

BLESSED LOUIS GUANELLA

1842-1915

"God helps those who help themselves" could have been the motto of Blessed Louis Guanella. The founder of the Servants of Charity, who care for the old, the incurable, and the mentally handicapped, he once said, "The Lord ordinarily wants everything here on earth to follow a natural course." For Blessed Louis, the ordinary course involved as much elbow grease as it did prayer. For instance, when he decided to reclaim some swampland, he used some of his mentally handicapped for the labor, with some of the elderly as supervisors. Within a few years, people were building homes in the area and Blessed Louis was honored with a medal from the minister of agriculture.

Although the saints show us miracles can and do happen all the time, we can't just sit back and wait for one. As Blessed Louis says, most of the time God lets things follow their natural course. Expecting God to perform miracles at our beck and call is presumptuous. When we take for granted that God will answer our prayers in the time and manner we decree, we are setting ourselves up for massive disappointment. Far better to heed the advice of Blessed Louis and go to bed every night tired out from honest labor. Then, if a miracle does occur, we will recognize it for the extraordinary blessing it is.

Do I ever decide ahead of time how God should help me? Am I disappointed when it doesn't turn out the way I expect?

·❧━━━━━━━━━━━━━━━━━━━━━❧·

I KNOW WHEN I DO MY PART, GOD WILL ALWAYS BE THERE TO HELP ME.

ST. JUDE

FIRST CENTURY

Sometimes in the personal section of newspapers, you see a notice, "Thank you, St. Jude, for favors received." Who is St. Jude and why are people publicly thanking him?

Jude or Judas was one of Jesus's twelve apostles. He is also called Thaddeus, to distinguish him from the Judas who betrayed Christ. Virtually nothing is known about him except his name, although he has been associated with the Letter of Jude in the New Testament.

The reason he gets notices in the personal columns even today is because he has become known as the saint of impossible or hopeless cases. One tradition says that if St. Jude answers your prayer, you should formally thank him. Since celestial mail service isn't possible, what better way to write a thank you note than in the newspaper?

The practice of writing thank you letters has slowly been eroding until now it is almost the exception rather than the rule. At one time it would have been unthinkable not to send off an immediate note for a wedding or birthday gift. Now, people write to advice columns asking if it's too late to acknowledge wedding gifts as much as five years later!

Writing thank you's is more than just an archaic duty. It's a way of maintaining a level of civility in an often uncivilized world.

While it's fine to verbally express your thanks, taking the time to express your gratitude in writing lets the other person know you care, not just about the gift, but about the giver as well.

How do I feel when I give someone a gift that is never acknowledged?

THE NEXT TIME I AM GIVEN A PRESENT, I WILL MAKE SURE I WRITE A THANK YOU NOTE RIGHT AWAY.

BARTHOLOMEW DE LAS CASAS

1474–1566

It isn't always easy to do the right thing, even when we know what the right thing is.

Bartholomew de Las Casas was a Spanish slave owner on the island of Hispaniola. For many years the idea of owning slaves seemed perfectly reasonable to him. Then he heard a Dominican friar preach against slavery and he began to realize the injustice of the system. He wasn't ready, however, to give up his own slaves. Even after he had a conversion experience and entered the priesthood, he merely turned his slaves over to one of his good friends. Not until almost eight years later, when he entered the Dominican Order, did he finally free his slaves and become one of the great champions of the Indians against their Spanish owners.

How often we are like Bartholomew de Las Casas. We know in our hearts what we should do, but we find it difficult to put our convictions into practice. We stall, hoping maybe the nagging of our conscience will go away if we ignore it long enough. Of course it won't and we end up making ourselves miserable. When we find ourselves in such situations, the saints tell us our best and only recourse is prayer. What we may not have the ability to do on our own, we will be able to do with the strengthening power of prayer.

As St. Teresa of Avila, another holy Spaniard, said, "Even if you are committing mortal sins, keep on praying and I guarantee you that you will reach the harbor of salvation."

Have I ever tried to ignore my conscience? What happened?

I FOLLOW MY BEST INCLINATIONS TO DO GOOD
AND AVOID EVIL.

ST. ALPHONSUS RODRIGUEZ

1533–1617

Sometimes saints, even the saints described in this book, get a little sanitized. Early hagiographies were often quite circumspect, leaving the reader with the impression that the worst temptation any saint ever faced was a momentary flicker, immediately routed by a quick prayer. Certainly any *real* temptations were nonexistent.

Not true. Saints were people before they were saints, and they often struggled with great and grave temptations.

St. Alphonsus Rodriguez went into the family woolen business at age twenty-three. Unfortunately, times were tough and the business failed. Not long afterward, Alphonsus's wife and daughter died. After a number of false starts, he ended up taking his final vows as a lay-brother with the Jesuits when he was fifty-four.

Once he was in the Order, St. Alphonsus was tormented by numerous sexual temptations and erotic dreams haunting him day and night. As if that weren't bad enough, at the end of his life he felt totally worthless, writing, "I am good for nothing. I do nothing for those in the house, nor for those outside, nor for myself."

Sometimes we feel like we are all alone when we struggle with our temptations. We don't dare tell anyone what we are *really* like because then they would know just how worthless we are. When we begin to fall into those self-incriminating patterns, we need to remember St. Alphonsus Rodriguez. Even though he was gravely tempted, his holiness was such that another great saint, St. Peter Claver, carried a notebook filled with St. Alphonsus's advice when he sailed to South America as a missionary.

Do I ever feel worthless?

WHEN I AM SUFFERING TEMPTATIONS OR FEELING SORRY
FOR MYSELF, I REMEMBER EVEN THE SAINTS HAD TO
STRUGGLE.

BLESSED BROTHER MUCIAN OF MALONNE

1841–1917

Do you have a deaf ear? Can't draw a straight line? While you might not be blessed with abundant artistic or musical talent, you can learn to develop whatever modicum of ability you do possess. If you're still feeling doubtful, Blessed Mucian of Malonne may change your mind.

Brother Mucian joined the Christian Brothers, but he was not a natural teacher. In fact, his classroom was so disruptive, the superiors doubted his vocation. A senior brother agreed to let Brother Mucian help in the art and music department. Although he had little natural ability, Brother Mucian was willing to learn. Following orders, he took up the harmonica and a number of other instruments. When he was very elderly, someone noticed he came to the music room every morning promptly at 9 o'clock to practice and asked him why. He replied that fifty years before he had been told to practice every day and he was still following his orders.

This is not one of those amazing stories in which the person discovered his or her true genius and went on to receive international recognition. Brother Mucian never became outstanding at either art or music, but he did become competent enough to teach others and bring joy to his own life.

Exploring the world of art and music may not bring you fame or fortune either. But, as Brother Mucian discovered, learning new, creative skills enriches our lives and makes us more appreciative of the talents of others. And who knows, maybe you will turn out to have more talent than you think.

*If I've always wanted to learn to play a musical instrument,
what's stopping me from trying?*

I AM NOT AFRAID TO LEARN NEW SKILLS.

ALL SAINTS

ALL SAINTS DAY

Today we honor all the saints, known and unknown, famous and not so famous. The saints in this book are just a few of the quite literally thousands of holy men and women who have been honored over the centuries. If your favorite isn't listed, it doesn't mean he or she isn't a saint. Saints are usually honored on the day of their death and perhaps your saint had the misfortune to die on the same day as someone famous, such as Francis of Assisi. Or maybe you've been looking for someone like St. Christopher, who was never formally canonized and whose life is so shrouded in legend that it's difficult to discover any facts about him. In those cases, another saint with more accessible information may have been chosen.

If your favorite isn't in this book, today is the day to celebrate him or her anyway. From as early as the fourth century, "all the martyrs" have been honored collectively. Certainly by the year 800, the feast of All Saints was firmly established as part of the Church year.

Today is a good day to remember all those people—in addition to all the official saints—who have touched your life. Your grandmother. Your parents. A beloved teacher. A good friend. Anyone who has made the love of God a reality in your life.

Right now, why not take a few minutes and give thanks for everyone in heaven whom you love and who loves you. In other words, blessed be all the saints!

Who are the saints in my life?

I WANT TO BE IN THAT COMPANY, WHEN THE SAINTS GO MARCHING IN.

ST. MARCIAN

C. A.D. 387

In *Anna Karenina*, Leo Tolstoy writes, "Happy families are all alike; every unhappy family is unhappy in its own way." Well, all the saints are said to be happy in the family of God, but few of them resemble one another. In fact, the hallmark of the saints might be uniqueness. And some are more unique than others!

St. Marcian was a hermit in the fourth century, when hermits were more popular than they are now. He lived in such a small cell he couldn't stand up straight or lie down flat and primarily ate bread. Despite his oddities, he attracted many followers and, at the end of his life, had to put up with people debating over which chapel he was going to be buried in.

In a day and age when you can drive the entire length of the country and see the same stores in the same malls, eat at the same fast food restaurants and see the same movies, the saints stand as a glorious tribute to uniqueness. No saint ever got to heaven by following the same path as another. Even though the saints often influenced each other (Blessed Jordan of Saxony and Blessed Diana D'Andalo for instance), they always remain vibrantly unique individuals

Sometimes we let ourselves get stuck in a pattern of conformity. We dress, not the way we might like, but the way we think we should. We eat the right foods, read the right books, watch the right TV shows. It may be comfortable to conform, but it's dull, boring, and not the least bit saintly.

Do I let others dictate my behavior?

I HAVE THE COURAGE TO BE THE UNIQUE INDIVIDUAL I WAS CREATED TO BE.

ST. MARTIN DE PORRES

1579 – 1639

St. Martin de Porres was the illegitimate son of a white Spanish nobleman and a freed black Panamanian. His father hated Martin and his sister for resembling their mother and soon abandoned them. At age twelve Martin was apprenticed to a barber-surgeon and learned both how to cut hair and how to administer medical treatment. Although he did not feel worthy, he entered the Dominican Order as a lay brother; nine years later, because of his obvious holiness, he was fully professed.

Of all St. Martin de Porres's remarkable abilities—including being able to cure the sick or injured simply by placing his hands on them—his love and respect for animals is one of the most appealing. He would let the mice and rats carry out their raids unmolested, excusing them on grounds that they were underfed. In a time when animals were not particularly well treated, he opened what amounted to a humane society for cats and dogs at his sister's house. (We aren't sure what his sister thought!)

Many of us share our lives with beloved pets. They enrich us in innumerable ways, yet we must remember when we bring a cat or dog into our homes, we become accountable for it. We have an obligation to see that our pets are well fed and properly housed. If we can no longer provide for them, it is our duty to see they are taken care of since, as Antoine de Saint-Exupéry writes in *The Little Prince*, "You are responsible forever for that which you have tamed."

Have I tamed my pets or have they tamed me?

IF I HAVE A PET, I ACCEPT JOYFULLY THE DUTIES AS WELL AS THE PLEASURES.

ST. CHARLES BORROMEO

1538–1584

With all our responsibilities, how tempting it is to procrastinate. Tomorrow I'll start my diet. Next week I'll write those letters. Next year I'll organize my closet. Yet none of us knows if we'll have a next year or a next week or even a tomorrow. The past is a dream and the future is a vision. All we have is today. The only reality is this moment.

St. Charles Borromeo knew what it was like to have too much to do and not enough time to do it. Not only was he deeply involved in the Council of Trent (he was responsible for the entire correspondence of the council), but he was also bishop of Milan, a diocese in deplorable state, since no bishop had lived there for more than eighty years.

Despite his strenuous workload, he understood the importance of living in the present tense. Once, when he was playing billiards, a friend asked what he would do if he knew he had only fifteen minutes to live. Barely pausing, St. Charles answered, "Go right on playing billiards."

God exists only in the present. If are to meet God, we, too, must learn to live only in the present. Only when we open ourselves fully to the moment at hand can God bless us fully.

In what ways do I cling to the past or fret about the future? What is keeping me from living in the present tense?

I WILL LIVE AS IF TODAY WERE THE ONLY DAY OF MY LIFE.

BLESSED ELIZABETH OF THE TRINITY

1880–1906

Sometimes we think of heaven as being up in the clouds or maybe out there beyond the stars. If we look for heaven in a physical location, we will end up like the Russian cosmonaut who declared he couldn't see heaven from outer space. That's because heaven isn't a location; it is a state of being.

Blessed Elizabeth of the Trinity was a Carmelite nun who spent her day in work and prayer. Upon the orders of her superior, she wrote down some of her thoughts on the nature of God and the Trinity. While many of her reflections fall directly into the category of mysticism, she was not an ephemeral person. She enjoyed life to the fullest (including eating pie) and was characterized by great happiness. Once she said she was so happy in her life work she believed she had found heaven on earth.

When we love what we do then, like Blessed Elizabeth of the Trinity, we too can experience heaven on earth. All too often, we think our work is supposed to be just that—work. We drag ourselves through our days, waiting for the weekends when real life can begin. When we squander five out of every seven days, just think how much of our life we are wasting.

If you don't love what you're doing, maybe it's time to do something else. If immediate change is impossible, then ask God to help you learn to love what you're doing. In either case, there's no point creating a hell for yourself when you could be having a taste of heaven.

On a happiness meter of 1 to 10, where am I right now?

I MAKE UP MY MIND TO BE HAPPY.

BLESSED ALPHONSUS NAVARRETE

A.D. 1617

Ideas seem to come in clusters. Often you'll read how two people came up with the same invention, like the telephone or the airplane, at virtually the same time. It's almost as if an idea has a particular time to be born. Who gets the credit for the invention almost seems to be the luck of the draw.

Spiritual ideas also seem to come in clusters. At about the same time St. Vincent de Paul was rescuing abandoned babies in France, Blessed Alphonsus Navarrete was doing the same thing in Japan. In fact, Blessed Alphonsus is sometimes called the St. Vincent de Paul of Japan for just that reason.

At times we become very protective of our ideas. We guard them, for fear someone else might steal them and use them to make a profit. We want everyone to know when a good idea is ours.

The saints remind us that ideas can't be copyrighted. What we do with our ideas—write a particular book, build a new invention, create a better mousetrap—can be protected, but the idea itself is free for the taking. The universe is filled with good ideas. The more you open yourself to their presence, the more ideas you will have. If you're ever in the situation where someone steals your idea, don't let it bother you. Just trust that another better idea will come to you. It always does.

*Do I realize ideas are like flower bulbs? The more I plant now,
the more blooms I'll have later?*

I DO NOT HOARD MY GOOD IDEAS.

ST. WILLIBRORD

658–739

St. Willibrord wanted to be a missionary to Germany and so, with great high hopes, he set out and successfully built churches and an abbey. St. Willibrord was doing fine in his original location. Then, for whatever reason, he decided he could do even better if he expanded his work into present-day Denmark. There he was a miserable failure. He baptized only thirty boys and while trying to return to his home, ended up landing on an island where one of his companions was murdered. St. Willibrord would have done far better if he had recognized his limits.

Knowing your limits isn't the same as placing limits on yourself. When you know your limits, you evaluate your talents and abilities fairly and set attainable goals. Knowing your limits means you don't get up one morning and decide to run ten miles when you haven't exercised for a month. It means you choose to buy a salad from the deli for the company potluck instead of staying up to the wee hours trying to make something from scratch. It means being reasonable in your expectations.

Placing limits is just the opposite. Instead of seeing what you can do and making a plan to do it in a reasonable manner, placing limits on yourself means you admit you're defeated before you even begin. It means you say you can't before you even try. If we are to lead full, productive lives, we need to know our limits, but we never need to limit ourselves.

Do I ever try to push myself beyond my limits?

⊱⊶⊶⊶⊶⊶⊶⊶⊶⊶⊷⊷⊷⊷⊷⊷⊷⊷⊰

I REALIZE PART OF SPIRITUAL MATURITY IS KNOWING HOW
MUCH I CAN DO . . . AND THEN DOING IT.

ST. GODFREY

A.D. 1115

Few things are more frustrating than knowing you're right, having people admit you're right, and then not do anything about it. St. Godfrey was a French monk and abbot during the twelfth century. Under his highly disciplined leadership, his monastery flourished. Then he was appointed bishop of Amiens and tried to apply the same discipline to the clergy there. He was not a smashing success. In fact, he was met with so much resistance, he was tempted to give up being bishop.

There's an old saying, you can lead a horse to water, but you can't make it drink. The same is true of spiritual matters; you can lead people to the truth, but you can't make them accept it.

When we've found the way to holiness that works for us, we sometimes make the erroneous assumption that it will work for everyone. St. Godfrey found his path to heaven through severe, inflexible discipline. When he tried to force others to use his same techniques, he encountered bitter opposition. It didn't matter that he was right about the need for discipline; what mattered was that he tried to make others do things exactly his way.

In all of life, not just spiritual matters, we have to give people room to make their own decisions. We can explain our position, but we can't force them to accept it, even if they admit we are right.

How do I react when someone says to me, you're right, but . . . ?

I MAKE MY OWN DECISIONS AND I GIVE OTHERS THE
FREEDOM TO DO THE SAME.

ST. BENEN

A.D. 467

St. Benen was the son of an Irish chieftain. When St. Patrick visited Benen's home on his travels, Benen was so impressed he asked to be allowed to accompany the saint as a missionary. He was given permission and became not only St. Patrick's disciple but also his successor. We don't know much about Benen, but we know he was noted for his fine singing voice. One of his nicknames is Patrick's psalmodist.

Singing is a natural activity. Listen to a baby just learning to talk. Along with the babble will be bits and pieces of baby-song. Children just naturally sing. It is only when we become adults and begin to compare our voices with professionals that we decide to keep our mouths closed. Singing is more than just something enjoyable to do while we are here on earth. It is said one who sings prays twice. The saints and the angels spend eternity singing God's praises. We, too, can use our lives to sing God's praises.

If you stopped singing because you don't have the greatest voice or someone once told you you can't carry a tune, it's time to make a change. If you truly believe people will wince if you sing in public, then sing when you are alone. Sing in the shower. Sing in the car. Sing while you are vacuuming. Starting today, make your whole life a song!

What's my favorite song? Can I sing it right now?

I SING THE GOODNESS OF THE LORD.

ST. LEO THE GREAT

400?–461

St. Leo the Great was pope when the Barbarians were preparing to storm the gates of Rome. When Attila the Hun first approached the city, St. Leo persuaded him not to attack but to accept an annual tribute. A few years later, the leader of the Vandals was not so easily dissuaded, but St. Leo managed to get him to agree not to burn the city. Although Rome was pillaged for two weeks, it was left intact. When the Vandals finally retreated, St. Leo began the enormous task of restoration.

You'd have thought St. Leo would have been discouraged when he looked out and saw all the work that had to be done, but the Lives of the Saints say because of his trust in God, he was never discouraged even in the most trying times.

Discouragement is almost always linked to distrust. When we're feeling the most discouraged, it's often because we don't believe God is with us. All we see is the enormity of the situation and our own inability. We *know* we can't do it by ourselves and so we slump into a morass of discouragement. That's exactly the point. We *can't* do it alone. But with God's help, we can do anything.

Jesus's disciples were often discouraged when they heard Jesus talk about what was needed to get to heaven. At one point they were so discouraged, they asked, then who can be saved? Jesus's answer is our answer, too: "With men this is impossible, but with God all things are possible."

Am I feeling discouraged right now? Have I asked God to help me?

WHEN I FEEL DISCOURAGED, I REMEMBER GOD CAN DO THE IMPOSSIBLE EVEN WHEN I CAN'T.

ST. MARTIN OF TOURS

316? – 397

Have you ever made a decision you thought was right at the time and then, when it was too late, second-guessed yourself? If you have, then you know what it's like to keep replaying your mental tapes. The fact that it's too late to make a change just adds to the torment. Where once you felt confident in your discernment, now you are dubious of all your decisions.

If you can identify with that picture, you need to get to know St. Martin of Tours. A soldier in the Roman army stationed in France, he left the army and studied under St. Hilary after he was baptized a Christian. At length he founded a monastery and became well known for his virtue. That's when the problem started.

A bishop by the name of Ithacius was putting heretics to death. St. Martin strenuously objected, saying excommunication was sufficient punishment. When Martin asked the emperor to spare the life of a man accused of heresy, Ithacius accused Martin of the same heresy. Although Martin's life was spared, the other man was executed. Martin then tried to cooperate with Ithacius on other matters but was always deeply troubled by his decision.

When we are in a similar situation, we need to remember hindsight is always 20/20 vision. If we look back and conclude we made the wrong decision, we also need to remember at the time we were deciding we did the best we could with the information we had.

When I make a decision, do I stick to it or do I keep second-guessing myself?

⟨⟨⟨⟨⟨⟨⟨⟨⟨⟨⟨⟨⟨⟨⟨⟨⟨⟨⟨⟨⟨⟨⟨⟨⟨⟨⟩

I KNOW I NEVER MAKE WRONG DECISIONS ON PURPOSE.

ST. JOSAPHAT

1580? – 1623

St. Josaphat has the distinction of being the first person in the Eastern rite churches to be officially canonized by the Vatican.

The archbishop of Polotsk in the seventeenth century, St. Josaphat faithfully followed the rituals and traditions of the Byzantine Rite but also remained loyal to the pope. Many people think the Roman Catholic Church is the only Catholic church, but in fact, nine rites exist in the Catholic Church, Roman being only one of them. The others are Byzantine, Armenian, Chaldean, Coptic, Ethiopian, Malabar, Maronite, and Syrian.

Rites (meaning sacred rituals and traditions) are deeply influenced by the culture and tradition in which they developed. The Eastern rite churches with their icons, for instance, are quite different in appearance from Roman rite churches with their statues. Many customs, such as the marriage of priests, the date for Easter, and others, vary from rite to rite. Nevertheless, all the rites share the same foundation based on the teaching of Jesus Christ. Only the outward appearance, not the inward expression differs.

More often than we would like to admit, we are inclined to make judgments based on outward appearance. We judge people by their clothes, their accents, their cars, their neighborhoods, and their jobs rather than by their hearts. When we do so, we not only do them a disservice, but we do ourselves one as well, for, as the Bible says, "For in the way you judge, you will be judged; and by your standard of measure, it will be measured to you." (Matthew 7:1)

How does it make me feel to think others judge me with the same standards I use to judge them?

I DO MY BEST TO LOOK BEYOND EXTERNALS WHEN MAKING DECISIONS AND JUDGMENTS.

ST. FRANCIS XAVIER CABRINI

1850–1917

In her best-selling book, *Feel the Fear and Do It Anyway*, author Susan J. Jeffers advises just that: doing what you have to do despite your feelings of apprehension. An athletic shoe company's slogan puts it more succinctly: Just Do It!

St. Francis Xavier Cabrini, the first American to be canonized, learned to just do it. For her, "it" was dealing with her fear of water. As a young girl she had fallen in a river and for the rest of her life she lived in terror of drowning, yet, because her work as foundress of the Missionary Sisters of the Sacred Heart required it, she crossed the ocean thirty times! She eventually died, not from drowning, but from malaria.

Sometimes we just have to do it—it being whatever we fear the most. It doesn't matter if our knees have turned to Jell-O or our heart is running a marathon, we just have to do it.

What "it" are you facing at the moment? You've probably already tried going around and over and under your fear. Now all that's left is going through with it. So take a deep breath . . . and do it!

Once you do, you'll probably discover that "it" wasn't nearly as bad as you thought it was going to be. More often than not, our apprehension and fear is much worse than the actual occurrence. When we plunge into our fears, we may never totally overcome them, but in confronting them, they will never totally overcome us either.

What do I fear the most?

WHEN I'M AFRAID, I ACKNOWLEDGE MY FEAR BUT DON'T LET MY FEARS PARALYZE ME.

ST. LAURENCE O'TOOLE

1128–1180

If St. Laurence O'Toole were better known, his life would make a good historical movie. As a ten-year-old boy he was taken hostage by one of his father's rivals. After two harsh years of captivity, he was turned over to the bishop of Glendalough. At age twenty-five, he was named the abbot of Glendalough and things were relatively peaceful for several years. (If his life were a movie, here's where the unrequited love interest would be inserted.) Then things heated up when a deposed Irish chieftain asked King Henry II of England to help him regain his lands. Roll the massive battle scenes, with St. Laurence rallying the troops and defending the castle against a barrage of archers. Fast forward through the next part of his life, since it consists mostly of negotiating treaties. Finally, St. Laurence would get a great death scene. On the way back to Ireland from France, where he had been detained by King Henry, he was taken ill. His last words were spoken as his beloved monastery came in view.

Just for fun, imagine your life is going to be made into a movie. Mentally film all your important events—giving yourself a starring role, of course. When you reach the present, imagine how you would like your movie to end. Give yourself the perfect "rest of the story." Once you've decided how you'd like your life to be, don't just stop there. Do all you can to make your imaginary perfect ending a reality.

If your life so far were filmed, would it be a comedy, a drama, or something in between?

I KNOW I CAN ALWAYS MAKE THE BEST OF MY FUTURE.

ST. ALBERT THE GREAT

1206–1280

Usually called Albert Magnus ("great" in Latin), St. Albert was one of the greatest teachers, thinkers, and scientists of the Middle Ages. Incidentally, Thomas Aquinas, no slouch in the mental department himself, was one of his students at the Dominican house of studies in Cologne.

Albert's interests were varied and he wrote on innumerable subjects, including botany, astronomy, chemistry, physics, biology, geography, meteorology, economics, politics, logic, mathematics, theology, Scripture, and philosophy.

If Albert had lived today, he undoubtedly would not have been able to explore as many subjects—not only because the amount of knowledge in each has increased exponentially, but also because we are increasingly encouraged to specialize. In medicine, for instance, the higher paid positions go to the specialists, not the general practitioners.

Having specialized knowledge is often necessary in today's society, but having *only* specialized knowledge is extremely limiting. Think of learning as though it were a can of salted nuts. You can pick out all your favorites, like the cashews, or you can just pour out a handful and take what comes. Today, why not pour out a handful of knowledge? Go to the library and grab a book off the shelf on a topic you know nothing about. Maybe Renaissance art. Or Creole cooking. Or auto mechanics. Or falconry (St. Albert the Great used to hunt with falcons). It doesn't much matter what the topic is so long as you know nothing about it. The point here isn't to further your knowledge of familiar subjects, but to break out of old patterns and to explore something totally different.

When was the last time I learned something totally new?

·⟨⟨⟨⟨⟨⟩⟩⟩⟩⟩·

I ALLOW MYSELF THE LIFELONG JOY OF LEARNING.

ST. GERTRUDE

1256–1301

St. Gertrude lived in the famous monastery of Helfta from the time she was a child. Creative and poetic by nature, her most famous mystical writing is *The Messenger of Divine Loving-Kindness.* St. Gertrude was a bit of a Medieval feminist. She adapted the writing of Scripture to fit her female audience, referring, for instance, to the prodigal daughter instead of the prodigal son.

The words we use have a great impact on the way we think. While some people take language sensitivity to an extreme—refusing to use the word "person" because it contains the masculine word "son" for instance—we all can be careful our words do not become isolative. It wouldn't have made much sense for St. Gertrude to talk about a prodigal son when the only people present were women.

Our image of God is also framed by the words we use. A missionary working among the disadvantaged inner-city poor couldn't understand why the children responded negatively when she described their loving Father in heaven. Finally, someone told her the children's image of a father was someone who did drugs and beat them. They couldn't identify with the concept of a loving father. Only after the missionary began speaking of God without using specific pronouns did the children begin to respond.

If it helps you to create a more loving image of God to use the traditional masculine pronouns then, by all means, use them. But if referring to God in male-only terms isn't helpful, then remember, God is neither masculine nor feminine. God is simply God.

What do I see when I picture God?

I KNOW I AM CREATED IN THE IMAGE OF GOD.

ST. ELIZABETH OF HUNGARY

1207–1231

Many of the saints—both male and female—seem hardly to have been able to wait until their spouses died so they could get on with entering monasteries, founding religious orders, and doing saintly things.

St. Elizabeth of Hungary was not one of them. She was madly, passionately in love with her husband, Louis IV, the Landgrave of Thuringia. She would hold his hand at night while he slept, and when he died in the Crusades she screamed and raved for days throughout the castle.

There is no one way to be a saint. Many, like Francis of Assisi, espoused radical poverty and isolation as the surest road to heaven. Others, like St. Elizabeth of Hungary, took a different approach. Instead of renouncing all the good things of the world, they reformed them. St. Elizabeth, for instance, was always depleting the castle stores to give alms to the poor, but her husband, who loved her as much as she loved him, never seemed to mind.

While it may be intriguing to read about saints who took their sanctity to extremes, most of us aren't interested in leaving everything and heading off to a monastery. Besides, there aren't many monasteries to join anymore. For most of us, holiness comes from living out our lives with the kind of lust for life that St. Elizabeth of Hungary exhibited. We will find sanctity, not amid sackcloth and ashes, but in the loving embrace of our spouse and the kisses of our children.

Do I ever get the idea that holy is just another word for boring?

·⟨⟨⟨⟩⟩⟩·

I REJOICE IN LIFE, LOVE, AND GOOD TIMES!

ST. ROSE PHILIPPINE DUCHESNE

1769–1852

For much of her life, St. Rose Philippine Duchesne wanted to be a missionary, most specifically a missionary working with Native Americans. Not until she was forty-nine was she able to leave her native France for America, and not until she was seventy-two was she allowed to establish a school for Native American girls in Kansas.

In a world of instant gratification, St. Rose Philippine Duchesne stands as a witness to the power of persistence. By age seventy-two, she might have given up hope of ever being allowed to go to the Native American missions. After all, she was well past the age of retirement, but, as the saying goes, where there's life, there's hope, and St. Rose never gave up hope. She never gave up looking for opportunities, either. She was ready when the chance came, and even though she was recalled after only a year in the mission school, she was ready to return, if the opportunity arose. To a friend she wrote, "I live in solitude and am able to employ all my time in going over the past . . . but I cannot put away the thought of the Indians, and in my ambition I fly to the Rockies."

Similarly, if we hold long-cherished dreams, we must never stop hoping they will come true but rather always be looking for the opportunity to make them a reality.

If I could have one wish, what would it be?
(No fair wishing for three more wishes!)

I WAIT EXPECTANTLY, WITH THE HOPE MY DREAMS WILL COME TRUE.

ST. MARGARET OF SCOTLAND

1046?–1093

They say opposites attract, and if that's the case, St. Margaret of Scotland and her husband King Malcolm III must have been very attracted to each other. Margaret was refined, cultured, and educated. Malcolm was rough, coarse, and uncouth. In almost fairy-tale fashion, they met when Margaret's ship wrecked off the coast of Scotland. The fell in love and lived pretty nearly happily ever after. Margaret helped Malcolm rule the kingdom and, in return, he helped her found several churches. Their eight children turned out just fine. One daughter married Henry I of England and became known as Good Queen Maud; their youngest son, David, became a saint.

Only the last four days of their life together were marred by tragedy. Malcolm and his son Edward were killed in a surprise attack on the castle and Margaret, who had not been well anyway, died four days later.

When we read the unexpurgated lives of the saints, most of them are pretty grim. After all, the surest way to get canonized is to be martyred, and martyrdom by its nature is grim. St. Margaret of Scotland shows us that it isn't always necessary to suffer to be a saint. Although her own life was rather austere, especially for a queen, she brought art, education, and culture not just to Malcolm, but to all of Scotland. Her steadfast good nature reformed her husband, and he remained passionately in love with her until the end.

When we feel like we just don't have what it takes to suffer our way to sainthood, let us remember St. Margaret of Scotland, who loved her way to heaven.

What is more in keeping with my nature—suffering or celebration?

I AM IN LOVE WITH LIFE.

ST. EDMUND THE MARTYR

841?–870

St. Edmund the Martyr was king of Norfolk and Suffolk in the ninth century. The records of his life are scanty. We know only that he fought against the Danish invaders in the winter of 870 and was killed when the Danes won the battle. More apocryphal stories say he was tied to a tree and shot with arrows when he refused to accept a treaty detrimental to his people and his faith.

Many of the stories of the early saints read more like novels than biographies. Part of the reason is that it's only been since the advent of photography and, more importantly, the invention of television (with their "you are here" qualities) that an emphasis has been placed on so-called objective reporting. Prior to that, accounts of distant events were crafted more into adventures than news accounts. With no one standing around with a video-recorder, it was much easier to remember glorious victories and noble defeats than it is today.

But technology hasn't totally driven out our natural tendency to turn events into stories. Now we can manipulate photographs and tapes to reflect a reality that never was. We can put movie characters into newsreel footage and enhance photographs via computer so someone looks entirely different.

Maybe the real lesson in all this is that sometimes looks can be deceiving. When you see something that's just too good to be true, it probably is.

Am I inclined to accept things on face value? Would I say I have a tendency to be gullible?

I DON'T BELIEVE EVERYTHING I SEE OR HEAR.

ST. ALBERT OF LOUVAIN

1166-1192

A number of saints started out life as soldiers and ended up becoming religious. St. Albert of Louvain took a different tack. He entered religious life at age twelve, but when he was twenty-one he became a knight. His foray into the military didn't last long, however, and he soon returned to work for the church.

Sometimes we get a notion to try something new and nothing will do but to give it a shot. As long as it isn't going to endanger our physical or spiritual well being, why not go for it!

Maybe you've always wanted red hair or perhaps you've longed to learn to skydive. What's stopping you?

Maybe you're afraid of others' disapproval. Undoubtedly St. Albert's fellow clerics were less than keen on his idea of joining a company of soldiers, but that didn't stop him.

Maybe you're afraid you'll make a mistake. It didn't take St. Albert long to figure out he wasn't meant for a soldier's life, but he never would have known if he hadn't tried.

Maybe you don't know where to begin. St. Albert approached a man who had been one of his family's most bitter enemies and asked to join his entourage. The man agreed and St. Albert got his wish.

St. Albert probably had all the same concerns you have, but his desire to try military life overrode his reluctance. It turned out he didn't like his new venture, but ultimately that didn't matter. What did matter was he tried.

So what's stopping you from trying?

Is there something I've secretly always wanted to do? Is there some serious reason I can't try it?

WHEN I FEEL RESTLESS, I PAY ATTENTION TO WHERE MY SPIRIT WANTS TO GO.

ST. CECILIA

SECOND CENTURY

St. Cecilia is one of those saints who have been honored since the beginning of the church but of whom nothing concrete is known. Her legends are charming but totally unreliable. For instance, she is said to have been given in marriage to a non-Christian by the name of Valerian. She told her husband she was guarded by an angel and if he would consent to be baptized, he could see the angel, too. Valerian was and did, immediately becoming as ardent a Christian as was his wife.

Perhaps because she listened to the voices of angels, St. Cecilia is honored as the patron of music, musicians, and poetry.

Poetry is one of those things we often feel guilty about not liking. While most people would freely profess to loving poetry, you don't see many books of poetry on the best-seller list. And unless you frequent the company of love-struck college students, you probably won't hear much poetry quoted in everyday life.

If you haven't read any poetry since you had to when you were in school, maybe it's time to pick it up again. As William Wordsworth wrote, "Poetry is the breath and finer spirit of all knowledge; it is the impassioned expression which is in the countenance of all Science." If you remember liking one poet even a little bit, go back and read some of his or her works. If you don't have a clue where to begin, you might consider asking St. Cecilia to help you. Who knows, you may discover you're a poet . . . and didn't know it!

Some prayers are almost poetry. Have I ever tried praying
a poem?

I GIVE THANKS FOR ALL THE ARTS, INCLUDING MUSIC
AND POETRY.

BLESSED MIGUEL PRO

1891–1927

Blessed Miguel Pro is one of the most contemporary martyrs for the faith. Born in Guadalupe, Mexico, he led the normal life of the son of a middle-class Mexican family. He tormented his sisters, fell in love, and played endless practical jokes. When he was twenty, he applied to the Jesuits, and after his ordination in Belgium, returned to Mexico at a time when any priest in that country could be arrested and prosecuted. Through his wit and skill, he managed to evade capture for nearly a year, but he was betrayed by a young boy and executed by firing squad for the crime of being a priest. He asked for only two things: to spend a few minutes in prayer and to die with arms outstretched in the form of a cross. As the shots rang out, he cried, "Viva Cristo Rey!" (Long live Christ the King!) His sister, who had obtained a stay of execution, was not allowed into the courtyard until it was too late.

Because his executioners believed that his death would prove the cowardice of Catholic priests, many reporters and photographers were present. Thus we have a complete photographic record not of Blessed Miguel's cowardice, but of his bravery. If a picture is worth a thousand words, then the pictures taken at the time of Blessed Miguel's death are worth tens of thousands of words in behalf of his unshakable courage.

May Blessed Miguel and all who have died for their faith give us the courage to live for ours.

What would I be willing to die for?

MAY I ALWAYS REMEMBER RELIGIOUS FREEDOM IS OFTEN PAID FOR IN THE BLOOD OF MARTYRS.

ST. ANDREW DUNG-LAC AND COMPANIONS

1820–1862

When you look up into the night sky, you see clusters of stars. The saints come in clusters as well. One such saint cluster consists of the 117 Vietnamese martyrs canonized in 1988. At least three waves of persecution occurred in Vietnam between 1820 and 1862, when a treaty with France gave religious freedom to Catholics. Of the 117 martyrs, 96 were Vietnamese, 11 were Spanish, 10 were French. Fifty nine were lay Catholics and 58 were clerics. St. Andrew Dung-Luc, whose name is listed first on the feast day, was a parish priest.

One of the most exciting things about the saints is that they come from every continent (except Antarctica). Moreover, they come from every walk of life—from servants to royalty. And they come from every nationality. Every personality type is represented and every possible type of personality. In short, the saints are a complete cross section of humanity.

Despite their enormous differences, the saints do have certain common characteristics. The first is their overriding love of God. They are first and foremost in love with the divine. Second, the saints are constantly telling us not to be afraid. As long as God is for us, who can be against us, they say over and over. Finally, the saints encourage us to become the unique individuals we were created to be. None of them are alike and neither should we try to be anyone but ourselves.

What lessons have I learned from the saints?

·⟨━━━━━━━━━━━━━━━━━━⟩·

I ALLOW MYSELF TO ENJOY THE COMPANY OF THE SAINTS.

POPE JOHN XXIII

1881 – 1963

On the first anniversary of his election as pope, Pope John XXIII mentioned that a man of seventy-eight doesn't have much of a future. John XXIII not only had a good deal of future left, he would also alter the entire face of the Catholic Church through the Second Vatican Council. More importantly, Pope John XXIII brought a spirit of hope and optimism to the entire world.

At the opening session of the council, Pope John spoke words that should continue to comfort and challenge us today:

"In these modern times, they can see nothing but prevarication and ruin. They say that our era, in comparison with past eras, is getting worse. And they behave as though they learned nothing from history, which is nonetheless the teacher of life . . . We feel that we must disagree with those prophets of doom, who are always forecasting disaster as though the end of the world were at hand . . . In the present order of things, Divine Providence is leading us to a new order of human relations."

Angelo Giuseppe Roncalli, the man who would be pope, came from humble peasant stock. Even when elevated to the highest office of the church, he took great delight in his family and friends. For him, faith was not something to be experienced on a theological level; it was something to be lived and celebrated.

When he convened Vatican II, he said he wanted to bring a "gust of fresh air" into the church. He did more. He brought a "gust of fresh air" into the entire world.

Am I ready to be swept away on a gust of fresh air?

I DO NOT LET PROPHETS OF DOOM DEPRESS ME.

ST. SILVESTER GOZZOLINI

1177–1267

Some people can really hold a grudge. St. Silvester Gozzolini's father must have been one of them. It's said he stopped speaking to his son for ten years when Silvester gave up studying law for theology. Apparently they restored the lines of communication, but ten years is a long time for the silent treatment.

Have you ever been the victim of the silent treatment? Has someone you care about refused to talk to you because of some real or imagined slight? Or perhaps you've been the perpetrator, refusing to talk to someone who has angered you by their words or actions.

Slamming the door shut on lines of communication may feel satisfactory for a moment, but like any door left unused, the hinges will grow rusty, the lock will stick, and the key will get lost. Then, when you want to start using the door again, it will be almost impossible to pry it open.

If you and someone you care about are on opposite sides of a stuck door, what better time than today to open the door? You may feel it's their responsibility to make the first move—and it may be— but take the initiative anyway. If you don't feel you can make contact in person, write a letter. You don't have to apologize or rehash old events. Just say you've missed them and would like to start over. Even if they don't respond, you will have the satisfaction of knowing that you've oiled the hinges from your side of the door.

What can I do to make amends with someone I've hurt or who has hurt me?

✦ I DO NOT LET DISAGREEMENTS RUIN MY RELATIONSHIPS.

ST. VIRGIL

A.D. 784

Ever know someone who got a little weird all of a sudden? Maybe he or she adopted a special diet and could talk only about rice cakes and tofu, or perhaps they became enamored of mountain climbing. Whatever it was, the obsession took over the person for a little while.

That apparently happened to St. Virgil. The administrator of the diocese of Salzburg, he did the usual clerical things. Then, all of sudden, he seems to have become obsessed with the idea that there is another world beneath this one, with people and a sun and a moon. Needless to say, St. Boniface, the archbishop of Mainz, was not thrilled and denounced him to the pope. Virgil apparently was tried and gave up his adventure in creative thinking sometime before he was named bishop of Salzburg in 767.

Maybe it's time for you to get a little weird. No, you don't have to start believing in subterranean worlds or espousing the virtues of tofu, but perhaps it's time to do something to shake up your complacency. Most of us are very good at being ourselves; at least at being the self we are expected to be. But what about the self that isn't being expressed? The child who still loves to tromp in mud puddles and swing upside down.

Now is a good time to let that child come out to play. Wear a new color and style of clothing. Take up a new hobby. Find something expressing a side of your personality you have never expressed before. Have a little fun!

Is there some aspect of my personality I keep hidden? Why am I afraid to express it?

TODAY I WILL DO THE UNEXPECTED.

ST. CATHERINE LABOURÉ

1806–1876

I'm Nobody! Who are you?
Are you—Nobody—too?
Then there's a pair of us!
Don't tell! they'd advertise—you know!

—Emily Dickinson

St. Catherine Labouré avoided publicity as much as Emily Dickinson did. She spent her entire adult life doing the most humble jobs, working in a hospice for old men, seeing to their physical and spiritual needs. She also tended the chickens and was responsible for answering the convent door. Yet she was privileged to have had a vision of Our Lady—one of the first people in the modern age to do so.

In late November 1830, St. Catherine saw the Virgin standing on a globe with the words "O Mary conceived without sin, pray for us who have recourse to thee." When the image turned around she saw an *M* with a cross and the hearts of Mary and Jesus. St. Catherine understood she was to have medals made of the model. Soon after the first medals were struck and distributed, they became known as the "Miraculous Medal." Today millions of people wear the medal St. Catherine first saw in her vision.

During her lifetime, when someone would suggest perhaps she was "the sister of the apparitions," she would just laugh. It was not until after her death that the world learned this humble sister was one of the great saints in heaven. Appearances can be deceiving. The next great saint may be living next door or working in the office beside you. For that reason, we must strive to treat all we meet as if they might someday be ranked among the highest in heaven.

Do I ever judge by appearances?

I RECOGNIZE THE INHERENT GOODNESS IN EVERY PERSON.

ST. RADBOD

A.D. 918

Even though a great many of the saints in this book were priests or nuns, priests and nuns don't have an edge on sainthood—but priests and nuns generally have religious communities that are able to promote their cause and keep to the necessary records for canonization.

St. Radbod is one of those saints who probably wouldn't have become a saint if he hadn't been a priest and bishop. Not that he didn't live a good and holy life, but he led a rather boring one. To be honest, the most interesting thing about St. Radbod is his great-grandfather, who said he would rather be in hell with his relatives than in heaven without them.

Without a religious community ready to vouch for his sanctity, St. Radbod probably would have slipped obscurely into heaven. As it is, he's now part of the official calendar of saints.

It's only human nature for us to like some people better than others, and the same is true of the saints. Of the 365 holy individuals in this book, perhaps you'll find one or two who really appeal to you. As you read about their lives, you get the feeling that you would really like to know more about this person. If that happens, take it as a personal invitation from the saint to be your special friend. Begin to talk to that saint and ask for his or her wisdom and insight. Ask the saint to pray for and with you. Let the saint share his or her love with you.

What saint would I like to get to know personally?

⋅⟨⸺⸺⸺⸺⸺⟩⋅

I CHOOSE ONE SAINT (OR LET ONE SAINT CHOOSE ME!) TO BE MY
SPECIAL FRIEND AND COMPANION ON THE ROAD TO HEAVEN.

ST. ANDREW

FIRST CENTURY

Many interesting books have been written on birth order. First-borns, for instance, are take-charge individuals who like to be in control. Because they are used to bossing their siblings, they tend to be bossy in other situations as well. Because last-borns are the babies of the family, they tend to be more dependent and can often be spoiled. Middle-children often have to fight to find their role in the family. Overshadowed by their older siblings and not as cute as their younger ones, they have a more difficult time carving out their own unique niche.

St. Andrew must have been a middle child. Although he was one of the first of Jesus's twelve apostles, he is almost always overshadowed by his more famous older brother—St. Peter.

Peter and Andrew could not have been more different. Peter was impetuous and excitable, ready to walk on water if Jesus asked him to. Andrew was more quiet and reserved; a typical middle child.

Despite his more restrained nature, Andrew is one of the most important figures in the gospel. First of all, he introduces Peter and Jesus. Second, he's the one who brought the boy with the loaves and fishes to Jesus. Finally, when the Gentiles wanted to see Jesus, they came first to Andrew.

Andrew's lesson for us is simple. It doesn't matter what your birth order; you still have your own, essential role to play in the drama of life.

Where do you fall in your family's birth order?

I WILL CELEBRATE MY PLACE IN MY FAMILY.

ST. EDMUND CAMPION

1540–1581

Phyllis McGinley called St. Edmund Campion "the most dashing holy man who ever played hounds and hare with fate." A Jesuit priest during the persecution of Catholics by Protestants in sixteenth-century England, he evaded capture through a series of daring escapes, disguises, and just plain luck. He was betrayed after saying a secret Mass at which a traitor was present. Tried on falsified charges of treason, he was sentenced to be hanged. Like St. Thomas More, St. Edmund Campion died professing his commitment to the crown but his greater commitment to his God.

Commitment is a word that's often bandied about in this world of disposable values. If a relationship doesn't work out, we look for someone else. If a job isn't to our liking, we turn in our resignation. While we certainly aren't obliged to stay in relationships or situations that are physically, emotionally, or spiritually destructive, we may sometimes be guilty of bailing out prematurely. We leave as soon as things get a little bit rough, rather than sticking with them to the end.

Of course, being committed to something or someone has its dangers. No one would have blamed St. Edmund if he had hopped the first boat to safety. But he was committed to serving the Catholic church and its members who were forced underground. It was his sense of commitment that kept him in England when it would have been much safer almost anywhere else. And it was his sense of commitment that got him executed.

When I think of commitment, do I think only of relationships?
What other kinds of commitments have I made in my life?

WHEN I MAKE A COMMITMENT, I STICK WITH IT.

VENERABLE CHARLES DE FOUCAULD

1858–1916

Are you in a desert place in your life right now? Does everything appear bleak and barren, with nothing but endless sand dunes stretching into your future?

As you mature spiritually, you discover the deserts of life are an essential part of growth. Often much of our best soul work occurs during our desert times. All the great saints have experienced deserts—symbolic and literal; some have even deliberately sought them out.

Venerable Charles de Foucauld, better known as Little Brother Charles of Jesus, spent the last ten years of his life dwelling as a hermit in the Algerian desert. As a young man, he had lived a fast and free life, telling each of his new mistresses, "I rent by the day, not by the month." At the end of his life he was able to pray, "By force of events, you made me chaste. . . . Chastity became a blessing and inner necessity to me." The desert became the fire in which Venerable Charles hardened the steel of his resolve and discipline.

We also need our desert experiences to harden our resolve. We need the desert because only when we are stripped of everything that we think will bring meaning to our lives are we able to find the One who brings true meaning.

Do I need to carve out some desert time in my life so I can be alone with my questions and God's answers?

I WELCOME THE DESERTS IN MY LIFE AS A TIME TO REEVALUATE AND GROW.

ST. FRANCIS XAVIER

1506–1552

Many a cruise has been ruined by seasickness, but can you imagine being seasick for five months? That's how long St. Francis Xavier was seasick as he made the voyage from Spain to India to begin his missionary career.

In the pantheon of saints, St. Francis Xavier is certainly one of the best known. With St. Ignatius of Loyola and six other men, he helped found the Jesuit Order. After his ordination, he spent the rest of his life preaching and teaching in India, Malaysia, and Japan. His dream was to go to China, but he died on an island about a half-dozen miles off the coast. Ironically, he had tried to take refuge on a Portuguese sailing vessel, but once again he became seasick. He came ashore and died in a fisherman's hut.

Often we may not be seasick but we can become *seesick*. We can become so sick of seeing all the pain and misery in the world that we put on mental blinders. We decide what we don't know won't hurt us, so we stop looking around. We pretend the problems of homelessness and injustice aren't really as bad as everyone says they are. When we choose not to recognize misery, however, we are in danger of not just being *seesick*, but of becoming blind to the opportunities we have to make the world a better place. There is, after all, none so blind as those who will not see.

When I find something difficult to accept, do I ever turn a blind eye?

˙⟨⟨⟨⟨⟨⟨⟨⟨⟨⟨⟨⟨⟨⟨⟨⟨⟨⟨⟨⟨⟩⟩⟩⟩⟩⟩⟩⟩⟩⟩⟩⟩⟩⟩⟩⟩⟩⟩⟩⟩⟨⟩˙

I CHOOSE SEEING LIFE OVER BEING BLIND TO OTHERS'
MISERY.

ST. JOHN DAMASCENE

A.D. 749

The story is told of a woman who had two children, one by birth, the other by adoption. When she was asked which was which, she replied with a gentle smile, I don't remember.

St. John Damascene was the son of the chief of the revenue department in the city of Damascus. His father had him tutored in the sciences and theology by an Italian monk. At the same time, the father also had his adopted son, Cosmas, taught by the same monk. Apparently, St. John's father treated both his natural son and his adopted son alike, for the two brothers became good friends. Together they entered a monastery near Jerusalem, where they wrote books and composed hymns. Cosmas, who also became a saint, was appointed bishop of Majuma, but St. John lived the rest of his life at the monastery.

Through adoption, we become a permanent part of a family. Each of us, whether we were raised by birth parents or not, has been adopted into the family of God. As children of the same God, we are shown no partiality. God loves each of us as much as if we were the only child in the family. Sometimes it's hard for us to imagine how God could love the people we dislike, but that is part of the divine mystery. We are selective in our affection, but God is indiscriminate in love.

Am I ever afraid to love?

⚬⟨⟩⚬

¶ RECOGNIZE THAT WE ARE ALL PART OF THE SAME
FAMILY OF GOD.

ST. SABAS

439–532

Much of our world is flooded with noise pollution. In the classic Dr. Seuss story *The Grinch Who Stole Christmas*, the Grinch hated the Whos for all of their celebration, but the one thing he hated the most was "the NOISE! NOISE! NOISE! NOISE!"

For most of us, our days (and our nights) are filled with noise. Silence is something we rarely, if ever, experience. While becoming a noise-hating Grinch shouldn't be our goal, we all need some silence for our souls.

St. Sabas loved silence. Perhaps he treasured it so much because he had so little of it as a child. His father and mother left him in the care of an aunt and uncle when he was very young. The aunt was so cruel, he ran away to another uncle when he was eight. This uncle and the first one then got into a series of lawsuits and discord over who should have the money from the Sabas's estates. The friction (and noise!) was so upsetting to St. Sabas, he ran away again to a monastery, where he could finally find the peace and quiet he wanted.

Sometime soon, find a quiet place where you can let the quiet rush over your being like a healing balm—a place where, along with Robert Browning, you can allow "Silent silver lights and darks undreamed of. . . . hush and bless [you] with silence."

Does silence make me nervous? When I come into an empty house, do I immediately turn on the TV or the radio?

⸱ ⸨▰▰▰▰▰▰▰▰▰▰▰▰▰▰⸩ ⸱

IN THE MIDST OF THE NOISE OF MY LIFE, I WILL FIND A TIME AND PLACE TO BE ALONE AND BE QUIET.

ST. NICHOLAS

A.D. 350?

Years ago, on the popular television show *To Tell the Truth*, celebrities would try to figure out which of three candidates was telling the truth about his or her occupation. At the end of the show, the host would ask, Would the real [fill in the blank] please stand up?

If Santa Claus were on the show, St. Nicholas would have to stand up.

St. Nicholas of Bari, the bishop of Myra in the fourth century, is the *real* Santa Claus. Exactly how a kindly cleric from present-day Turkey got associated with an overgrown, red-suited elf from the North Pole is hard to figure.

The real Santa Claus was well known for his kindness and generosity, especially to the poor. One legend says he tossed bags of gold in the open window of a poor man's house to help with his daughters' dowries. The gold is supposed to have landed in stockings dangling on the corners of the beds, which would account for the custom of hanging stockings for Santa Claus to fill. At any rate, St. Nicholas was linked with gift giving, and, in many countries, children still put out their shoes on his feast day to be filled with presents.

Santa Claus has become a symbol for the Christmas holidays, but Santa is a commercial contrivance. St. Nicholas, the real Santa, is just that—real. As we move into the holiday season with its excitement and bustle, let us take a few minutes to remember that love and joy won't magically appear unless, like the real Santa did, we make them happen.

How can I be a St. Nicholas to someone needy this Christmas season?

· ⟨⟨⟨⟨⟨⟨⟨⟨⟨⟨⟨⟨⟨⟨⟨⟨⟨⟨⟨⟨⟨⟩⟩⟩⟩⟩⟩⟩⟩⟩⟩⟩⟩⟩⟩⟩⟩⟩⟩⟩⟩⟩⟩ · ·

I LET MYSELF BE FILLED WITH THE JOYS OF
THE HOLIDAY SEASON.

ST. AMBROSE

340?–397

St. Ambrose is recognized as a doctor of the church for his teaching, but he is also remembered as the man who converted St. Augustine. Among his other abilities, he possessed a talent for using the ideas of the great philosophers, such as Cicero, to support Christian truth. Afraid of no one, he even took on the emperor. When Emperor Theodosius wiped out an entire town for the murder of some royal officers, Ambrose made him do public penance.

St. Ambrose obviously had two sides to his personality: the public Ambrose, who would do battle with anyone, including the emperor, and the private Ambrose, who could quietly and calmly convince a skeptic like St. Augustine.

We too often have a public and a private side to our personality. However, unlike Ambrose, who seemed to have shown his best side to his closest acquaintances and his harshest to strangers, we sometimes demonstrate our best qualities in public and our worst at home. We've all read about public figures who were much loved by their fans but who exercised all manner of vice and even cruelty to their families.

As we grow and develop spiritually, let us strive to integrate the various aspects of our personalities into one, cohesive whole—with the emphasis on the good parts, of course! We can begin by treating those who are the closest to us with the same courtesy we use with strangers.

Do I reserve my best behavior for the outside world? Am I ever rude or harsh with those I am supposed to love the most?

I WILL BE AS POLITE IN PRIVATE AS I AM IN PUBLIC.

ST. ROMARIC

A.D. 653

When St. Romaric's father lost all of his property (and his life) at the hands of Queen Brunehilda, Romaric became a homeless wanderer. Eventually, though, he turned his fortunes around and became a wealthy landowner with many slaves. Then one day he met St. Amatus and decided to willingly renounce what had previously been taken forcibly from him. He gave up his property, freed his slaves, and entered religious life.

In a sermon the night before he was assassinated, Dr. Martin Luther King, Jr., said that if he could choose to live in any time of history, he would visit all the momentous periods, including the day when Abraham Lincoln signed the Emancipation Proclamation, but he wouldn't stop at any of them. Instead, Dr. King said, he would select the second half of the twentieth century, despite the horrendous problems plaguing humanity. He would choose that time period, he said, because it is only when it is darkest out that you can see the stars.

St. Romaric undoubtedly saw only darkness when he lost his home and property. But in that darkness, he was able to see a star, a star leading him not only to a restored fortune, but eventually to spiritual renewal as well. Likewise, when our futures seem the darkest, that is precisely the moment we need to look up and see the stars. If your life seems particularly dark right now, have you checked to see if there is a star rising on the horizon?

When I am stressed or fearful, what do I do? Where do I focus
my attention: on the problem or on the solution?

I KEEP WATCH FOR THE FIRST STAR OF NIGHT.

BLESSED JUAN DIEGO

1474–1548

A poor Aztec Indian who lived near Mexico City, Juan Diego was fifty-seven years old when the Virgin Mary appeared to him. When the local bishop would not believe his story, Our Lady told Juan to climb to the top of a hill and gather the roses growing there. Despite the fact that it was winter, Juan did as he was told and collected the flowers. When he opened his cloak to show the roses to the bishop, a life-size image of Mary also appeared. Juan Diego's cloak with the picture of Mary still hangs in the Basilica of Our Lady of Guadalupe.

When Our Lady spoke to Juan Diego, she told him, "Do not let anything bother you, and do not be afraid of any illness, pain or accident."

We all worry about illness, pain, and accidents, but the message of the saints throughout the ages has always been, "Don't worry." From Julian of Norwich's prayer "All will be well and all will be well and all manner of thing will be well" to Mother Teresa of Calcutta's total trust in God's provision ("Where there is great love, there are always great miracles"), the saints tell us that despite outward appearances, we have nothing to fear.

Fear and worry nibble the edges of our peace, destroying our confidence and composure. Only when we replace them with the trust that all is unfolding according to divine plan will we be able to experience the serenity we are meant to have. As Jesus himself said, "Do not let your hearts be troubled. Trust in God and trust in me."

Am I ever afraid to trust God?

I BELIEVE. GOD, HELP MY UNBELIEF.

ST. GREGORY III

A.D. 741

St. Gregory III was elected pope by popular acclamation when the people carried him off from the funeral procession of his predecessor. As pope he had to deal with a rather nasty controversy over the use of sacred images in churches, but once that settled down, so did Pope Gregory. During the period of peace following the brouhaha about icons, he wrote a letter to the English tribes consisting mainly of quotations from the Bible; it was, as one writer put it, "not very meaningful to its heathen recipients."

Has someone ever offered to help you but ended up giving help that wasn't very meaningful? Perhaps they actually made more work for you?

We all want to be helpful, but sometimes the best help we can give is to stay out of the way. St. Gregory wrote his letter to help St. Boniface, who was working as a missionary in England. St. Boniface was doing fine in his work, and it's not inconceivable that the letter did more harm than good. At any rate, it wasn't helpful. Had St. Gregory asked St. Boniface what he really needed, a letter consisting of biblical quotations probably would not have been high on the list.

When someone asks us what they can do to help, we need to tell them. We can't assume they will figure it out on their own. Although we often may hang back for fear of appearing bossy, we actually do everyone a kindness when we speak up. We don't waste our time receiving useless help and we don't waste the time of the helper either.

When I want to help, do I make sure my help is really helpful?

⸱⟨⟨⟨⟨⟨⟨⟨⟨⟨⟨⟨⟨⟨⟨⟨⟨⟨⟨⟨⟨⟨⟨⟨⟨⟨⟨⟨⟩⟩⟨⟩⸱

1 EXPLAIN THE KIND OF HELP 1 NEED.

ST. DAMASUS I

305?–384

Digging in the dirt hasn't been the same since Indiana Jones went searching for the lost Ark of the Covenant in the movie *Raiders of the Lost Ark*. Actor Harrison Ford gave archaeology—and archaeologists—a definite boost in popularity. While the profession might want to adopt Indy as its patron saint, archaeology already has a patron—St. Damasus I.

Pope St. Damasus may be best known for commissioning St. Jerome to work on his famous translation of the Bible, but he also is remembered for the care he took in restoring the catacombs and caring for the relics of the early martyrs. For doing the latter he was named patron of archaeologists.

While archaeologists explore our common past, we can all become archaeologists of our own individual pasts. We can uncover those events and people that have shaped our lives and see how they continue to influence us today.

Digging into your own past doesn't have to mean intense psychotherapy and problem solving. If the past is too painful, then let it stay buried. If and when the right time to excavate arrives, you'll know it. An easier kind of personal archaeology means learning where your ancestors came from, what your parents were like as children, and how certain family customs developed. Find out the story behind the painting in your aunt's dining room. Look through old family pictures and try to find resemblances. Make a genealogy chart and see how many different countries your family members have come from. Have fun uncovering your own life.

What is the funniest story I know about my family?

MY LIFE MAY NOT BE PERFECT, BUT IT'S MY LIFE AND I
CELEBRATE IT JUST THE SAME.

ST. JANE FRANCES DE CHANTAL

1572–1641

One of the great friendships between saints is that of St. Jane Frances de Chantal and St. Francis de Sales. After her husband died, Jane and her six children moved in with her father-in-law, a difficult and tyrannical old man. During this stressful period, she met St. Francis de Sales, who became her spiritual director and close friend. Eventually, he and Jane founded a religious community of women: the Sisters of the Visitation of Holy Mary.

At one point, Jane was consulting Francis about the possibilities of such an endeavor. Looking at her fine jewelry, he asked if she was contemplating remarriage. When she vehemently assured him she was not, he suggested, "Why not lower the flag then?"

Our closest friends can sometimes say things to us no one else can. That's because, as Alexander Pope says, "In every friend we lose a part of ourselves, and the best part." Making a close friend is a little bit like falling in love. There's an almost mystical quality to the process that transcends explanation.

When you meet someone who is destined to be an important part of your life you just *know*. It's as if the name of that person has been written on your heart from all eternity and you've just now been able to decipher it. St. Francis de Sales felt that way about St. Jane. "It seems to be that God has given me to you," he wrote to her. "I am assured of this more keenly as each hour passes." Would we all could find such a friend!

Who are my closest friends? Who is my best friend?

·⟨≈≈≈≈≈≈≈≈≈≈≈≈≈≈≈≈≈≈≈≈≈≈≈≈⟩·

I TREASURE MY FRIENDS.

ST. LUCY

A.D. 304

Have you taken your Vitamin See today? No, not your Vitamin C, your *Vitamin See*. Just as we all need Vitamin C to stay well and healthy, we also need a daily dose of Vitamin See.

What is Vitamin See? Vitamin See is the ability to view things, not just with our earthly eyes, but with heavenly insight. Vitamin See is the capability of looking beyond the mundane and ordinary to see the divine light infusing all of us every day.

Because her name means light, St. Lucy is the patron of those with eye trouble, but she could be the patron of Vitamin See as well. Determined to remain a virgin, St. Lucy refused marriage. Her suitor had her banished to a brothel, but even there she remained steadfast. Finally, tradition tells us she was tortured and stabbed to death.

If St. Lucy hadn't had her eyes fixed on heaven by virtue of Vitamin See, she would certainly have chosen the easier route of marriage. But Lucy was willing to risk all, even death, because she could see beyond the present to the eternal.

Often we get so caught up in the hustle and bustle of life we forget that we, too, should have our eyes focused on heaven. That's when we need a dose of Vitamin See.

But Vitamin See can't be purchased in any store. We have to manufacture it for ourselves through spiritual reading, prayer, and quiet times alone with God.

Have you had your dose of Vitamin See today?

WITH THE HELP OF THE SAINTS, I EXPAND MY VIEW TO SEE
BEYOND MYSELF AND MY PROBLEMS.

ST. JOHN OF THE CROSS

1541?–1591

A good friend of St. Teresa of Avila and, with her, a reformer of the Carmelite Order, St. John of the Cross was misunderstood and mistreated throughout his life. Even the consolation of God was denied him for long periods, and his struggles with scrupulosity and spiritual emptiness are recorded in his great work, *The Dark Night of the Soul.* While he was unfairly imprisoned for nine months in a tiny cell where the only light came from a window so high up he had to stand on a stool to read, St. John came to understand that the things imprisoning us are not always obvious. "A bird can be held by a chain or by a thread, still it cannot fly," he wrote.

When we are bound by major chains, like addiction or an unhappy relationship, we recognize them for what they are. But what about the threads of selfishness or disinterest? The thin cords of boredom and pride? The irony in the threads imprisoning us is we often don't realize how effective they are at holding us earthbound. Because they are light and slight, we believe we can break them any time we want. But, of course, we don't, and they hold us as firmly as if they were made of forged steel. Today, let us ask for the wisdom to see the threads imprisoning us and the courage to cut them so we can be free to fly.

Do I ignore the threads holding me back just because they aren't as painful as chains would be?

⟨ ⟩

1 SEVER WHATEVER KEEPS ME FROM FINDING GOD,
WHETHER IT IS A CHAIN OR A THREAD.

ST. MARY DI ROSA

1813–1855

St. Mary di Rosa was endowed with more than her fair share of common sense. While many saints seem to have had their heads so far in the heavens they tripped over their own feet, St. Mary di Rosa was eminently practical. When the abandoned girls she was working with didn't have a place to sleep at night, she found them one. When nurses were needed on the battlefields, she sent her sisters out with bandages. When a horse bolted and threatened to overturn its carriage, St. Mary rescued the occupants.

When St. Mary saw something to be done, she did it.

All too often, when we face problems, our first reaction is to sit back and study the situation. If you've ever served on a committee, you know that's what committees inevitably do. While the committee is thinking about the overall problem, smaller sub-committees are often formed. The upshot, of course, is nothing ever gets done.

While it isn't a good idea to race off half-cocked, neither does it do any good to sit around and wait for someone else to come up with the answer. Often the solution is obvious. We just have to implement it. If St. Mary had waited for a committee to decide what to do about the need for nurses on the battlefield, hundreds would have died. Instead, she saw what had to be done and did it. Such is the virtue of common sense.

When I see something to be done, do I roll up my sleeves
and do it?

I USE MY COMMON SENSE.

ST. ADELAIDE

931–999

Many a joke has been made about mother-in-laws. Undoubtedly, St. Adelaide was the brunt of more than one of her daughter-in-law's jabs. To put it bluntly, her daughter-in-law Theophano hated her. She managed to turn her husband, Emperor Otto II, against his mother and to drive Adelaide from the royal court. When Otto died, Theophano took over as regent for their son and made certain that Adelaide wasn't welcome.

Despite the harsh treatment, St. Adelaide apparently was so forgiving she was able to overcome her enemies and detractors. In fact, before his death, Otto reconciled with his mother and begged for her forgiveness. St. Adelaide didn't just forgive; she was also able to forget past injustices.

Often when someone has hurt us, we forgive them but we cling to the memory. We forgive, but we never forget. Forgetting past wrongs isn't the same thing as not remembering them. If we don't remember the past, we are doomed to repeat it. But forgetting the past means we no longer hold it against the person. We no longer extract our little bits of revenge by reminding them of their past mistakes.

Forgiving and forgetting means we let go of our hurts so their memory no longer has any power over us. When we cling too tightly to painful memories, we have no room to build new memories. We forget, in order to make room for love.

When I forgive someone, do I forgive and forget,
or do I just forgive?

WHEN SOMEONE MISTREATS OR INSULTS ME, I FORGIVE
THEM, EVEN IF THEY DON'T ASK ME TO.

BLESSED HYACINTH CORMIER

1832–1916

Blessed Hyacinth Cormier dedicated his entire life to two main principles: prayer and study. To that end, he built the new college of the Angelicum for the Curia in 1909. Pope John Paul II, who beatified Blessed Hyacinth in late 1994, is a former theological student of the Angelicum.

Blessed Hyacinth was an exemplary religious, but he almost didn't make it. When he expressed a desire to become a Dominican, he was told he had "no vocation; or an immature one." Fortunately he wasn't dissuaded by the rash judgment and persisted in his desire.

We don't realize what a profound effect our cutting remarks can have on others. We may say we are just being honest or funny when, in fact, our words are intended to sting and wound. If we're candid with ourselves, we will realize that using the coverup of honesty or humor is still a cover up.

Apparently the priest who made the remark about his vocation to Blessed Hyacinth thought he had a legitimate criticism. Even when we believe we have a legitimate criticism, we can still choose our words with care. For instance, when we have to correct someone, we can soften the impact by beginning with a few words of praise before launching into our complaint. It's much easier for someone to accept a correction beginning, "I really appreciate the way you started this. However, I think we could improve it if we . . ." rather than "This is terrible. Do it over." If we must criticize, let us do it as if we were the one on the receiving end.

Am I critical by nature?

·⟨⟨⟨⟨⟨⟨⟨⟨⟨⟨⟨⟨⟨⟨⟨⟨⟨⟨⟨⟨⟨⟨⟨⟨⟨⟩⟩⟩·

1 DO NOT LET CONSTRUCTIVE CRITICISM BECOME JUST PLAIN CRITICISM.

ST. FLANNAN

A.D. 642?

St. Flannan was a Celtic bishop in the seventh century. Although he was of royal descent, he dreaded becoming king and is said to have prayed for a deformity that would prevent him from ascending the throne. According to the stories, his face immediately became covered with scars and rashes and boils. While the deformity could have been the miracle St. Flannan asked for, it sounds more like a severe case of acne. If he had lived today, undoubtedly the court physician would have prescribed antibiotics and acne cream and St. Flannan would have had to face the possibility of becoming king. St. Flannan managed to luck his way out of his responsibilities, but not all of us are as fortunate.

Facing up to our responsibilities is an important part of being an adult. If we are to become spiritually and emotionally mature, we must recognize that we have to become adults.

Being an adult isn't the same as being a grown-up. We're all called to be adults, to take responsibility for our actions and our decisions. We have to become adults, but we don't have to become grown-ups. Grown-ups don't just take life seriously; they are serious. Grown-ups are so wrapped up in the important business of life they have forgotten how to have fun. The saints may agree it's time for you to become an adult, but they guarantee you never have to be a grown-up.

Do I know the difference between taking things seriously and being serious?

·⟨҉⟩·

EVEN WHEN I GROW UP, I'M NEVER GOING TO BE A
GROWN-UP.

ST. ANASTASIUS I

A.D. 401

When you apply for a job, often you are asked for the names of references. While you could write down your mother and best friend, it's a lot more useful if you know someone in your profession who could give you a recommendation.

If St. Anastasius had needed references to become pope, he could have listed some great names as references. Among his friends were St. Jerome and St. Augustine, as well as St. Paulinus of Nola. St. Jerome said he was "a distinguished man, of blameless life and apostolic solicitude." Having friends in important places never hurts. Even if we don't know any movers and shakers here on earth, all of us can have friends in high places—the saints.

The saints are ready and willing to be our friends. Because they are already in heaven, they have clearer insight than we do into what is best for each of us. When we ask them for their help and friendship, they are always there for us. When you make friends among the saints, you get to know kings and queens as well as housewives and laborers. You can spend time with some of the greatest minds the world has ever known, as well as with some of the greatest eccentrics. You can be friends with people you would never have a chance to meet here on earth.

John Keats wrote, "Wherein lies happiness? In that which becks/Our ready minds to fellowship divine,/A fellowship with essence." When we become friends with the saints, we indeed take part in a fellowship divine.

Has my concept of sainthood changed as I've read this book?

I WILL LEARN MORE ABOUT MY FAVORITE SAINT.

ST. ANASTASIA

A.D. 304

As is the case with so many of the early martyrs, we know virtually nothing about St. Anastasia except that she died for her faith. She was tortured and burned alive in the year 304. Numerous legends, however, have surrounded the rather spartan details of her life. She is said to have been miraculously rescued not once, but twice, by St. Theodota. The most amazing rescue supposedly happened when Anastasia was put on a ship and abandoned at sea. St. Theodota appeared on board and piloted it to safety. (Apparently, one isn't supposed to question where St. Theodota, a reformed prostitute who was stoned to death, got her sailing experience.) Not only that, all the non-Christians on board were supposedly converted by the experience.

When we hear about miraculous events, we are often inclined to be skeptical. After all, many so-called miracles do turn out to be frauds. But miracles happen to each of us every day. We just don't always recognize them. Your heart, pumping millions of gallons of blood over the course of your lifetime, is a miracle. The sunrise is a miracle. A birdsong is a miracle. You are a miracle.

Today, as you go through your usual activities, begin to look for miracles. You'll soon discover it's a little like learning a new word. After you learn a word for the first time, it seems like it suddenly crops up everywhere. The same is true of miracles. Once you look for them, they'll appear everywhere. You just need to start looking!

What would it take to make me believe in miracles?

I WILL OPEN MY EYES TO THE MIRACLES SURROUNDING ME
EVERY DAY.

ST. PETER CANISIUS

1521–1597

If St. Peter Canisius ever gets named as a patron saint, he should be the patron of the overworked. Born in Holland, he got his master of arts degree at age nineteen and never slowed down until his death, nearly sixty years later. A preacher and teacher (he became a Jesuit priest after his graduation), he founded colleges, did missionary work, cared for the sick, and wrote—incessantly. His letters alone fill eight volumes! When someone (undoubtedly exhausted from just watching him) asked him how he coped with his work load, St. Peter replied, "If you have too much to do, with God's help you will find time to do it all."

St. Peter was right. God does help us when we ask for help. The problem is we often fail to recognize the help when it comes. The story is told of a man who prayed to be rescued from a flood. A rowboat, a powerboat, and a helicopter all came by and offered him a ride, but he said he was waiting for God. When he drowned and entered heaven, he asked God why he wasn't rescued. God replied, I sent a rowboat, a powerboat, and a helicopter. What more were you waiting for? When we ask God for help, we can trust it will always arrive; we just have to be on the lookout for the form it will take.

Do I ever make more work for myself? Do I take on tasks I don't need to because they make me feel needed or necessary?

·⟨⟩·

WHEN I FEEL OVERWORKED, I WILL ASK GOD TO HELP ME
FIND A WAY TO GET IT ALL DONE. (AND I'LL BE SURE
TO LOOK FOR THE ANSWER!)

ST. IRMINA

A.D. 710

The story of St. Irmina seems to have come directly from a fairy tale book. A princess, she was set to marry a count. One of her retainers, who was in love with her, somehow managed to get the unlucky groom to stand near a cliff, where he promptly pushed him over the side. The unhappy suitor then jumped himself. St. Irmina, understandably distraught by this turn of events in the midst of her wedding preparations, seems to have entered a convent her father founded for her. The only other thing we know about her is that she was a great supporter of the missionary St. Willibrord.

St. Irmina's life didn't turn out anything like she expected. While some people can hitch their life wagons to a precise star from childhood on, others of us sort of meander. We start out thinking we want to be one thing and then end up doing something quite different. If you look back over the important crossroads in your life, the places where, in the words of Robert Frost, "two roads diverged in a yellow wood," you will discover that if you hadn't chosen the road you did, you wouldn't have the blessings you have now. Of course, no life is without difficulties, and the road you have chosen undoubtedly has its share of rocks, but along with the rocks are the blessings. We can't have one without the other, no matter how hard we might try.

How can I make the most of the road I have chosen?

I AM THANKFUL FOR THE CHOICES I'VE MADE AND THE BLESSINGS I'VE RECEIVED BECAUSE OF THOSE CHOICES.

ST. MARIE MARGUERITE D'YOUVILLE

1701–1771

Are you familiar with the old saying, they who laugh last, laugh best? Although some saints were definitely lacking in humor and wouldn't be anyone you'd like seated next to you at a dinner party, St. Marie Marguerite d'Youville understood that a sense of humor is often the best mediator in difficult situations.

St. Marie had more than her share of difficulties. Her husband, Francis d'Youville, was a French Canadian trader who spent most of his time gambling and trying to cheat the Native Americans. When he died, St. Marie had to sell everything she owned to pay his debts. Totally destitute, she opened a sewing shop to support herself and her children. Gradually she attracted other women who helped her with her charitable works, which included caring for the poor and sick.

Because she was the wife of Francis d'Youville, who was well known as a ne'er-do-well. St. Marie was often distrusted. She and her group were blamed for the drunks who hung around their house and were derisively called the tipsy Sisters. With a great show of good humor, St. Marie had the sisters dress in gray habits and call themselves the "Gray Nuns" because of a play on words between the French word for "tipsy" and the word for "gray." If you find it difficult to see the humor in a situation, ask St. Marie Marguerite d'Youville for help. After all, in the end it was St. Marie who not only had the last laugh, but the best one!

Do I take myself so seriously that I can't appreciate a joke at my own expense?

I WILL BE THE FIRST TO LAUGH AT MY OWN MISTAKES.

ST. CHARBEL MAKHLOUF

1828–1898

One of St. Charbel Makhlouf's favorite sayings was, pray without ceasing. Since he was a monk, he was able to spend long hours in the chapel doing just that. But St. Charbel isn't the only saint to make that recommendation. St. Paul says the same thing in his letter to the church at Thessalonia, "Rejoice always; pray without ceasing; in everything, give thanks."

Who has time to pray without ceasing? There are meals to be prepared and work to be done and families to be tended to. If any of us suddenly announced we were going to spend the rest of our lives in church praying, we probably would receive an icy reception, to say the least. But that's precisely what we are called to do. The difference is that we aren't called to pray without ceasing *in church*. We are called to turn our entire lives into a prayer.

Praying isn't kneeling down, saying words; it's lifting our hearts, minds, and activities to God and letting God's love turn them into something holy. Thus, everything from scrubbing toilets to running off memos can be a prayer.

Unceasing prayer is closely linked with gratitude. Giving thanks opens your life to overflowing blessings. When you are grateful for everything, even the bad things, you acknowledge the fact that good always triumphs. Even those things which seem to be horrendous may contain lessons we need to learn or opportunities to grow in holiness. When we give thanks for them—even before they happen—we help make them become a reality in our lives.

What difficulties of my past life can I look back on and be grateful for?

I MAKE MY LIFE INTO A PRAYER OF THANKSGIVING.

JESUS CHRIST

When Tinkerbell is dying in the play *Peter Pan*, the audience is asked to clap if it believes in fairies. The implication is clear: if the audience doesn't clap, Tinker Bell will die. Of course, the audience always comes through, and Tink always goes on to do whatever it is fairies do.

At times we act as if Tinkerbell and God are alike. With our rather egocentric points of view, we behave as if God *needs* us. God doesn't need us. We need God, but God doesn't need us. Even if the entire universe stopped believing, God would still exist. That doesn't mean we aren't important to God. God loves us—and love is a good deal more valuable than need.

It's amazing that God, who created everything, loves each of us as individuals. God loves us so much, as Christians have believed for nearly two thousand years, God sent Jesus to live among us, to teach us and to put a human face on God's love.

Even those who do not accept Jesus Christ as God-made-man agree he is the most influential person ever to have lived. Most of the facts of his life are uneventful; the effects of his life are overwhelming. Jesus's message is simple to state but often takes a lifetime to comprehend: Love the Lord your God with your whole heart, your whole mind and your whole soul and love your neighbor as yourself. The saints in this book dedicated their lives to living out those principles. They ask each of us to do the same.

Am I living a life of love?

WHEN I CHOOSE LOVE, I CHOOSE ALL.

ST. VICENTA LOPEZ

1847–1890

Ralph Waldo Emerson wrote, "Some of your hurts you have cured, and the sharpest you have survived, but what torments of grief you've endured from evils that never arrived."

Undoubtedly St. Vicenta Lopez would have concurred whole-heartedly with Emerson. In a letter to her mother, she wrote, "Come and stay with us, and your ills will certainly mend. Imagination plays a large part in them, and here there are so many distractions that you will have no time to think."

St. Vicenta's advice to her mother is good for us as well. When we are busy we have no time to worry and fret over evils that may well never arrive. Worry is one of the most insidious of all bad habits. When we worry, we *feel* like we are quite busy; after all we are *worrying!* But worry is a sham activity. It drains our energy, destroys our hope, and leaves us with empty hands and aching hearts. When you are feeling worried, you have two choices. First, if there's something you can do about your worry, then do it. If for instance, you're worried your snow tires are getting bald, have them checked. Don't just stew and fret wondering if they are getting worn. Second, if there's nothing you can do—say your college-age son is driving home over mountain passes—then say a prayer, give your worry over to God and find, as St. Vicenta recommends, something practical to distract your mind.

Am I a worrier? Has my worry ever solved anything?

IF I AM A WORRIER, STARTING TODAY I WILL BEGIN TO
REPLACE MY WORRY WITH TRUST THAT GOD IS TAKING
CARE OF ME AND THOSE I LOVE.

ST. JOHN THE EVANGELIST

FIRST CENTURY

While we might not admit it out loud, most of us put our friends in echelons. We all have an inner circle of our closest friends. These are the people we love and who love us no matter what we do, or what we fail to do. In the most real sense, these are the friends who own a part of our hearts, now and forever.

In the next level are our close friends, people we care about but with whom we don't have quite the same level of intimacy. Finally, most of have a third circle of friendly acquaintances, people we enjoy being with but who aren't an essential part of our lives.

When Jesus lived on earth he was no different than the rest of us in this respect. While he had great love for everyone, he also had his closest, dearest friends. St. John the Evangelist was one.

John was a fisherman working alongside his brother, James, and father, Zebedee, when he met Jesus. From then on, he seldom left Jesus's side. At all the important events—the raising of Jairus's daughter from the dead, the Transfiguration, the Agony in the Garden—John was there. Finally, when Jesus died on the cross, he asked John to take care of his mother, Mary.

Having different degrees of friendship is part of human nature. We can't be equally close to everyone, but in order to be fully human, we must be close to someone. If you've never told your best friends how important they are to you, why not do so today?

How do I classify my friends?

I LET MY CLOSE FRIENDS KNOW HOW MUCH I LOVE THEM.

ST. ANTHONY OF LÉRINS

C. A.D. 520

St. Anthony of Lérins is one of many early saints who followed a rather predictable pattern. They entered monasteries, became well known for their virtue, and finally ended their lives by living as hermits. Like most other hermits, St. Anthony prayed and studied, but he also loved his garden.

Dorothy Gurney wrote, "One is nearer God's heart in a garden than anywhere else on earth." Most gardeners would agree. Even though this time of year the weather is bleak and the ground frozen, gardeners are active. Pouring over their seed catalogs, they order starts to be delivered in the spring and look forward to the days when they can once again feel the soil beneath their shovels.

Not all of us have the time or the inclination to be gardeners, but we can all appreciate gardens. Is there a public garden or park near your home? Next year, make it a habit to visit it regularly to rejoice in the ever-changing, never-ending cycle of life. Watch the bare bones of the bushes and trees fill with the mouse-ear-sized leaves of spring, the full bloom of summer, and the vivid colors of fall. Then, finally, give thanks as winter once again folds its hands over the garden.

What season is taking root in my soul right now? What season would I like it to be in my heart's garden?

EVEN IN WINTER, I CARRY THE PROMISE OF SPRING.

ST. THOMAS BECKET

1118–1170

St. Thomas Becket was the archbishop of Canterbury during the reign of King Henry II. Once the king's great friend, his life and death have been immortalized in T. S. Eliot's *Murder in the Cathedral*. It was, indeed, in the cathedral where St. Thomas died, the victim of King Henry's rage. When Thomas defied the king's wishes regarding the coronation of his son, Henry swore, "Who will free me from this troublesome priest?" Four knights took the request literally and murdered St. Thomas as he was praying. For his part in the murder, King Henry performed public penance after St. Thomas's canonization.

St. Thomas Becket was a man of regular habits. Rising early to read the Scriptures, he worked until early afternoon, when he regularly took a nap. Resting in the afternoon isn't a sign of sloth; it's often the best thing you can do. A brief catnap can refresh and restore you so you can think more clearly and work more efficiently. All too often, we ignore our bodies' signals. When our brain is sending the message, let me rest! we ignore it and give it just what it doesn't want—a jolt of caffeine. Then we wonder why we become jittery and crabby.

St. Thomas Becket paid attention to his physical needs. He got up early, but he also rested in the afternoon. We need to do the same. After all, when you burn the candle at both ends, you're likely to end up with singed fingers.

What do I do to restore my spirits when I'm fatigued?

I LISTEN TO MY BODY'S MESSAGES.

ST. EGWIN

A.D. 717

Sometimes too much of a good thing can be, well, too much. Eating a whole box of chocolates, for instance, would be too much of a good thing. On occasion, enthusiasm and zeal can also be too overwhelming. St. Egwin, the bishop of Worcester in the eighth century, was so earnest about stamping out vice that some of his parishioners complained to the pope. In order to answer the charges, St. Egwin was forced to make a pilgrimage to Rome. It's not certain exactly what transpired at the Vatican, but when he got back, St Egwin does not seem to have returned to ordinary pastoral work. Instead, he founded a monastery.

Many of the saints were extremely strict with themselves, but most exercised moderation when dealing with others. St. Egwin is the exception. Apparently he was consistently strict with everyone!

Consistency is a valuable trait . . . to a point. While being indecisive and wishy-washy won't get you anywhere, being consistent to the point of rigidity isn't helpful either. If you're the kind of person who knows what's right and expects everyone else to get with the program, maybe you should take a lesson from St. Egwin. He ended up with what certainly seems to have been a papal reprimand.

Learning when to hold fast and when to let go isn't easy, but it's one of those lessons we can learn either the easy way or the hard way. St. Egwin chose the hard way. Which one will you choose?

Do I ever claim to be consistent when I'm just being plain stubborn?

1 UNDERSTAND THE DIFFERENCE BETWEEN BEING CONSISTENT IN DIFFICULTIES AND BEING CONSISTENTLY DIFFICULT.

ST. SYLVESTER I

A.D. 335

Today is a day of endings. The end of a month. The end of the year. The end of this book. Endings are always tinged with sadness, but as the saints so often remind us, things are seldom what they appear to be.

St. Sylvester I was the first person to be honored as a saint who was not a martyr. In one sense, his canonization marked the end of the era of early martyrs, but in another it marked the beginning of the broader company of saints—the celestial company each one of us has a chance to join. Likewise, today may appear to be an ending, but it's also a beginning, the beginning of the rest of your life.

The lessons of the saints are many and varied. From fun-loving St. Philip Neri to dreary St. Jerome, the saints come in every possible variation. Some were serious; others fun-loving. Some gave up all worldly goods; others lived more ordinary lives. The only thing they had in common was their incredible, overwhelming love of God.

We are all called to be saints. We can spread our spiritual wings and fly, no matter how earthbound our feet seem to be. We are born, not to be part of the ending, but part of the beginning—the beginning of a new and eternal life.

Today and all the days of your life may you walk in the glory of God and may you always travel in the company of the saints!

Am I ready to soar with the saints?

I GIVE THANKS TO GOD FOR ALL THE SAINTS I HAVE
KNOWN AND HAVE STILL TO MEET.

INDEX

Brigid of Ireland, February 1
Brother André, January 6
Brother Mucian of Malonne,
    October 31
Bruno, July 18

Casimir, March 4
Catherine of Bologna, May 9
Catherine Labouré, November 28
Catherine of Genoa, September 15
Catherine dei Ricci, February 13
Catherine of Siena, April 29
Cecilia, November 22
Ceclia Caesarini, June 8
Cedd, October 26
Ceslaus of Poland, July 17
Charbel Makhlouf, December 24
Charles Borromeo, November 4
Charles de Foucauld, December 2
Charles Lwanga and Companions,
    June 3
Christina the Astonishing, July 24
Clare, August 11
Cloud, September 7
Colette, March 6
Cornelius, September 16
Cosmas, September 25
Cuthbert, March 20
Cyril of Alexandria, June 27
Cyril of Jerusalem, March 18

Damasus I, December 11
Damien, September 25
Damien de Veuster, April 15
David, March 1
Diana D'Andalo, February 15
Dominic, August 8
Dunstan, May 19

Edmund Campion, December 1
Edmund the Martyr, November 20
Egwin, December 30
Elizabeth Ann Seton, January 4
Elizabeth Bichier des Ages,
    August 26
Elizabeth of Hungary,
    November 17
Elizabeth of Portugal, July 4
Elizabeth of Schönau, June 18
Elizabeth of the Trinity,
    November 5
Emily de Rodat, September 19
Ephrem of Syria, June 9
Etheldreda, June 23
Euphrasia, March 13

Fabian, January 20
Felix of Cantalice, May 21
Fidelis of Sigmaringen, April 24
Flannan, December 18
Fra Angelico, February 18
Frances of Rome, March 9
Francis of Assisi, October 4
Francis Borgia, October 10
Francis (Ascanio) Caracciolo,
    June 4
Francis of Paola, April 2
Francis de Sales, January 24
Francis Solano, June 14
Francis Xavier, December 3
Francis Xavier Cabrini,
    November 13

Gabriel, September 29
Gabriel Possenti, February 27
Galdinus, April 18
Gaudentius, October 25

Gemma Galgani, April 11
Genevieve, January 3
George, April 23
Gerard, September 24
Germaine of Pibrac, June 15
Gertrude, November 16
Gianna Beretta Molla, M.D.,
    October 7
Gildas the Wise, January 29
Godfrey, November 8
Gonzaga Gonza, May 27
Gothard, May 4
Gregory III, December 10
Gregory the Great, September 3
Guy of Anderlecht, September 12
Guy of Pomposa, March 31

Hedwig, October 16
Helen, August 18
Henry II, July 13
Hilary, May 5
Hilary of Poitiers, January 13
Hildegard of Bingen, September 17
Honoratus, January 16
Hormisdas August 6
Hugh, April 1
Hyacinth Cormier, December 17
Hyacintha Mariscotti,
    January 30

Ignatius Azevedo, July 16
Ignatius of Antioch, October 17
Ignatius of Loyola, July 31
Imelda Lambertini, May 13
Irenaeus, March 24
Irenaeus, June 28
Irmina, December 22
Isaac Jogues, October 19

Isidore Bakanja, August 22
Isidore the Farmer, May 15
Isidore of Seville, April 4
Ita, January 15

James the Greater, July 25
Jane of Aza, August 2
Jane Frances de Chantal,
    December 12
Jeanne de Lestonnac, February 2
Jerome, September 30
Jerome Emiliani, February 8
Jesus Christ, December 25
Joan Antida Thouret, August 24
Joan of Arc, May 30
John the Almsgiver, January 23
John the Baptist, June 24
John Baptist Rossi, May 23
John Baptist de la Salle, April 7
John Before the Latin Gate, May 6
John of Beverley, May 7
John Bosco, January 31
John de Brébeuf, March 16
John de Britto, February 4
John Capistrano, October 23
John Chrysostom, September 13
John of the Cross, December 14
John Damascene, December 4
John Dominici, June 10
John of Egypt, March 27
John Eudes, August 19
John the Evangelist, December 27
John Gaulbert, July 12
John of God, March 8
John Joseph-of-the-Cross, March 5
John Marie Vianney, August 4
John Neumann, January 5
John Ogilvie March 10

John of Sahagun, June 12
Jordan of Saxony, February 15
Josaphat, November 12
Joseph, March 19
Juan Diego, December 9
Juan Macías, September 18
Jude, October 28
Julian of Norwich, May 8
Juliana Falconieri, June 19
Julie Billiart, April 8
Julius I, April 12
Junípero Serra, July 1
Justa and Rufina, July 20
Justin I, June 1

Kateri Tekawitha, July 14
Katharine Drexel, March 3

Laurence Giustiniani, September 5
Laurence O'Toole, November 14
Lawrence, August 10
Lawrence of Brindisi, July 21
Léger, October 2
Leo IX, April 19
Leo the Great, November 10
Leobinus, March 14
Louis, August 25
Louis Bertrand, October 9
Louis Guanella, October 27
Louise de Marillac, March 15
Lucy, December 13
Luke, October 18
Lutgardis, June 16
Lydia, August 3

Macrina, July 19
Madeleine Sophie Barat, May 25
Mamertus, May 11
Marcian, November 2
Margaret of Castello, April 13

Margaret Clitherow, March 25
Margaret of Cortona, February 22
Margaret of Scotland, November 19
Marguerite Bourgeoys, January 12
Maria Goretti, July 6
Maria of Jesus Crucified, August 15
Maria Magdalena Bentivoglio,
    August 12
Mariana of Jesus, May 28
Marie Marguerite d'Youville,
    December 23
Marie Poussepin, October 14
Marie Rose Durocher, October 6
Mark, April 25
Martha, July 29
Martin de Porres, November 3
Martin of Tours, November 11
Mary, January 1
Mary MacKillop, August 5
Mary Magdalene, July 22
Mary di Rosa, December 15
Mary Soledad, October 11
Mary Theresa Ledochowska,
    June 6
Matt Talbot, June 7
Matthew, September 21
Matthias, May 14
Maximilian, March 12
Maximilian Mary Kolbe, August 14
Mechtildis of Edelstetten, May 31
Meletius, February 12
Michael, September 29
Miguel Pro, November 23
Monica, August 27
Montanus, February 24
Mother Teresa of Calcutta,
    August 29

Nereus and Achilleus, May 12
Nicholas, December 6

Nicholas Owen, March 22
Nicholas Pieck and Companions, July 9
Nicholas of Tolentino, September 10
Notburga, September 14

Oengus, March 11
Onesimus, February 16
Opportuna, April 22
Osanna of Mantua, June 20
Otto, July 2
Our Lady of Lourdes, February 11

Pammachius, August 30
Pantaleon, July 27
Paphnutius, September 11
Paschal Baylon, May 17
Patrick, March 17
Paul, January 25
Paul Miki and Companions, February 6
Peregrine Laziosi, May 1
Perpetua and Felicity, March 7
Peter, June 29
Peter Canisius, December 21
Peter Chrysologus, July 30
Peter Claver, September 9
Peter Damian, February 21
Peter Manrique de Zúñiga, March 2
Peter Mary Chanel, April 28
Peter Orseolo, January 10
Philip, May 3
Philip of Heraclea, October 22
Philip Neri, May 26
Pier Giorgio Frassati, July 7
Pierre Toussaint, June 30
Pius V, April 30
Pius X, August 21

Polycarp, February 23
Pope John XXIII, November 25
Prisca, January 18

Radbod, November 29
Raphael, September 29
Raymond of Capua, October 5
Raymund of Peñafort, January 7
Richarius, April 26
Rita of Cascia, May 22
Roch, August 17
Romanus, February 28
Romaric, December 8
Rose Hawthorne Lathrop, July 8
Rose of Lima, August 23
Rose Philippine Duchesne, November 18
Rose of Viterbo, September 4
Rupert, March 29

Sabas, December 5
Samson, July 28
Sava, January 14
Scholastica, February 10
Sebastian de Aparicio, February 25
Serapion of Thmuis, March 21
Seven Founders of the Servite Order, February 17
Silvester Gozzolini, November 26
Sixtus II, August 7
Stephen Harding, April 17
Stephen of Hungary, August 16
Sylvester I, December 31

Teresa of Avila, October 15
Teresa Benedicta of the Cross, August 9
Teresa of Portugal, June 17
Thais, October 8
Theodore of Heraclea, February 7

Theodosius the Cenobiarch, January 11
Theodosius Pechersky, July 10
Theodotus, May 18
Thérèse Couderc, September 26
Thérèse of Lisieux, October 1
Thomas, July 3
Thomas Aquinas, January 28
Thomas Becket, December 29
Thomas Cantelupe, October 3
Thomas More, June 22
Thomas of Villanova, September 22
Thorfinn, January 8
Timothy, January 26
Titus Brandsma, July 26
Turibius de Mogrovejo, March 23
Tutilo, March 28

Valentine, February 14
Vicenta Lopez, December 26

Vincent, January 22
Vincent Ferrer, April 5
Vincent of Lérins, May 24
Vincent de Paul, September 27
Virgil, November 27

Waldetrudis, April 9
Wenceslaus of Bohemia, September 28
Wilfrid, October 12
William of Eskilsoë, April 6
William of Toulouse, May 29
William of Vercelli, June 25
Willibrord, November 7
Wulfric, February 20
Wulfstan, January 19

Zita, April 27
Zosimus, March 30